PRAISE FOR
PREDICTIVE ANALYTICS
FOR MARKETERS

'This book is an invaluable aid in the journey from big data to smart data usage, which is where competitive advantage rests. Leventhal delivers lashings of common sense based on erudition and experience, making this a very pragmatic and useful work.' **Jane Frost CBE, Chief Executive Officer, Market Research Society**

'A comprehensive, engaging and accessible introduction to the increasingly important field of predictive analytics and marketing from one of the leading practitioners. Each chapter underlines the fundamental aspects to keep in mind – user needs, experimental set-up, validating results – across a wide range of scenarios and data sources, and the book is packed with real-world case studies. Leventhal takes each of the main application areas in turn and focuses on how to generate value from data for your organization.' **Tom Smith, Managing Director, Office for National Statistics Data Science Campus**

'This volume provides a comprehensive overview of a cutting-edge technology that can transform a merely good company into an outstandingly successful one. Leventhal masterfully presents a complex subject in a highly accessible way, liberally illustrating the material with real-life examples from his own experience.' **David J Hand, Emeritus Professor of Mathematics, Imperial College London, and Chief Scientific Adviser, Winton Group**

'Data and customer analytics now sit at the heart of driving every successful business. The battle for customers in a digital world brings challenges, but equally provides great opportunities to those businesses able to identify and respond at pace to their needs. Leventhal has distilled his wealth of rich practical experience into a clear and comprehensive text, sharing best practice in methods for collecting data, building models, and operationalizing and leveraging the power of data to maximize economic value. A mandatory book for anyone working with customer data or predictive analytics.' **Paul Cushion, Customer and Digital Associate, KPMG Management Consulting**

'Leventhal has written an authoritative book on the use of data analysis in marketing and beyond, with clear case studies and a focus on the pragmatic usage of analytics. I highly recommend this book both to those starting out in a career in marketing and to those seasoned marketers in need of some new tricks if they are to stay relevant. A marketer who has understanding of all of the techniques covered in this book will be a highly prized asset to any organization.' **Giles Pavey, Head of Data Strategy, Department for Work and Pensions, and former Chief Data Scientist, dunnhumby Ltd**

'*Predictive Analytics for Marketers* is an engaging, comprehensive and practical framework for the application of advanced analytical techniques in market research. The case studies are relevant and informative, and neatly support the key principles outlined in the text. A very useful guide for organizations, big and small, aiming to get the best out of their data.' **Dr Emma White, Chair of the Market Research Society Census and Geodemographics Group, and Assistant Director, Administrative Data Research Centre for England, University of Southampton**

'In a world teeming with data, competitive advantage now firmly lies in how effectively data is analysed. This book provides a comprehensive guide on how to approach, execute, evaluate and get the most out of predictive analytics. It is very easy to read – even for the non-statistically minded. Each chapter contains real case histories and rounds off with a summary of the key points made, and the final chapter details the top tips for gaining business value from predictive analytics. *Predictive Analytics for Marketers* will prove to be an essential handbook for navigating and gaining insight from our growing data mountains.' **Lynne Robinson, Research Director, Institute of Practitioners in Advertising (IPA)**

'If you think predictive analytics is not for you, think again. It is vital for anyone in any management capacity. Every organization has mountains of customer data which, properly mined, can lead to a fuller understanding of customer and market behaviour. Leventhal's *Predictive Analytics for Marketers* is required reading for anyone who needs to understand the latest practical methods to segment and analyse data, whether for the public or the private sector, or to predict future success or understand reasons for failure.' **Roger Holland, Executive Chairman, JICPOPS (the Joint Industry Committee for Population Standards)**

'With a clear focus on the actionability of predictive analytics, this is a hugely valuable book for all marketers who want both a comprehensive introduction to what predictive analytics is and how it is enabled, and who also want to make sure that they focus on the business outcomes and benefits of such an approach, which is where the real value kicks in. As Leventhal points out, to avoid analytics for analytics sake, getting all the stakeholders on board focused on a key business problem is key to a successful project.

The book doesn't just focus on the techniques that are at the cutting edge of analytics, but also gives air time to the analytics standards that continue to be hugely valuable business tools – the message being use the right technique for the right problem. Leventhal sets out an end-to-end analytics journey – from tips about the preparation of data to avoid "garbage in" to robust measurement of the outcomes of any analytics project to ensure business benefit is realized – and to ensure that stakeholders remain onside and want to continue the journey.

We are also encouraged to think about the ethical and data protection framework that all analysts and the users of analysis should consider throughout the analytical journey and to consider the impact that their analysis can have on the individual.

Throughout, this is a very practical guide, with a number of marketing-focused case studies bringing the power of the analytical techniques discussed to life. A book that's very definitely not just for the shelf!' **Paul Cresswell, Head of Data Governance, Experian Marketing Services – Targeting**

'*Predictive Analytics for Marketers* clearly explains the analytics process and its commercial context in language understandable to managers, marketers, IT specialists and analysts. It addresses the essential areas of communication between these specialisms, giving lucid accounts of the process of planning an analytics project, the importance of framing the business problem, and the need for its alignment with appropriate methods. The book examines the strengths and weaknesses, and the areas of applicability, of a wide range of methods, reinforced by a selection of real-world examples in financial services, telecoms, retail and the public sector. The topics covered include data preparation, sampling, project planning, the continuing importance of statistical principles, choice of technique, survival analysis, customer segmentation, price optimization, demand forecasting, the value and challenges of big data, data protection law, testing outcomes, and social network analysis, always retaining an emphasis on commercial needs. Leventhal's book is a welcome addition, covering current topics in analytics clearly and insightfully.' **David Harris, Product Development Partner, CACI Ltd**

'This publication is much more than a lucid and comprehensive textbook on predictive analytics. From the rarely documented aspects of data collection and preparation through to model building and evaluation, Leventhal's profound expertise shines through as he shares his thoughts from a practical as well as a technical point of view. For businesses that wish to be data driven, this unambiguous and wise advice will provide an accelerated path to success.' **Gordon Farquharson, Director of Analytics, more2 ltd**

'In the conclusion to the book, Leventhal prompts the reader to ask the question, "Where would predictive analytics add value?" This book is a great resource to answer that very question. This comprehensive review of the inherent possibilities of predictive analytics is packed full of pithy insights and common-sense observations based upon Levethal's wide-ranging and meticulous experience. It will help many a practitioner to step back from the intricate details of each methodology and set each technique in a useful context, thereby enabling each organization to see the wood for the trees.' **Dr Tim Drye, Director, Data Analysts User Group**

'This much-needed book examines how to make effective use of the data that organizations now routinely accumulate on customers, products and transactions. Leventhal helpfully clarifies key concepts and gives sound and practical advice, drawing on his extensive experience in marketing. No matter how much you think you know about analytics, I suggest you read this book, apply it, and benefit from it!' **Paul Allin, Visiting Professor in Statistics, Imperial College London**

'Leventhal's *Predictive Analytics for Marketers* explains the need for robust research designs and reproducible analysis, providing tested and established statistical models and analytical approaches in order to answer old and new questions. No matter what your job role or background is, if the application of your analysis relates to marketing activities, *Predictive Analytics for Marketers* is a must-have.' **Claudio Calvino, Senior Data Scientist, Capgemini Ltd**

Predictive Analytics for Marketers

Using data mining for
business advantage

Barry Leventhal

KoganPage

First published in Great Britain and the United States in 2018 by Kogan Page Limited

2nd Floor, 45 Gee Street
London EC1V 3RS
United Kingdom
www.koganpage.com

c/o Martin P Hill Consulting
122 W 27th St, 10th Floor
New York, NY 10001
USA

4737/23 Ansari Road
Daryaganj
New Delhi 110002
India

ISBN   978 0 7494 7993 0
E-ISBN   978 0 7494 7994 7

British Library Cataloguing-in-Publication Data

A CIP record for this book is available from the British Library.

Library of Congress Cataloging-in-Publication Data

Names: Leventhal, Barry, author.
Title: Predictive analytics for marketers : using data mining for business
  advantage / Barry Leventhal.
Description: London ; New York : Kogan Page, 2018. | Includes bibliographical
  references and index.
Identifiers: LCCN 2017060508 (print) | LCCN 2017050352 (ebook) | ISBN
  9780749479947 (ebook) | ISBN 9780749479930 (alk. paper)
Subjects: LCSH: Marketing research. | Consumer behavior. | Data mining.
Classification: LCC HF5415.2 (print) | LCC HF5415.2 .L483 2018 (ebook) | DDC
  658.8/302856312–dc23

Typeset by Integra Software Services, Pondicherry
Print production managed by Jellyfish
Printed and bound by CPI Group (UK) Ltd, Croydon, CR0 4YY

CONTENTS

ABOUT THE AUTHOR

Dr Barry Leventhal is a consultant statistician with extensive experience in helping organizations use data to solve their business problems. He has previously worked in market research, collecting and analysing consumer panel data, and in geodemographics primarily using census statistics. Since 1991 he has focused on customer analytics and has worked with data-rich companies in sectors such as financial services, telecommunications and retail.

In 2017, Dr Leventhal was awarded the Market Research Society's Gold Medal for signal service to the profession, by chairing the MRS Census and Geodemographics Group. He chaired the group for over 25 years and stepped down in June 2017.

Dr Leventhal studied statistics at University College London (UCL) and graduated with first-class honours. He took the Diploma in Computer Science at Cambridge before returning to UCL to do a PhD in Bayesian statistics. He is a Freeman of the Worshipful Company of Marketors and has been awarded the Freedom of the City of London. He is also a Fellow of the Market Research Society, the Royal Statistical Society and the Institute of Direct Marketing.

He has published widely and in 2003 was awarded the MRS Silver Medal for best paper in the *International Journal of Market Research*. The same paper received an Emerald Citation of Excellence. His first book, *Geodemographics for Marketers*, was published by Kogan Page in 2016.

CONTRIBUTORS' BIOGRAPHIES

Wajid Shafiq

Wajid has over 30 years' experience of delivering complex technology programmes across both the private sector (with a range of blue-chip organizations) and the public sector (across central and local government). From a public-sector perspective this has included the development and deployment of hosted technology solutions to over 200 local government organizations.

He founded Xantura in 2008 specifically to address the need for improved partnership working across the public sector – with particular emphasis on how to improve outcomes for the most vulnerable in society. Xantura's Fusion platform has been designed to support this aim and this platform is now deployed to over 100 councils across the UK, supporting a range of agendas from fraud prevention to safeguarding.

In this context, Wajid's main interest is helping public-sector clients to navigate unique complexities so that advanced analytics can be brought to bear in a way that improves outcomes for vulnerable groups and delivers quantifiable benefits for public services that are under intense financial pressure.

Dr Atai Winkler

Atai gained a first-class honours degree in chemical engineering and a PhD from Imperial College of Science and Technology. He was awarded a prize for the best thesis submitted in that year. His interest in statistics and modelling started during his PhD.

Atai is an experienced predictive analytics, data mining, forecasting and simulation consultant with project management experience. He has worked in a number of business sectors, including utilities, telecoms, database marketing, retail, advertising, education, health and local government. He is familiar with many widely used analysis and modelling techniques, including descriptive statistics, regression (many different types), segmentation, forecasting, survival analysis and missing value imputation.

Atai has passed the IBM Professional Certification Program for giving training courses on IBM Statistics (SPSS). He has developed two software products: proMISS – a unique and advanced tool for imputing missing values in large databases; and PAM – a system that uses advanced predictive analytics for optimizing asset management (engineering, not financial) at the operational and tactical levels.

His clients have included Sainsbury's, Tesco, Orange, Cisco, South West Water, Royal Bank of Scotland, Cannon Avent, Ohal (a specialist econometrics consultancy), AlphaPlus, Petainer, the London Borough of Newham and a number of niche consultancies.

FOREWORD

Predictive analytics have been put to use in marketing for years. As it happens, my first job nearly 25 years ago focused on predicting the behaviour of telephone customers. However, even with the rising usage and influence of predictive analytics, it is not well understood outside of the small (but ever growing) community that focuses on predictive analytics for a living. In fact, with all of the attention and hype that predictive analytics has received in recent times, it may well be that it is *misunderstood* by even more people today than in the past! Many people read a few articles or see a few models applied in their organization's marketing efforts and they think that they fully understand what predictive analytics is all about. Alas, just as with any discipline, building accurate, useful, appropriate predictive models is much more complex than it seems to someone just learning about it.

In *Predictive Analytics for Marketers*, Barry Leventhal provides an easy-to-read summary of everything you need to know about predictive analytics in the marketing realm. The book is not loaded with formulas and theory, but rather focuses on much of the common-sense information that one must be familiar with to become properly grounded in how predictive analytics can be applied in a marketing setting. The book provides an overview of the common techniques utilized for predictive modelling, as well as the relative strengths and weaknesses of each. The point is rightly made that no single technique will perform best in all situations. A lot of work and exploration must be done to find the best path for any given situation. This is one area where people unfamiliar with predictive analytics often underestimate the skills and effort required to be effective.

The sections focusing on defining a business problem properly, and framing the related analytics effort effectively, are critically important. These steps are often shortchanged in the haste to start an analysis – and that is unfortunate. Small changes to how a business objective is defined, or how an analysis is framed, can lead to big differences in what analytics are developed and what outcomes are achieved. A seemingly simple change from a focus on the number of customers responding to the total dollar value of sales from their responses will lead to completely different methodologies and potentially very different assessments of each customer with respect to the goal.

Another key theme that the book hits upon is that classic statistical methods are still as relevant as ever and are still the primary drivers of analytics in the business world. This is especially true in marketing. It is also true that the types of data and breadth of business problems to which we now apply predictive analytics is constantly growing. However, many of the same fundamental approaches that have been used for business benefit for years are continuing to drive benefits today. This made Barry's review of classic sampling and experimental design techniques especially refreshing for me. Many people assume that with so much data in our hands we don't have to worry about such things any more. However, as the book lays out, this is not true.

Marketing is not purely about predicting who will take what action at which point in time. There are also other areas of interest such as identifying customers with similar profiles, understanding the relationships between customers, or identifying how long it may be before a given customer defects. Barry provides an overview of common techniques to address these issues such as segmentation models, social network analysis and survival models. Survival models in particular are worth considering if an organization has not yet done so. Long used in health and insurance settings, survival models have become much more widely adopted in marketing settings to look at issues such as customer churn. The cross-pollination of techniques from one industry or discipline to another has been increasing in recent years. The adoption of survival techniques for marketing has been one area that has seen a lot of success.

Predictive Analytics for Marketers is a terrific summary of the important topics that must be understood to succeed in one's own predictive analytics efforts. The book is written at a level that enables people who are not formally trained in the gory details to understand the concepts. While there are formulas shown periodically, they are used more to illustrate the concepts than to be a technical deep-dive. The practical examples that surround the formulas will help readers stay at a level of technical depth that they are comfortable with.

It is impossible to succeed in marketing today, or more broadly in business, without embracing predictive analytics. The marketing arena was one of the earliest and most enthusiastic adopters of predictive analytics. As a result, it is critical that anyone with responsibility for the success of marketing endeavours be versed in the basics of predictive analytics. This book is a terrific resource, whether you are learning for the first time or looking to refresh your knowledge. I predict that you will enjoy the read and I wish you luck!

Bill Franks
Chief Analytics Officer, The International Institute for Analytics
Author, *Taming the Big Data Tidal Wave* and *The Analytics Revolution*

PREFACE AND ACKNOWLEDGEMENTS

The subject of this book – predictive analytics – has been an invaluable tool throughout most of my career. In the 1980s I was applying the science to build neighbourhood classifications and store location models, mainly based on statistics from the 1981 census. In the 1990s I was developing targeting models and segmentation systems, using customer data and market research. And in the 2000s I was analysing and modelling data stored in vast data warehouses.

My main aim in writing this book has been to share my experiences, to explain the use of predictive analytics on customer data and summarize the understanding gained from hundreds of projects conducted over the last 30 years. Some of the most interesting projects have made it into the book as case studies.

However, this book would never have been written by itself – it took another publication to act as a 'trigger'. At the start of 2016 Kogan Page published *Geodemographics for Marketers* – my first foray as a solo author – which had come about, in no small part, at the suggestion of my wife Hazel. In the excitement of the launch, I felt that another book was lurking inside me on my experiences with customer analytics, and so *Predictive Analytics for Marketers* was born. I am very grateful that Kogan Page agreed again to be my publisher.

While this book is written largely from personal experience, I would like to thank a couple of industry experts who have contributed articles to it. My thanks go to Wajid Shafiq and Atai Winkler for sharing their knowledge of two important applications of advanced analytics.

I am particularly grateful to Peter Furness for fact checking my entire manuscript and for the many suggestions he made. Of course, all errors and omissions are entirely my responsibility; please let me know if you spot any, just in case Kogan Page ever decides to publish a second edition.

I must thank everyone involved at Kogan Page, especially Jenny Volich, Charlotte Owen, Philippa Fiszzon and Amanda Dackombe, as well as their external reviewers.

Lastly, special thanks go to my family – Hazel, Matthew and Laurence – without Hazel suggesting my first book, I would never have written a second.

Introduction to predictive analytics

We all create data. Through the products we purchase, our financial activity, our calls and texts, our e-mails and online behaviour, we produce a continuous stream of transaction records, text files and images. Our various service providers capture this data and use it to run their businesses – from delivering their services through to collecting our payments.

Predictive analytics is the science that converts data into predictions about the future. By storing our data, together with those from other customers, companies can make use of predictive analytics to identify new opportunities, minimize their costs or manage their risks.

In the early days of data-driven marketing – which, in the UK, was in the 1970s – only the largest companies, with millions of customers, employed predictive analytics – companies such as Reader's Digest targeted their direct mail campaigns using statistical models. Over the years, as computer resources, analytical software and customer management systems have become more widely available, the use of predictive analytics has broadened and become a mainstream activity.

The main aim of this book is to explain the concepts of predictive analytics to marketing professionals in companies that hold customer data. Our goal is to help marketers to understand how analytical solutions are developed, so that they may work with their information technology (IT) and analytical colleagues to achieve equivalent benefits. Equally well, the book will help other professionals in those businesses to understand the techniques and how they are being applied.

Furthermore, this book will also help IT professionals to gain a better understanding – for example of the data required by their analytical colleagues, the reasons for their strange requests, and the requirements for implementing their models.

The approaches we discuss may be followed in any country and for any business that holds customer data on computer, so the scope is fully international. Also, we do not assume or require you to be using a particular system architecture or software package – we remain independent of all software products at all times. The methods will be applicable irrespective of whether your data are stored in a cloud, a lake, a warehouse, a server or just on your desktop computer!

The book is organized along the lines of a journey to explore the wonderful world of predictive analytics. We have selected some important places to visit; however, new destinations are continually being discovered; for example, the internet of things will become an essential area for analytics in the near future. At the same time, revolutionary methods of travel are constantly being invented, such as the Cloud.

As with any journey, it is always nice to have an idea of where you are headed – therefore Chapter 1 provides an overview of the subject area, presents a series of examples to illustrate the benefits, and discusses key data protection and privacy issues.

The next four chapters explain the main components of a predictive analytics solution. Chapter 2 discusses the process that converts data into patterns known as 'models'; this process – known as 'data mining' – is a 'step-by-step' approach for creating and deploying an analytical model. Having understood the process, Chapter 3 focuses on the data that will be needed, the format required and the data preparation steps for creating the necessary analytical dataset. Chapter 4 examines modelling techniques – it introduces and explains the concepts of the methods that are most widely employed with customer data. Chapter 5 identifies different types of software solutions that enable you to apply these techniques in your IT environment.

From Chapter 6 onwards, we start to discuss applications to different types of business problem. Chapter 6 considers prediction of customer behaviour – it takes you through the steps involved in predicting the likelihood of an event such as product purchase or attrition, or for estimating quantities such as future spending. Chapter 7 concerns the analysis of *time*, such as time till churn, or the interval between purchases. This chapter demonstrates that the same techniques may be used in completely different spheres and applications, for example to predict the time remaining before the failure of a machine. A contributed article by Atai Winkler describes this application.

Another area where predictive analytics gets widely applied is for segmentation – to identify distinct groups within your customer base that would benefit from different marketing strategies or treatments. Chapter 8 discusses the most frequently used approaches for developing and implementing a segmentation system.

The next three chapters look at analytical applications that go slightly beyond the traditional idea of a customer. Chapter 9 reviews the use of predictive analytics in the banking, mobile telecoms and retail sectors; also, it discusses the use of analytics in the public sector, with the help of a contributed article by Wajid Shafiq. This chapter includes a section on analytics for business-to-business (B2B) marketing, identifying key differences that apply in the B2B world.

In Chapter 10, we focus on the retail sector and show how similar techniques may be applied to analysing products; we discuss, in more detail, approaches for price optimization, markdown pricing and forecasting demand. Chapter 11 examines how relationships between people may be measured, using social network analysis. This chapter has wide-ranging applications – from customer databases through to online social media platforms.

The most powerful way to prove the benefits from predictive analytics is to carry out a business experiment. Chapter 12 explains how to set up and interpret marketing tests, and introduces the use of advanced experimental design for getting the most out of your tests. The chapter closes with a section that identifies approaches being applied for testing in the online world.

Finally, the concluding chapter offers a reprise of the main messages and some final tips to help you on the journey.

Throughout the book, we present case study examples to demonstrate the applications; these are based on actual projects; however, client names and detailed results are omitted for obvious reasons.

Also throughout the book * is used as the symbol for multiplication, except where otherwise stated.

How can predictive analytics help your business?

01

Introduction

Predictive analytics involves bringing together resources and skills in a creative way, for the benefit of your company. The essential resources include business users, analytical experts, data and information technology (IT). In subsequent chapters we discuss how these elements work together, but in drilling down to the detail it will become more difficult to keep in mind the big picture of what can be achieved, particularly for new users.

For this reason, this opening chapter aims to provide an overview of predictive analytics in action, in particular to:

- Define and explain key terms associated with predictive analytics.
- Discuss some of the ways in which companies can benefit from these techniques.
- Provide examples of cases where analytics made a difference.
- Identify data protection and privacy issues and recommend the best ways to comply with them.

What is predictive analytics?

Predictive analytics is an umbrella term for the application of mathematical techniques to predict customer behaviour. The outcome is typically a score or code for each customer, which in some way indicates their likely future behaviour. For example, the score could represent their likelihood of purchasing another product from your company. Alternatively, the code could place customers into groups that are likely to have differing needs for management and communications, or for your products and services.

The main benefit of producing this information is that it enables customers to be treated or managed in different ways, according to their needs. For example, the score could be used to identify people with the highest chances of responding to a direct marketing campaign. Alternatively, it could pick out those with the least likelihood of purchasing, who would be best excluded from marketing.

Either way, by making use of each customer's response probability when selecting prospects for a campaign, marketing activity can be targeted to achieve a greater success rate than would ever be possible if prospects were selected at random. And we will show, later on in this book, that just a small improvement in success rate can deliver a substantial increase in profitability.

Predictive analytics is actually a subset of a wider set of activities known as **advanced analytics**. In 2010,[1] advanced analytics was defined by independent research firm Forrester (see Kobielus, 2010), as:

> Any solution that supports the identification of meaningful patterns and correlations among variables in complex, structured and unstructured, historical, and potential future datasets for the purposes of predicting future events and assessing the attractiveness of various courses of action. Advanced analytics typically incorporates such functionality as data mining, descriptive modelling, econometrics, forecasting, operations research optimization, predictive modelling, simulations, statistics and text analytics.

This broadens the use of analytics into areas such as deriving new data by decoding web logs, or by interpreting unstructured text or through analysis of social networks and customer networks. In practice, there is often little difference between predictive analytics and advanced analytics, and the two terms will be used interchangeably throughout.

Key point

Predictive analytics in marketing is usually applied to customers – we will make this assumption throughout, unless stated otherwise. However, it could also be applied to other things – including, for example:

- prospects, or people who are not yet your customers;
- lapsed or lost customers, who you might want to win back;
- businesses, including corporations, large companies, small and medium-size enterprises (SMEs);

- subscribers, eg of a phone company or cable TV service;
- accounts, eg of a bank or building society;
- shopping baskets or transactions in a retail outlet;
- citizens, eg residents in a local authority;
- assets, eg motor cars acquired by your customers;
- computers and devices such as mobile phones and tablets;
- machines and appliances connected to the internet of things (IoT);
- geographical areas such as census output areas.

There is really no limit to the application of predictive analytics, subject to the availability of useful data on the customers or audience of interest. Some example applications are presented later in this chapter.

The process of developing and applying predictive analytics is known as **data mining**. An end-to-end process for data mining is set out in Chapter 2; the process has been designed to ensure that predictive analytics delivers real business benefits that can be measured and replicated.

In recent years, the term **data science** has come to the fore, and **data scientist** has been described as the 'sexiest job of the 21st century' (Davenport and Patil, 2012). Data science essentially combines data mining with the information technology required to create meaningful data. It is particularly associated with **big data** sources such as online searches and e-mail files; these often require IT solutions such as cloud computing in order to handle them, due to their size and complexity.

In Chapter 2 we discuss the relationship between data mining, data science and statistics, while in Chapter 3 we consider **big data** and how it sits alongside more traditional **small data** sources.

The analytical model

At the heart of the predictive analytics process a formula is calculated or a set of rules is applied in order to obtain the score or code for each customer. This **algorithm** – be it a formula, rule set or any predefined calculation – is known as an **analytical model**. It makes use of pieces of information or **variables** that are known for each customer.

Analytical modelling works by using mathematical techniques to identify meaningful relationships between the customer variables. These relationships are then harnessed to create the model, which might predict an outcome, such as 'will the customer respond to a direct marketing campaign?' The model can then be employed to predict the likelihood of response for customers who have yet to be included in that campaign, enabling the marketer to identify the best (or the worst) prospects.

Models are employed throughout many fields, including science and medicine, economics, fraud detection and financial services. Every model is a simplification of the real world, summarizing how an outcome of interest is likely to depend upon key inputs, and often ignoring other factors that are either unknown or unmeasured.

For example, in 2012 *The Times* included an article on the mathematics of weight loss, which discussed daily calorie limits and diet (The Times, 2012). The article used the following model, which predicts basic calorie need for men and women:[2]

For a man:

basic daily calorie need = (4.545 * weight in pounds)
+ (15.875 * height in inches)
− (5 * age in years) + 5

For a woman, the equation is similar:

basic daily calorie need = (4.545 * weight in pounds)
+ (15.875 * height in inches)
− (5 * age in years) − 161

The beauty of this model is its simplicity – it can be applied to any adult using three easily measurable variables. So, for a 170-pound, 70-inch-tall man aged 50, the basic daily calorie need would be (4.545 * 170) + (15.875 * 70) − (5 * 50) + 5, giving 1,639 calories.

Extensive research may have gone into developing this model, examining many more pieces of information across a large sample of men and women. However, the end result summarizes the relationship between calorie needs, weight, height and age in one simple formula for each gender, which is straightforward to apply using just three variables. This model is known as the Mifflin-St Jeor equation (see Mifflin et al, 1990). Marketing models share some of the same features as this non-marketing example. They are obtained by analysing large datasets containing many facts about each customer. They reduce this data down to a formula requiring a much smaller number of variables – albeit often more than three. And this formula can be applied to make predictions for other individuals.

'All models are wrong, but some are useful'

The eminent British statistician George Box is famous for saying 'Essentially, all models are wrong, but some are useful' in his 1987 book on model building (Box and Draper, 1987). By this, Box meant that every model is a simplification of reality, and therefore is certain to be wrong. However, simplifications can still be useful, and so a model can help us to understand the world and make predictions.

In science, models may be only slightly wrong – they may ignore small effects. For example, the daily calorie model may leave out other factors but it gives a useful guideline. However, in marketing, models attempt to predict a customer's future behaviour, such as their response to a campaign, from highly incomplete information. Even with the best marketing database, the marketer usually knows very little about the customer's demographics, products needs or intention to purchase. And the marketing database invariably has no information about products that the customer has bought from other companies.

So there can be no field in which Box's maxim is truer than in marketing. And yet marketing statisticians have been using models for over 40 years and businesses have been reaping the rewards. And predictive analytics has spread from being a 'high-tech corporate' activity to a business practice that many companies can adopt. Why is this? It is because a small improvement in targeting efficiency, resulting from a model, can produce a substantial financial benefit. Therefore, provided that the model's results are real and sustainable, then its application should be worthwhile. Later chapters explain how to measure the benefits and monitor model performance.

Two types of model – predictive and descriptive

While there is a large body of statistical and mathematical techniques for analytical modelling, they broadly split into just two main types of model – predictive and descriptive.

Predictive models

A **predictive model** is designed with a particular outcome in mind, in order to predict that **target variable** for each customer. This type of model is sometimes also known as *directed*.

The campaign response model is one example of a predictive model. Another example, from the insurance industry, would be a model to predict whether a customer will renew or lapse their policy when it comes up for renewal. This model will identify which customers are most likely to renew their policies and which are the least likely – all customers can be scored on this basis, and assigned a marketing treatment according to their predicted renewals. Therefore, predictive models are highly action-able, and are often employed on a tactical basis in marketing.

Several further marketing applications of predictive models are shown in Table 1.1, together with the business questions that would typically be addressed.

The role of a predictive model

Figure 1.1 illustrates how a predictive model works, in the context of a model to identify which customers are most likely to purchase a product or service. There are three main steps in this example, which are described in turn below.

Step 1 Suppose that the company has carried out a marketing trial on a sample of its customers. For this group of people, the company knows

Table 1.1 Examples of situations where predictive models can be applied

Marketing application	Business question
Customer recruitment from a prospect database	Which prospects are most likely to purchase a product/service?
Cross-sell/up-sell campaign	Which customers of Product X are most likely to purchase Product Y? Which customers of Product Z are most likely to purchase more of Product Z?
Next-best offer	Which product/service is each customer likely to purchase next?
Customer retention	Which customers are most likely to lapse or attrite?
Customer lifecycle management	How long before each customer becomes likely to lapse or attrite?
Win-back campaign	Which past customers are most likely to respond to a win-back offer?
Customer future value or lifetime value	What is the predicted future value of purchasing, or contributions to profit, for each customer?

Figure 1.1   The role of a predictive model

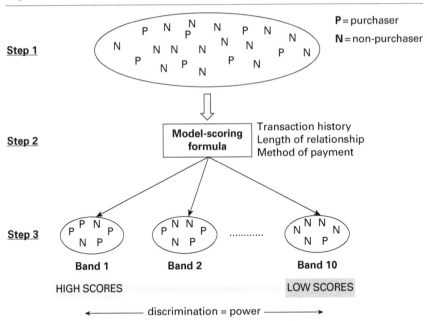

whether each customer was a purchaser (P) or non-purchaser (N). In addition, a number of attributes are known for every customer, eg their length of relationship, previous transaction history, usual method of payment, and so on. These are the available **predictor variables**.

Step 2 These pieces of information are examined by your analyst to produce a scorecard or scoring formula; the scorecard weights and combines the most useful variables to calculate a model score for each customer, such that purchasers are assigned high scores and non-purchasers receive low scores.

Step 3 The list of customers is sorted from highest down to lowest model scores, and is typically divided into 10 score bands based on this ranking. Your analyst then looks at band 1 (highest scores) and finds that it contains a high number of purchasers. Not everyone has purchased, but the purchase rate is perhaps three or four times the overall average. In band 2, the purchase rate is also well above average, but not quite as high as for band 1. Similarly, the purchase rate continues to decrease in subsequent bands – by band 10, the rate is very low; however, band 10 still contains a small number of people who made a purchase for some unknown reason.

Armed with this scorecard your analyst is able to calculate the corresponding scores for every customer, and can assign them to the 10 ranked bins based on model scores. The company is now in a position to control its marketing activities better – it could target its offer to customers who are most likely to take it, in bins 1 and 2 (say). Or it could market more widely and exclude, or deselect, those who are least likely, in bin 10. Chapter 6 discusses in more detail how these decisions can be made.

Descriptive models

A **descriptive model** is designed to give a better understanding of customers or their behaviour, without being directed to predict a particular outcome. Therefore, this type of model is sometimes known as *undirected.*

The applications of descriptive models tend to be more strategic; for example, subdividing the customer base into groups or **segments**, each containing customers who are similar in terms of behaviour, needs or attitudes, say, is a classic case. The resulting customer segmentation can help you to plan your marketing strategy and track its success. Table 1.2 provides some examples of situations where descriptive models can be applied and the business questions addressed.

The examples in Table 1.2 are mainly focused on customer relationship management (CRM) and growing value through increasing sales to customers. These are just a few of the situations where predictive analytics can add value. The following section discusses more ways in which this can happen, using the profitability seesaw.

Table 1.2   Examples of situations where descriptive models can be applied

Marketing application	Business question
Customer segmentation (1)	What are the underlying factors that explain differences between customers, eg on their purchasing behaviour?
Customer segmentation (2)	How does the customer base divide into groups, containing similar individuals according to criteria relevant to marketing? (eg purchasing behaviour)
Product affinities	Which products are more likely to be purchased together in the same transaction (or in sequential transactions)?
Product recommendation	For a customer who has purchased product X, which other products are product X buyers also likely to purchase?

The profitability seesaw

The profitability seesaw, illustrated in Figure 1.2, demonstrates that there are two possible ways in which the profitability of a business or activity can grow – by increasing revenues or by decreasing costs. If analytical modelling can help to improve either revenues or costs, then an increase in profits will naturally follow. This assumes, of course, that the company is geared up to implement predictive analytics efficiently and that its deployment costs do not outweigh the gains.

Example

One of the core applications of models has been for targeting direct mail, including cold mailings and cross-sell offers to customers. However, large-scale campaigns are expensive, in terms of mailing packs and postage costs. Essentially, cross-sell models enable mailings to be reduced in size, by only contacting customers who are predicted to be more likely to respond, or by excluding those who are least likely. By reducing the list of customers mailed, the total response and resultant revenue are reduced; however, this is more than offset by the cost savings due to the smaller mailing – leading to an increase in profitability.

Figure 1.2   The profitability seesaw

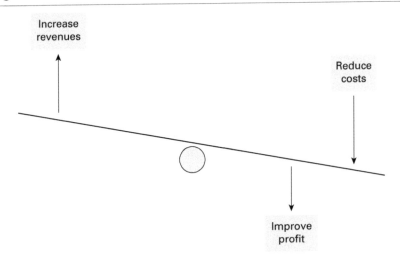

Applying predictive analytics to e-mail marketing

In recent years, we have all seen the take-off in e-mail marketing; one of the great advantages of e-mail, of course, is that the cost of each communication is negligible; therefore marketers are able to contact their entire lists without worrying about the costs and so achieve maximum numbers of responses and resultant sales.

In practice, this means that customers get bombarded with large numbers of messages, many of which are irrelevant to them, leading to declining interest in receiving e-mails, and decreasing response rates. The ideal solution would be to send only the most appropriate messages to each customer and exclude the irrelevant ones. Alternatively you might still decide to e-mail everyone, but you could personalize the message according to the customer's segment. Another option is to identify which products are likely to be of most interest to a customer who has bought Product X, based on other Product X buyers. This approach, known as a **recommender system** (see Chapter 11), is taken by online retailers such as Amazon and Netflix for suggesting products or movies to their customers.

Making a difference – eight examples of useful models

The eight case studies presented in this section demonstrate some of the applications of advanced analytics, illustrating ways in which analytics can make a difference to its users.

Targeting customers of a retail bank

A European retail bank had invested in a new data warehouse, and was keen to show quick wins by leveraging its data for customer management. Using the available customer data, a set of six analytical models were developed to predict likelihoods of product purchase for the bank's core financial products. These models were applied in combination, to improve the customer contact planning process and for call-centre operators to select next-best products to offer.

The models worked well and the majority of them continued to be used for making customer selections, for some years. The case study and models are discussed more fully in Chapter 9.

Assessing customer potential in financial services

In the financial services industry, customers tend to spread their product holdings across several providers. So, for example, an insurance company may not know which of its policy holders are likely to be interested in investment products.

To address the issue, a market-wide segmentation model was developed for the UK consumer financial services industry. This model assigned each adult individual to a segment, according to his or her life stage, wealth and portfolio of financial products. A number of companies used the segmentation to manage their customer base, target cross-sell campaigns and assess their share of wallet.

The segmentation was built and assessed using a market research survey on consumer financial services. After gaining acceptance, the segments were assigned to customers and prospects with the help of predictive models. This survey-based approach to customer segmentation is described more fully in Chapter 8.

Managing mobile phone customers over their lifetimes

A mobile phone company introduced a predictive approach to managing customer lifecycles through the use of survival modelling, a technique for analysing events that take place over time.

Separate models were created for pre-pay and post-pay customers and these were implemented to produce a predicted survival curve for each customer, which showed how the likelihood of retention changed over time. The model developments also provided insights into the factors that affected customer longevity.

Using the survival curves, key points in the lifecycle could be identified where the churn rate increased significantly. The phone company designed interventions to manage and retain customers through those risky periods. The technique and this case study are discussed more fully in Chapter 7.

Evaluating effects of an in-store promotion

A supermarket retailer analysed its basket data to measure promotional buying behaviour, and evaluate one of its seasonal promotions.

Each year, the supermarket ran an in-store promotion across its range of baby products and evaluated the results in terms of meeting top-line financial targets. However, these results gave little insight into the types of customers who had taken part and contributed to a successful outcome.

To achieve greater insights, the retailer developed a customer segmentation of its baby-product shoppers, which identified six shopper segments. The purchasing behaviours of these segments were then tracked before, during and after the promotion, to see how their buying patterns changed.

The analysis demonstrated the benefits of taking a customer-centric approach to promotion evaluation. The results caused the retailer to change their advertising strategy for future campaigns in this product category.

Measuring availability of products in supermarkets

A supermarket retailer wished to develop a measure of product availability using its electronic point of sale (EPOS) transaction data. The classic problem with tracking sales of a specific product in a particular store is that zero sales will occur naturally and do not necessarily imply a problem with availability.

A probability model was created in order to flag periods where zero sales were unlikely to have occurred by chance. This formed the basis for a credible measure of product availability and for deriving estimates of the sales that were lost during periods of non-availability.

Generating estimates of market size at neighbourhood level

Accurate small area estimates of demand for the 'eating out' market were required by a retailer that operated a number of different restaurant chains for different types of meal occasions.

Market research data were analysed as a source of consumer demand, and a demographic model was built for each market. Neighbourhood profiles from the Census were used to generate demographic cell counts corresponding to the variables employed in each model. Finally the models were applied to the demographic counts, to obtain neighbourhood market sizes, and the results were calibrated to known national market sizes.

The analysis gave a set of market sizes at neighbourhood level, which were significantly more accurate than the usual estimates obtained via traditional geodemographic classification systems. This case study is described more fully in Leventhal (2016).

Benchmarking the results of the EU referendum in the UK

On 23 June 2016, a referendum was held in the UK on its membership of the European Union (EU) – should the country remain or leave? Although the outcome was that 'Leave' won by 52 per cent to 48 per cent, the results were announced by local authority on referendum night. Unlike election polls, this referendum was a one-off event – so there were no results from 'last time' against which to interpret the outcome in each area and say whether it represented a 'swing' to Remain or Leave.

To overcome this problem, the BBC employed a benchmark that predicted the results in each local authority. This used a predictive model developed by John Curtice and Stephen Fisher (2016), based primarily on analysis of over 61,000 interviews about people's attitudes towards the EU. These interviews were conducted in Great Britain by YouGov between March 2015 and March 2016.

The benchmark enabled the BBC to rank the areas from 'most likely to vote Leave' through to 'most likely to vote Remain' and hence comment on the actual results as they came in. Figure 1.3a shows the top 10 local authorities where the benchmark suggested that Leave would do best, together with the actual Leave percentages – these were all strong Leave areas as predicted, with an average Leave vote of 71 per cent. Similarly, Figure 1.3b shows the corresponding results for the top ten Remain areas, which all proved to be Remain strongholds. Figure 1.3c shows the 10 areas in the middle of the ranking – the actual Leave vote varied from 45 per cent to 58 per cent in these areas, with an average of 51 per cent.

Therefore, the benchmark provided a useful tool for assessing the referendum results as they were announced, in the absence of other information.

Going beyond business reports

A study was conducted to identify scenarios where advanced analytics could be of value for a fleet maintenance organization, with a fleet of 200 vehicles to maintain. The organization mainly relied on business reports that described the state of the fleet, the numbers of repairs conducted and parts replaced.

One particular scenario was that a modification had been introduced in order to extend the life of the hydraulic pump; however, the business reports gave no information on whether the modification was effective or not.

Figure 1.3   EU referendum results (with actual percentages of those who voted Leave) for top predicted Leave areas, top predicted Remain areas and areas in the middle

a) The top 10 predicted Leave

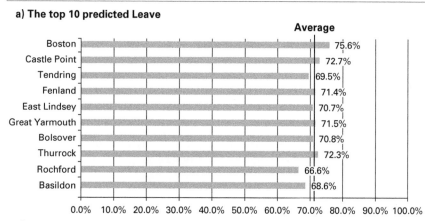

b) The top 10 predicted Remain

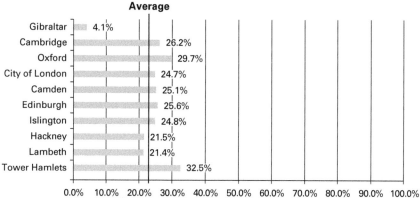

c) The 10 in the middle

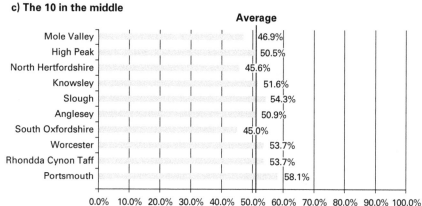

A descriptive survival analysis (see Chapter 7) was carried out in order to compare the survival rates of pumps pre- and post-modification. This analysis took account of the use of those pumps that had already failed, as well as the ages of pumps that were still working. It found that, going beyond a certain length of operation, there were higher survival likelihoods and lower failure rates on those pumps that had received the modification.

This project demonstrated that there was potential in applying advanced analytics for fleet maintenance, which might have seemed unlikely at the outset – and the study illustrated some of the business questions that could be answered.

You may be wondering how this case study is relevant to marketing analytics – exactly the same approach could be used to test whether a major modification to a car engine, say, is beneficial for customers and to quantify the improvement in engine lifetime. The car marketer would certainly be interested in the results!

Generating customer knowledge

The mobile phone case study, described above, can be thought of as a specific example of using advanced analytics for **generating customer knowledge** – in this case, the lifecycle of each customer. More generally, if customer profitability is driven by a certain variable, then it can be helpful to predict that variable, and hence segment customers on their likely profitability.

A good example of generating customer knowledge occurs in the roadside assistance market. For companies that operate in this market, customer profitability is likely to depend on the number of times that the insured car breaks down and requires roadside assistance. Customers with no breakdowns will be highly profitable, while those incurring multiple breakdowns are likely to be heavily loss-making. Therefore, when taking on a new (or renewing) customer it can be useful to predict the likely number of breakdowns that their car will incur over the coming year, using factors such as age of vehicle and annual mileage. The 'number of breakdowns' model may then be applied to estimate the likely profitability of each customer.

Competing on analytics

Tom Davenport coined the phrase '**competing on analytics**' to describe companies that exploit advanced analytics to achieve superiority in the ways that they operate their internal systems and serve their customers.

Integrating predictive models to drive enterprise-wide business processes is the ultimate level of adoption by companies, which Davenport and Harris (2007) term as 'analytical competitors'. Well-known examples of analytical competitors include:

- Amazon, which makes recommendations based on past browsing behaviour and also purchases by other customers who bought the same product.

- Netflix, provider of streaming films and television series, which forecasts customers' preferences and offers these as 'top picks'.

- Capital One, which continuously runs experiments on all the 'levers it can pull' such as interest rates, incentives and packaging, to improve the uptake and return from its credit-card customers (see Chapter 12).

- Google, which continuously analyses big data and conducts experiments to improve the performance of its search engine.

Data protection and privacy issues

In order to achieve sustainable benefits from predictive analytics, your company will need to comply with the appropriate data protection and privacy legislation. Going beyond the legislation, it is important to earn and maintain the customer's trust, through the ways in which their information is stored, handled and used.

In the UK, at the time of writing, the Data Protection Act 1998 (DPA) governs the processing of personal data. By *personal data*, the DPA means any data that can be used to identify a living individual. Under the DPA, individuals and organizations that process personal data must register with the Information Commissioner's Office (ICO) in order to declare their uses of personal data. The DPA sets out eight data protection principles to be followed in the acquisition, processing and use of personal data – these are principles such as fair processing, accuracy and security (see ICO, 2017a).

The EU has developed a new legal framework for data protection, known as the General Data Protection Regulation (GDPR). The GDPR is being introduced in the UK from 25 May 2018, superseding the DPA, and will continue to apply after the UK has left the EU. The principles of the GDPR are similar to those of the DPA, with the addition of a new principle of **accountability**, meaning that organizations must show how they comply with the data protection principles.

In connection with analytics, the ICO (2017b) has made six key recommendations for helping organizations to achieve data protection compliance and address privacy issues – in brief, these are:

1 Use **anonymized** data which does not identify individuals, instead of personal data, wherever possible.

2 Be transparent about the processing of personal data, by providing meaningful privacy notices to customers.

3 Identify privacy risks by carrying out privacy impact assessments.

4 Build privacy measures into analytics activities, eg covering data security and minimizing the amount of information that needs to be held.

5 Develop ethical principles to help reinforce key data protection principles.

6 Develop analytical algorithms that are auditable, in order to explain and check the performance of the algorithms.

The first recommendation, of anonymization, is particularly important in predictive analytics. All of the analytical applications discussed in this book are developed using anonymized data – customer names and addresses, or identifiers, are unnecessary when it comes to building a model. Certain elements may, however, be used for deriving potentially useful attributes such as geodemographic codes from postcodes or genders from titles.

Recommendation 6 above applies particularly to 'black box' machine-learning systems such as neural networks, which are discussed in Chapter 4.

As the recommendations imply, compliance with legislation alone is not sufficient – it is important to protect the privacy of individuals and gain their trust in how their data are being used. Principles such as data security, openness and transparency are key here, along with giving individuals options about how their information will be used. Linklaters (2014) discuss privacy issues in the context of social media data; however, the same principles apply to all types of personal data.

Conclusion

In this chapter, we have seen that:

✔ Predictive analytics leverages relationships between customer variables to predict outcomes and assign customers to segments.

✔ A predictive model is directed towards a particular target variable, enabling that activity to be predicted for each customer.

✔ A descriptive model is undirected, and may be used to create segments of customers based on multiple criteria.

✔ Predictive analytics brings business benefits by helping company resources to be assigned more efficiently – either to increase revenues or reduce costs.

✔ There are many ways in which predictive analytics can make a difference – for example in improving internal business processes, taking customer-facing actions and interpreting complex behaviour patterns.

✔ Compliance with data protection legislation is essential when processing personal data; at the same time, it is important to protect the privacy of the individual and gain their trust in how their data are being used.

Notes

1 Forrester updated this definition in 2014 as follows: 'Analytic techniques and technologies that apply statistical and/or machine-learning algorithms that allow firms to discover, evaluate, and optimize models that reveal and/or predict new insights.'

2 Throughout this book * is used as the symbol for multiplication, except where otherwise stated.

Using data mining to build predictive models

02

Introduction

Sometimes, predictive models can be obvious and require little effort to build or apply them. For example, certain markets are driven by a single dominant variable or attribute, such as the age of the customer. If that were the case, then a simple analysis of purchasing rates by age would identify the most important age group – if not already known. The same principle extends to two or three attributes – a cross-analysis could identify the priority groups. However, customer databases often store hundreds or even thousands of attributes, therefore in most cases a more sophisticated approach is needed to identify the model.

In this chapter, we discuss the end-to-end approach of converting data – which may be 'messy' or held in an unsuitable format – into a model. The complete process is best known as data mining, although nowadays the 'sexier' label of data science is often preferred – this chapter will explain why!

The main aims of this chapter are to:

- Introduce and review the data-mining process.
- Discuss the issues and requirements within each data-mining phase.
- Identify the main parties involved in data mining, and the roles that they play in the process.
- Consider the relationships between data mining, data science and statistics.

What is data mining?

In order to achieve real and sustainable benefits from predictive analytics, a process is required that will take you on a journey – starting from your business problem and the data to tackle it, and finishing with a proven solution that is ready to be implemented. This process of converting data into useful information is known as data mining.

More formally, data mining can be thought of as a *process of discovering and interpreting patterns in data to solve business problems*. The data-mining process *converts data into information* in the sense of creating model predictions that you can put into action.

Data mining is often associated with large amounts of data, containing millions of records and thousands of attributes held for each record. Sophisticated software is necessary to identify meaningful relationships and harness them to create analytical models.

The related term 'knowledge discovery' (KD) is sometimes also used – knowledge discovery is the process of discovering potentially useful information from a collection of data. KD encompasses all types of data and does not necessarily involve analytical modelling, while data mining is taken to include creating predictive or descriptive models. Frawley et al (1992) present an overview of the knowledge discovery process, approaches to KD and associated issues.

While we are going through definitions, another term you will sometimes meet is 'business intelligence'. Business intelligence, or BI, is an umbrella term that refers to a variety of software applications used to analyse an organization's raw data. As a discipline, BI consists of several related activities, including database querying, reporting tools and data mining. It tends to be mainly used by IT departments, in the context of a company's analytical systems.

Who are the stakeholders?

Data mining invariably implies a team effort because it involves different functions in your company – typically business operations, analytics and IT. Therefore, for any project, the data-mining team will typically comprise:

- a business person – who fully understands the problem to be tackled and the desired outcome;
- an IT person – who is responsible for the IT infrastructure required to supply data to the project, deploy models and manage the outputs;
- a data analyst – who possesses the skills and software tools to build models.

These three parties are jointly responsible for the success of a project, and so are sometimes known as the 'stakeholders' in data mining. We shall consider their involvement in the process later on in this chapter, having first discussed the process itself. In some companies, one person will have multiple roles – for example, he or she may be responsible for both IT and data analysis. Nevertheless their separate skills will be involved in different stages of the process.

Why do we need a data-mining process? The main reason is that there are many potential traps for the unwary, along the road from data to information. By carefully following an end-to-end established process, you can be more confident that your findings will be valid and that real business benefits will be delivered.

The data-mining process

In the late 1990s, a consortium of software providers and analytics users combined to agree on a standard approach to data mining. The outcome was CRISP-DM – the Cross Industry Standard Process for Data Mining (see Chapman et al, 2000). The full CRISP-DM methodology is described in a hierarchical way, with four levels in the hierarchy. At the top level, the data-mining process is divided into six phases, which are illustrated in Figure 2.1 and summarized briefly below.

Figure 2.1   The data-mining process

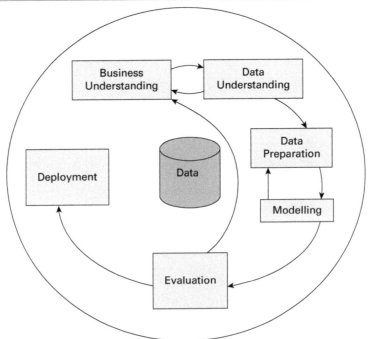

SOURCE Cross Industry Standard Process for Data Mining (CRISP-DM)

As we see in Figure 2.1, a cylinder of data sits at the centre – this represents all the systems and sources that are available to contribute data to the project. The following six phases then form the data-mining process.

Business understanding

This initial phase focuses on understanding the project objectives and requirements from a business point of view, and then converting this knowledge into a data-mining problem definition and a preliminary plan designed to achieve the objectives. If the requirement is for a predictive model that will need to fit in with existing processes, then it is essential to understand exactly how these processes operate and any constraints that will apply to the model's inputs and outputs. For example, if the business need is for a segmentation of customers into no more than five groups, then it will be no use building a solution that delivers 10 segments – this will almost certainly be rejected, even though 10 subsets might be more accurate than five.

The main tasks and issues within business understanding are:

- Determine business objectives:
  - What does the business really want to achieve from the data-mining project?
  - What are the success criteria – from a business point of view?
- Assess situation:
  - Identify all resources available for the project – primarily these will be people, computer systems, software tools and data.
  - Specify all requirements, assumptions and constraints, such as the number of segments required.
  - List the risks and contingency plans to mitigate them.
  - Construct a cost–benefit analysis – what is the expected return on investment (ROI), assuming that the project is successful?
- Determine data-mining goals:
  - Define success criteria in data-mining terms – what does the data analyst need to do in order to show that the project has been successful?
- Planning:
  - Produce a project plan and perform initial assessments of the available data-mining tools and techniques.

A crucial component of this phase is framing the business problem in order to achieve a solution that is useful, both analytically and for the business. There are usually alternative problems that could be addressed and the choice of 'best' problem is often a combination of 'science' and 'art'. These issues are discussed more fully, for predictive models, in Chapter 6.

Data understanding

The understanding phase is designed to help the analyst to become familiar with the data, by examining its quality and exploring whether it would support the objectives decided at the previous phase.

It is often the case that data are sourced from multiple places, each with a different owner. For marketing information, this might be a marketing database, while a data archive might be required for historic transactions; additionally, the analyst might go to external suppliers for lifestyle and web-usage data. These multiple sources potentially complicate the data understanding phase, and certainly create more work when it comes to data preparation. However, the analyst will want to examine all available sources since the performance of the model will depend primarily on having truly predictive data.

The main tasks in this phase are as follows:

- *Collect initial data*
  The analyst acquires initial data, from each available source, identifying and resolving any problems concerning data access.

- *Describe data*
  The analyst describes the data, including its format and the quantity of records and attributes in each file. A first assessment is made as to whether the information satisfies the relevant requirements for the project.

- *Explore data*
  The exploration task delves more deeply into the data, examining aspects such as the values of key attributes, such as the outcome that the model will be designed to predict. Additionally, relationships between attributes may be explored and properties of any important subsets of customers.

- *Verify data quality*
  This task examines data quality, such as data completeness, presence of errors and incidence of missing values. Solutions to data-quality problems are identified and considered.

The existence of good metadata is important here – metadata is information that documents a set of data, including how the attributes have been constructed, the values they can take and how their format may have changed over time.

In Figure 2.1, the arrows go both ways between business understanding and data understanding, reflecting the fact that insights from this phase will sometimes cause the project plan to be revisited and updated. This, in turn, can lead to further data sources being obtained and explored, to support the data-mining objectives.

If the project objective is to build a model using a source that has already been analysed and well understood, then the requirement for data familiarization and quality checking is likely to be reduced. On the other hand, if a previously unused source is to be employed, such as a feed from another part of the business, then a detailed assessment known as a data audit becomes essential – see Chapter 3.

Data preparation

The data preparation phase consists of all tasks to create the dataset that will be used for the analysis and modelling phases. When building a predictive model, the analytic dataset (ADS) will contain potential predictor variables, measured over a historic period, together with one or more target variables measured over a subsequent outcome period. Therefore it is important to understand and design the time periods on which the ADS is based. This issue is discussed in more detail in Chapter 6.

Typically, up to five manipulation steps are carried out in the data preparation phase:

1 Data selection – to select the data sources and attributes within each source that are to be included in the project.
2 Data cleansing – to correct or remove errors and inconsistencies in the selected data, such as erroneous or missing values.
3 Constructing data – for example, creating records that summarize customer behaviour and deriving new attributes.
4 Integrating data – merging separate sources into a single set of data.
5 Formatting data – reformatting the dataset so that it can be read into the analysis and modelling software.

Due to the detailed nature of these tasks and the large quantities of records and fields that are likely to be involved, around 60–70 per cent of the work effort in a data-mining project will typically be required for the data preparation phase. The ADS created in this phase is a file or table containing all the data to be used for analysis and modelling.

Key point

The data preparation phase is critical to the success of your data-mining project – the predictive power of the data is more important than the choice of modelling technique. Therefore it is essential that all insights gained from the business and data-understanding phases are fully leveraged, and that as much information is 'squeezed out' of the data as possible.

Modelling

A better title for this phase would be 'analysis and modelling' – analysis to help understand the present situation and modelling to create a useful predictive model or segmentation accordingly. Sometimes the project will be ground-breaking within your company, in the sense of bringing together sources from different parts of the business for the first time. In that case, analysis of the combined data may uncover new insights and guide the requirements for a model.

Often, the modelling will suggest that different or recoded data should be included, which will necessitate returning to the data preparation phase. Hence there tends to be a high level of iteration between these two phases.

Key point

A successful project may not require a model – it may be that, by bringing data together in a novel way, a new insight is generated that obviates the need for a model. In that case, it is better to keep the project simple and apply the insight, rather than overcomplicate matters by building a model.

Assuming that a model is actually required, this phase includes the following tasks.

Select modelling techniques

As Chapter 4 shows, there are usually several different analytical techniques to choose from for any data-mining problem. Therefore, in the modelling phase, appropriate techniques may be selected and applied, and their results compared to select the most useful model. Also, any technique can usually be applied in various ways – in which case these will be tested in order to arrive at the final model.

The choice of techniques also implies selecting a modelling tool containing those methods – typically a statistics package, data-mining system or statistical programming language. A large and ever-increasing number of software products are available, which are discussed in Chapter 5.

Generate test design

In order to assess the quality of the model, the ADS is randomly split into subsets for model development and validation. And sometimes a third subset is created for the evaluation phase. This separation of the data means that some records do not contribute to building the model and are only used to evaluate its performance. So as to evaluate the performance of the model accurately, it is important that the evaluation subset is kept completely apart from the model development process.

Build model

The analyst runs the modelling tool on the ADS to create one or more models for consideration. For each model, the tool will produce a series of numerical and graphical outputs that aid in interpretation and assessment. The analyst interprets the model parameters, reviews the outputs and continues to build models, until an outcome is produced that satisfies the data-mining objectives and makes sound business sense.

It may be the case that the ADS is used to build one model, particularly when the approach is being tested in the early days of your data-mining activities. However, a single ADS may sometimes be used to generate a series of models, by analysing different subsets of customers – for example, to construct a separate model for each region and/or brand.

Assess model

The model is assessed by comparing the accuracy of its predictions between the development and validation subsets. Also it gets evaluated against the data-mining goals that were set in the business-understanding phase. If necessary, the build-and-assess model phases are repeated, refining the input variables and parameters until an acceptable model is obtained. Again, this refinement process should not involve the evaluation subset.

Evaluation

As the final stage in its development, the performance of the model is evaluated against the objectives and success criteria that were set by the business, during the business-understanding phase – to establish whether the outcome is potentially useful or is deficient in some way. Ideally, if timescales and budgets permit, the usefulness is confirmed by conducting a 'live test' – see key point box below.

The process is reviewed in order to identify key findings and any improvements that should be made for future projects. Finally, next steps are agreed – in particular: whether to implement the model, or carry out further work to improve it, or initiate a new data-mining project.

Key point

No matter how well the data-mining team has done its job and built a model that appears to be predictive, at this stage it is based on a particular set of data collected over a certain period of time. The 'acid test' is whether the model works sufficiently well for other time periods and conditions, and justifies the resources that will be required to implement it.

It is all too easy to build a model that works well on its development data and performs acceptably on the validation subset. These two subgroups are formed from the same ADS, and so are likely to contain similar relationships. Therefore, a further more stringent method of testing is needed, before you take the risk of applying the model across your business.

The ideal scenario – timescales and budgets permitting – is to carry out a trial implementation using test and control groups. The test group, targeted using the model, should contain a relatively small proportion of your customers in order to limit the risk whilst still giving statistically reliable results; the control group should continue to apply your standard approach, across the remaining customers. In Chapter 12, we discuss the construction of test and control groups, and also introduce more advanced methods for testing multiple options within a single experiment.

If live testing is not feasible, then it can sometimes be simulated by applying the model retrospectively to data from an earlier time period or to another related source.

Deployment

The earlier phases will hopefully have generated valuable new insights; however, the direct financial benefits of employing the new model are only achieved when it actually gets implemented. This phase is primarily concerned with planning how the deployment will take place, and how the model will be monitored and maintained over time.

Key point

Building and deploying the model are separate phases in the data-mining process. The build occurs once (until a model update is required), while deployment typically takes place many times over the model's lifetime. Therefore, ideally, the deployment method should be efficient, automated and self-monitoring. Since deployment is where long-term resources will be needed, start planning how the model will be deployed when you design the project plan – back in the business understanding phase.

Monitoring is essential if the model is going to be used to make automated selections or decisions for you. Remember – and document – that the model was built using customer data captured over a particular period of time. A number of external and internal factors are liable to change in the future, such as market dynamics, the way that customers purchase your products, and the information recorded by your operational systems. Any of these changes are liable to affect predictions given by the model. Therefore a method of monitoring its effectiveness and detecting unplanned changes should be designed as part of the deployment. The way to achieve this is to employ a control group of customers who are randomly selected and independent of the model, in order to provide a benchmark for evaluating its performance.

By this stage, you will doubtless want to target your entire campaign using the model, so it may seem wasteful and unnecessary to include contacts chosen at random. However, control groups are the only way of monitoring and proving the effectiveness of your targeting. The majority of the campaign can be targeted with just a small random control group. Its size can be planned to be as small as possible, while still giving statistically reliable results – see Chapter 12 for further details.

Involvement of the stakeholders

The three stakeholders in data mining – business, analyst and IT – share the responsibilities for operating the process that has just been outlined. The typical main areas of involvement for each party are summarized in Table 2.1, which considers key tasks within each phase.

As Table 2.1 shows, the analyst is the lynchpin in the process and is involved in all six phases. By definition, the business takes the main role in the first phase that initiates the project and then returns to evaluate its success and take over ongoing operation. IT supports the process by

Table 2.1 Stakeholders in the data-mining process and their main areas of involvement

		Stakeholders		
Phase	**Task**	**Business**	**Analyst**	**IT**
Business Understanding	Determine business objectives	X		
	Assess situation	X	X	
	Determine data-mining goals	X	X	
	Planning		X	X
Data Understanding	Collect initial data	X	X	X
	Describe data		X	
	Explore data		X	
	Verify data quality		X	
Data Preparation	Data selection		X	X
	Data cleansing		X	X
	Constructing data		X	X
	Integrating data		X	X
	Formatting data		X	X
Modelling	Select modelling techniques	X	X	
	Generate test design		X	
	Build model		X	
	Assess model		X	
Evaluation	Evaluate results and review next steps	X	X	
Deployment	Plan deployment, monitoring and maintenance	X	X	X

providing the infrastructure and tools associated with the required data and the eventual deployment of the model and its scores.

The relationship between data mining, data science and statistics

The term data science was put forward by William Cleveland (2001) as an enlargement of the technical work required in the field of statistics. IT solutions are an important component in data science – New York University (2017) defines this discipline as follows:

> At its core, data science involves using automated methods to analyse massive amounts of data and to extract knowledge from them. With such automated methods turning up everywhere from genomics to high-energy physics, data science is helping to create new branches of science, and influencing areas of social science and the humanities.

Data science is often associated with technical approaches for analysing big data – sources such as the web, which require projects to go beyond traditional single processor solutions.

Davenport and Patil (2012) have labelled data scientist as the 'sexiest job of the 21st century'; they described data scientists as curious, self-directed and innovative – a rare combination of skills that are in great demand. It is hardly surprising that data miners, data analysts and others have been rebranded as data scientists in order to increase their status and marketability. The job title is not really important, however – a similar set of skills applied to data miners, business analysts and other such job titles before data science was invented.

Both data mining and data science depend on statistics – *the art of collecting and analysing sample data in order to obtain information about the population from which it was drawn*. The origins of statistics go back to the late 19th and early 20th centuries, before the advent of computers, for making inferences based on small samples drawn from larger populations. Statistical calculations could be undertaken because both the number of records and the number of attributes per record were much smaller than we generally see nowadays.

Nowadays, the entire customer population is likely to be accessible and huge numbers of variables are liable to be stored – for example, each customer's volumes and values of transactions by product, brand, channel and time period. Therefore, automated tools become necessary for data preparation and model development. In the early days of data mining, traditional statistical models were often applied to large-scale databases, requiring analysts to deploy those tools in appropriate ways. In data science, the focus starts to be on use of machine-learning algorithms that rely less on the underlying statistical distributions in the data.

Even though data scientists have access nowadays to vast amounts of information and big data can provide many of the answers, the principles of statistics should continue to underpin data collection and analysis to ensure the integrity of the results. Failure to consider statistical concepts can lead to flawed projects, irrespective of the impressive size of the big-data source.

For example, Lazer et al (2014) discuss traps in big-data analysis, citing problems in Google Flu Trends – Google's flu-tracking system – that made headlines in 2013. This was immediately followed by Tim Harford (2014) who widened the warnings to include other potential problems with analysing big data. Based on these articles, a couple of fundamental health warnings on big-data analysis are included in Chapter 3.

Conclusion

In this chapter, we have seen that:

- ✓ Data mining is a process of converting data into analytical models that will be of benefit to your business.

- ✓ The data preparation phase is likely to take 60–70 per cent of the project's work effort and is crucial to success. The predictive power of the data is more important than the choice of modelling technique.

- ✓ No matter how good the results appear, it is essential to carry out a live test on a separate period, campaign or part of your business, and measure whether the model delivers real business value.

- ✓ Building and deploying models are separate phases in the data-mining process. Building takes place once, whereas deployment is repeated many times. Therefore start planning your deployment from the outset.

- ✓ Data science involves using automated methods to manage massive databases, and is often applied to analysing big data with the aid of technical solutions. It is nonetheless important to maintain a watchful eye on statistical concepts, rather than assume that data science is a substitute for traditional data collection and analysis.

- ✓ A successful project may not require a model. By bringing your data together in an innovative way, you may unlock a new insight that provides sufficient business value. If possible, keep the project simple rather than overcomplicating with an unnecessary model.

Managing the   03
data for predictive
analytics

Introduction

The benefits of predictive analytics to your business will depend crucially on the data that you have available on your customers – the data that can be leveraged is more important than choosing a highly sophisticated modelling technique. Therefore, your analyst will want to extract maximum value from your data, which implies identifying the types and sources of information that are likely to be beneficial, developing a good understanding of their content and creating a useful set of variables.

The main aim of this chapter is to consider data requirements:

- To identify the data sources that will be most useful for predictive analytics and where you are likely to find them.

- To discuss the different types of data that you are likely to encounter.

- To introduce the data audit as a tool for exploring the quality of your data.

- To set out the main data preparation steps involved in creating your analytic dataset for a data-mining project.

The roles of data

As we saw in Chapter 2, customer data can be used in many ways – in fact, playing up to three separate roles in the analytical process. We term these roles *development*, *deployment* and *description*; they have differing information requirements, as we shall see. These roles are illustrated in Figure 3.1 and are discussed below.

Figure 3.1   The roles of data in predictive analytics

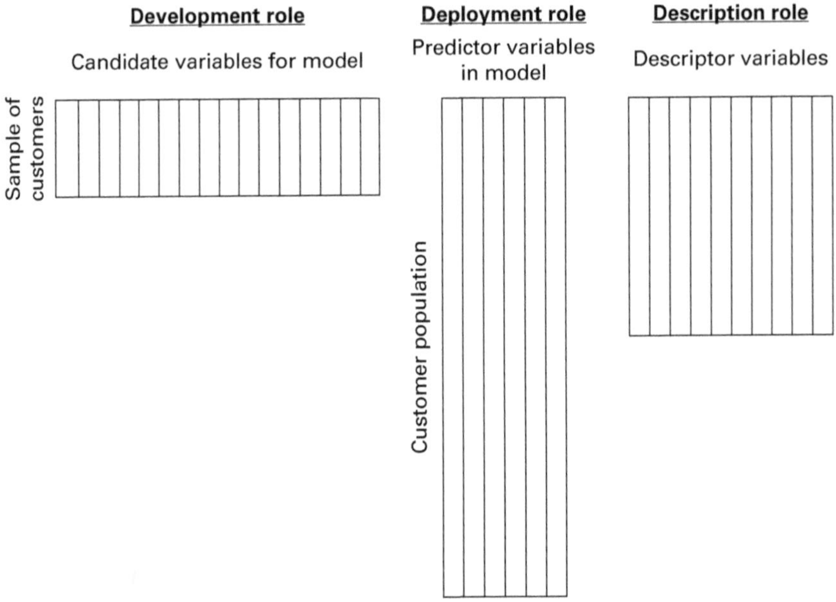

Development role

During the modelling phase in data mining, a large number of attributes – also known as fields or variables – in your data are examined and the most predictive are used to build an analytical model. It is essential that these fields are present and consistently coded throughout your customer base. For large companies with millions of customers, a representative sample will usually be selected for this development role. At the same time, there may be hundreds or even thousands of variables stored for each customer, therefore the development dataset is said to be 'short and fat' – 'short' because it will contain a relatively small number of customers, and 'fat' because it will include all available variables.

Deployment role

Once the model has been built and evaluated, in order to deploy it across your customer base the set of predictor variables that were used in the model will be required for every customer to be scored. Again, the variables will need to be present and consistently coded, in the same way as for the development role, across your customer base. For this purpose, the deployment dataset is 'tall and thin' – 'tall' because it will contain records for all of your customers, and 'thin' because the number of predictor variables used in the model is likely to be relatively small.

Description role

The third role is to use data to profile the customers that the model has assigned to each score band or segment, in order to build up your understanding, make sure that the segments make intuitive business sense, and plan how you will market to them.

This segment description process is essential when developing a customer segmentation system, and is used to create 'pen portrait' descriptions and meaningful names for the segments. The data can come from sample surveys as well as from your customer database – because in this case the information is being used solely for descriptive purposes.

Depending on the source of this descriptive dataset, it may be 'short' or 'tall' and 'fat' or 'thin'. For example, it could be a satisfaction survey that asked a wide range of questions for a small sample of customers. Alternatively, it might be a dataset with a few variables describing internet usage for a high proportion of customers.

The useful data for predictive analytics

Three broad types of data generally prove to be most useful for the above roles – demographics, behaviours, and attitudes and lifestyles.

Demographics

By 'demographics' we mean characteristics of customers such as age, gender and marital status, together with relationship attributes such as recruitment method and channel. Demographics are particularly important in defining which products are likely to be of potential interest to each customer – for example, needs for financial services products such as mortgages, savings, investments and pensions depend on factors such as life stage – the combination of age, marital status, presence of children, and working status. Some demographics can also be strong predictors – for example, household income is an indicator of 'ability to purchase', and so is helpful in predicting uptake in many markets. And many outcomes depend on age – including, for example, interest in technology products and online social media.

Demographics tend to be 'slow moving' – the values for each customer are likely to be unchanged from one month to the next. When there is a change, then it is liable to be important, since other things are likely to be changing at the same time. For example, if the customer moves home, then they will suddenly need numerous different products and services, depending on whether they have moved to a brand new dwelling or to an existing property. So they may need to purchase home-improvement products, furniture, garden equipment and so on, and possibly obtain finance for these items. Therefore, it can be useful to identify changes in circumstances when these occur, and utilize them to trigger follow-up marketing activity.

Behaviours

'Behaviours' imply data on what customers do – this covers a very wide area and it generates the largest number of data items – for example on purchase transactions and product usage. Online behaviour is of increasing interest, eg web browsing and use of social media such as Facebook and Twitter.

As we all know, customer activity can alter quickly in response to new needs and life changes, therefore behavioural data can sometimes be more predictive than demographics. Also, by tracking behaviour patterns you can sometimes get a first indication of other changes. For example, if the customer has bought a new mobile phone on a different network, then there will be a sharp reduction in calls made on their previous network. Similarly, if a new supermarket opens in a town, then this will have an obvious impact on levels and values of transactions with existing stores. At a more subtle level, even a change to a mobile user's size of calling circle (the number of other phone numbers called) can be indicative of a more significant event.

For this reason, behavioural data are ideally captured for each customer as events occur, eg call detail records (CDRs) for mobile phones and individual transactions by retailers. For use in analytical models, the behaviours are regularly aggregated into, say, monthly summaries of activity levels.

Behavioural variables are ideal for predictive analytics, as they should be accurate and available for all customers of that product or service. Their major drawback is that they tell us 'what the customer is doing' but not 'why they are doing it' – the causes often have to be discovered by other methods, including market research.

Attitudes and lifestyles

Attitudes focus on the beliefs, motivations and values that people hold, while lifestyles are generally concerned with their hobbies and interests. An understanding of customer attitudes and lifestyles can help in planning marketing communications, and the style and tone of messages that are likely to work best.

However, attitude data usually have to be captured specially, using sample surveys, and so will not be available for the entire customer population.

Therefore these data are most useful for describing segments and for planning how to market to them, rather than for developing and deploying analytical models.

Lifestyle data are typically collected by commercial lifestyle surveys used primarily for direct marketing. Their applications to segmentation projects are discussed towards the end of Chapter 8.

As we have started to see above, the data items that are captured and stored will vary from sector to sector, particularly in terms of behavioural data. Table 3.1 gives examples of behaviour data that would be typically

Table 3.1 Examples of behavioural data used in different sectors

TYPICAL VARIABLES HELD AT CUSTOMER LEVEL		
Retailer[a]	**Mobile phone operator**	**Retail bank**
Transactions (baskets) Date of last transaction Value of transactions Number of transactions – by day/time – by channel (store/ online/telephone) **Purchases** Number of items purchased – by product groups Amount paid – by product groups – by method of payment Discount amount Loyalty points earned/ redeemed	**Calling behaviour** Numbers and durations of calls by type (voice/ SMS/MMS) – by outbound/inbound – by on-net/off-net[b] – by destination type (mobile/fixed line/ international/roaming) – by source type (mobile/fixed line/ international/roaming) Usage by type by outbound/inbound – by day (weekday/ weekend) – by time of day **Revenue** – by outbound/inbound **Calling circle**[c] – by outbound/inbound – by on-net/off-net **Data** Data usage, app usage, websites visited	**Products held** – counts by product types – balances by product types **Transactions** – by product types – numbers and value by types of transactions – and split by channels (branch/ATM/online/ telephone) – numbers and values **Credit** Credit scores, days overdrawn Delinquency indicators

Notes
[a] Assumes that retailer operates a loyalty card, examples are for loyalty card holders.
[b] On-net is within the company's network, off-net is outside the company's network.
[c] Calling circle is the number of other phone numbers contacted.

held for each customer for companies in three highly 'information-rich' sectors – retailer, mobile phone operator and retail bank.

Data sources that can be leveraged

Internal data

The most useful source of data, for most companies, will be their internal systems that capture and store the information required for operational purposes. These systems will provide primarily behavioural data, covering all the different aspects of the company's relationship with its customers. Applicable sources will depend on the industry sector – some examples are:

- Sources of behavioural data, eg electronic point of sale (EPOS) system for retailers; transaction systems for retail banks; call detail records for phone companies.
- Loyalty system – for retailers that operate them, loyalty cards enable customer transactions to be linked together over time, to build a more complete picture of each customer's purchasing.
- Customer demographics and products purchased.
- Web-log data for your company's website.
- E-commerce data for online purchasing.
- Call-centre data for interactions with your customers via the call centre.
- Direct marketing campaigns data.
- Customer surveys – stored responses to survey questionnaires.
- Social media tracking/listening system.
- Complaints handling system.

Companies that have been working with predictive analytics for some time, or are advanced in data-driven marketing, will have already identified and extracted their most useful sources. They are likely to have built a central repository, such as a marketing database, data mart or data warehouse, for fast access to their most widely used data.

If your company is at the early stages of using predictive analytics, then it is more likely that you will need to access information from source systems, with the help of your IT colleagues, and put together your own set of customer data – according to the business problems that you are planning to tackle.

Not all companies have data on their ultimate customers, for example manufacturers of consumer products know their shipments to retailers, but not the purchases made by consumers. For businesses in this position, external information will be the priority – including the sources listed below.

External data

Your internal data will hopefully paint a detailed picture of your customers, their purchase histories and interactions with your company. Where this picture will be incomplete lies in what they do outside your company, for example:

- Do your customers also purchase products from your competitors? If so, how much of their total spending goes to your company – this key metric is known as share of wallet – and how much goes elsewhere?
- Do your customers have needs for other products and services that your company could offer?
- What are their circumstances, and how are their needs likely to change over time?
- How do their demographics and circumstances affect the business they give to your company?

These kinds of questions may only be addressed with external sources – lists and data held by third-party suppliers, which can be purchased or licensed for use by your company. Commonly available sources include:

- Demographics and lifestyle data – large-scale databases containing demographic attributes, leisure pursuits, interests, and other information collected from large lifestyle surveys.
- Geodemographics systems – classifications that describe the types of people living in every neighbourhood of the country. Leventhal (2016) explains how geodemographic classification systems are constructed and provides a guide to applying geodemographics in a variety of sectors.
- Census data – small-area statistics from the census of population, describing the demographics of people living in each area.
- Market research surveys – responses to market research (MR) questionnaires, conducted on a confidential basis by MR agencies.
- Social media monitoring/listening – including Facebook and Twitter.

Key point

Keep in mind the difference between actual and modelled data

Some of the available external sources include *modelled* data – that is predicted data for each individual, obtained by the supplier using their own models. Examples could include variables on financial holdings such as likelihood to hold loans, savings, investments and so on.

Modelled data are the supplier's best estimates for those variables; however, as with any model, they will not always be correct. Therefore keep in mind that *actual* data have been captured from the individual and so should be true (when collected) while modelled data will not be as accurate.

For companies such as manufacturers, who hold little information on the end users of their products, the analytics challenge is to find useful business questions that will enable them to gain value from external data. For example, this could be to target their products on a geographical basis, or to use social media analysis to increase the effectiveness of their messaging.

Key point

Testing external data

A cost is usually associated with obtaining external data, therefore potential users are well advised to test any source before deciding to acquire it. Suppliers are normally willing to provide sample extracts free of charge; the 'acid test' should be: does the incremental benefit of the dataset justify its cost?

Bringing in big data

Over the past few years, the volumes of data generated by the internet have been increasing at a massive rate – this is the most significant example of big data. Big data is a generic term for datasets whose size exceeds the capacity of typical computer systems and therefore very different technical solutions are required in order to access, manage and analyse these sources. Looking beyond the internet, big data are continuously being generated in every industry where sensors, embedded microprocessors and other devices are being used to monitor behaviour. Some instances of online and offline sources of big data are given in Table 3.2, together with examples of their business applications. Bill Franks (2012) discusses the many opportunities that advanced analytics of big data can bring.

Data, such as web logs for online searches, is highly specific to each consumer in terms of the product search being conducted at a point in time. Therefore, this data can provide a powerful means of displaying adverts for the same product back to that consumer.

Table 3.2 Examples of big-data sources and their business applications

Source	Example application
Utility company smart reader readings	Network management; control of consumer consumption
Telematics – capturing vehicle journey information	Understanding driver risk; setting insurance premiums
Geolocated Twitter data	Measuring mobility
Online product searches and browsing	Targeting online advertising
Online abandoned shopping baskets	Targeting offers to complete purchases
Postings on social media websites	Early identification of product problems/ faults
Text data from consumer comments	Measuring consumer sentiment about a company or product
Text data from insurance claims	Insurance fraud detection
Prices on supermarket web sites	Collecting prices for calculating consumer price indices
Time and location data from mobile phones	Location-based targeting
RFID[a] data in retail and manufacturing	Tracking items through the retail supply chain; stock control
Social network data in mobile phone industry	Identifying influential customers with high numbers of connections
Sensor data in engines and equipment	Fault diagnosis and correction

[a] Radio frequency identification data.

As business questions become more sophisticated, the online search data (in this example) will need to be merged with other sources, such as those discussed in this chapter, in order to create the required analytical solutions. For example, big data could identify the customer's interest in a product, internal sources could quantify their ability to purchase, and geodemographics could describe their circumstances. Then a more tailored offer could be made to the prospective buyer. This will require an integration of big-data systems with conventional database technology, which the solution providers are well placed to provide.

A common theme with big data is that a source collected for one reason may often also be used for other completely different purposes. For example, supermarket websites include prices for packaged groceries, so that consumers can make price comparisons and shop online. The same prices are being scraped from the websites of Sainsbury's, Tesco and Waitrose, by the Office for National Statistics (ONS), as input to their calculation of consumer price indices – see Breton et al (2016).

The reuse of any data for a different purpose always needs to be undertaken with particular care, taking possibilities such as measurement errors and population biases into consideration. This concern applies no less to big data – just because the dataset is vast does not necessarily mean that it will be accurate – and the same caveat goes for online sources. The following 'health warnings' go into further detail.

Key point

Some 'health warnings' on big data

Big data can be a valuable resource; however, as with any powerful tool, it needs to be handled with care. In particular, it should not be assumed that an impressive big-data source will be able to replace a small statistically designed sample. Statistical considerations continue to apply with big data – even more so, since there is vastly more data that could potentially be unrepresentative and misleading.

One set of 'health warnings' come down to the inherent bias in any dataset that has been generated by the internet. For example, the worldwide number of Facebook accounts was 2 billion as at April 2017 (see Statista, 2017). While this number is vast, it would be wrong to imagine that the Facebook user base is representative of the world population. Think about all the people who are not on Facebook – how likely are they to have different demographics and attitudes from those held by Facebook users? Mellon and Prosser (2016) examined this question in the context of Twitter and Facebook users in the UK, by comparing their profiles against a representative national survey. They found that users of both platforms are likely to be younger and better educated than non-users. They are also likely to have differing political attitudes, for example users are more likely to support the Labour Party. Therefore, a pre-election opinion poll conducted on Facebook would need to allow for this difference, in any predictions of the election outcome. This is one reason why pollsters do not rely on Facebook or any social media sources to carry out their surveys. They know that a properly conducted sample survey on 1,000 voters will be more accurate than an uncontrolled internet poll of 1 million or even 2 billion people who use social media.

Another batch of warnings are associated with performing large numbers of comparisons within big data. This activity is sometimes known as '*data trawling*' – searching all relationships in a big dataset, looking for significant correlations. An example occurs in financial markets and concerns the problem of predicting future prices of assets such as stocks, bonds, futures and options. If the analyst simply trawled through all assets, looking for those showing significantly good price predictions last year, they are liable to find large numbers of strong performers. However, look at them again this year, and the results are likely to have changed – either because the historic relationship was never real, or circumstances have changed. Just searching for significant changes, without understanding their underlying causes, is insufficient to generate useful knowledge.

Having the right data

No matter how many data items are available and how well they describe your customer base, it is essential to have the *right* data – in the sense of example cases that are representative of all the possible outcomes that your model will be designed to predict.

For example, in order to build a cross-sell model to identify which customers are likely to purchase a particular product, examples of known purchasers and non-purchasers will be required – as illustrated in Figure 1.1. This is essential in order to identify characteristics that differ between the two groups and create a scorecard based on these characteristics.

Likewise, if you need to predict which customers are likely to leave you (sometimes known as a churn or attrition model), examples of previous leavers and stayers will be required. Without direction, it is possible that an efficient IT department might decide to delete leavers from its system, in the misguided belief that non-customers are no longer of value to the company. However, this would make it impossible to build a churn model to target future leavers – therefore, it is far safer to keep all leavers on the system until some years have elapsed.

Types of data – structured and unstructured

Structured data

Analytical modelling requires that the dataset is held in a structured form, which means that each attribute or measurement has a fixed type and format. This is the usual way in which data are formatted in spreadsheets and databases.

The ways in which data can be analysed depend on the data type of each item – does the item represent a quantitative value such as customer age, number or value of transactions? Or does it represent a categorical attribute such as gender, region or occupation code? The most commonly used data types are:

- **Numeric quantitative values** such as counts, monetary amounts, ages and durations – the values may be whole integers (eg number of products purchased) or may be decimal numbers (eg exact expenditure or duration).
- **Categorical values** such as gender, social class and region codes – the categories are represented by letters (eg M or F for gender) and/or numbers (eg 0 to 9 for region codes), and a list of possible values exists for all the categories.
- **Date values** such as customer date of birth, date of first purchase and of most recent purchase. Sometimes date and time are required, especially for short-term targeting during, for example, web journeys.

Unstructured data

It has been estimated that the majority of data held by companies is actually unstructured – data with no fixed format, which can vary from record to record in terms of content. Unstructured data include *text* such as documents, customer comments, e-mails, chatbot interactions and web logs – all of which have no defined format and are of variable length. Unstructured data cannot be directly input into analytical modelling; however, there are approaches for analysing unstructured text, extracting meanings and deriving structured information from it – see, for example, Struhl (2015).

Unstructured data also include non-textual information such as images, audio and video. These are sometimes stored as binary large objects (BLOBs) – examples of analyses that can extract information from BLOBs are given by what-when-how (2016).

Data quality checks – the data audit

An understanding of the quality of your data is an essential prerequisite for predictive analytics. A wide-ranging audit of quality is recommended, before starting to rely on your data to predict customer behaviour. And, similarly, data audits should be conducted for new sources and feeds as they become available.

A **data audit** is a collection of analyses to examine the attributes in a dataset. It usefully consists of the four descriptive analyses shown in Figure 3.2, which are applied in combination, according to the data type of each item. Analyses (a) to (c) are used for numeric data while (d) is employed primarily for categorical data.

The audit should start with a review of documentation and metadata, in order to establish the definitions, units and formats used for the data attributes, any changes in these over time, and any known issues. You are then ready to carry out the four analyses, which are discussed in turn below and illustrated in Figure 3.2.

Note that the formats used for these analyses differ slightly from one software tool to the next; however, the same key metrics are generally provided. These are statistical measures for summarizing data – see an introductory statistics text for further explanation, such as Townend (2002) or Graham (2017):

a The **values analysis** measures whether each variable is well populated with values, and shows how many values are zero, positive or negative. If all or most of the values are missing or null, then the values analysis will identify this. Figure 3.2a gives an example values analysis for customer income, indicating that incomes are present for all cases, but are zero for a small proportion.

Figure 3.2 Example data audit analyses

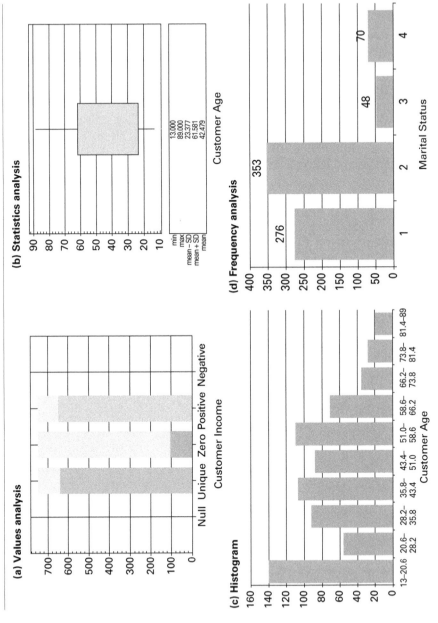

(a) Values analysis

(b) Statistics analysis

min	13.000
max	89.000
mean – SD	23.377
mean + SD	61.581
mean	42.479

Customer Age

(c) Histogram

Customer Age

(d) Frequency analysis

Marital Status

b The **statistics analysis** presents key measures such as the minimum, maximum, mean and standard deviation for each variable, and will identify the range of values present; in some cases, the analysis will also indicate whether the dataset contains any outliers or extreme values. Figure 3.2b shows an example analysis on customer age; in this example, the vertical line indicates the range of customer age values in the dataset, from 13 to 89. The shaded box at the centre of the chart represents the range given by the mean, plus or minus the standard deviation (SD): typically, the majority of values should fall within this range.

c The **histogram** splits the values taken by each variable into ranges or bins, and displays the number of cases falling into each bin. Figure 3.2c shows an example histogram for customer age, exploring further the data analysed in the statistics analysis above. We see a distribution of age values that could not have been inferred from the statistics analysis alone. A large number of cases belong to the first age range (13–20.6); following this range, the age distribution follows a more usual pattern – starting small, building up to peaks in the middle age groups, and then decreasing for higher age groups.

d The **frequency analysis** (Figure 3.2d) lists all the values taken by the selected data attribute, and counts the number of cases that have each value. It can be useful for detecting possible issues such as too many different values or codes being present, or values that would be expected are missing from the dataset. The example in Figure 3.2d shows a frequency analysis for marital status, revealing that there are four possible categories, with the majority of customers having marital status codes 1 or 2. The initial documentation review would have identified the meanings of the four codes.

The data audit is an excellent starting point for exploring a data source, and invariably leads to further analysis that drills down to examine issues with the data. Any findings that appear to be incorrect or that fail to accord with expectations should be investigated in more detail, to check whether they are due to errors or shortcomings in the data. If any problems are found, these should be considered further and corrected as appropriate.

Now that we have reviewed the importance of data for predictive analytics and the kinds of data that are likely to be involved, the second half of this chapter discusses the data preparation processes that convert this data into a useful form for analysis and modelling.

Data preparation

The data preparation phase starts with the data sources that have been selected for detailed analysis, and converts them into a useful format. In this section, we review the series of tasks undertaken as part of this process.

Data preparation has been estimated to take around 60–70 per cent of the effort in a data-mining project. A further surprising fact is that this level of effort still applies even if the data already resides in a well-managed database – if the sources have to be extracted from different systems, or if errors need to be rectified before use, then the work effort will be even greater. And inclusion of historical data from archives also adds to the work involved.

The analytic dataset

The main purpose of data preparation is to define and create the analytic dataset (ADS) that will be used for the modelling and evaluation phases of your project. Modelling software tools tend to read data in a particular format known as a data matrix – in which each row of data represents a case (eg a customer) and the columns correspond to data attributes, which are known as variables.

An example data matrix layout is shown in Figure 3.3 for an ADS containing 2,000 cases. This has been designed for building a model to predict a binary (0 or 1) variable Y, which represents a 'yes' or 'no' outcome, such as 'purchased or not purchased'. As Y is the outcome that the model will be designed to predict, it is often known as the target variable. In statistics, it is also known as the dependent variable.

The ADS also contains variables A, B, C and so on, through to X. These are other attributes known for each customer, from which the model will be created. They are the potential predictor variables that will be included in the model to predict the target variable. The values in these columns are not shown in Figure 3.3; however, they are likely to contain numeric data, character codes and date or time fields. Also, there is an identifier code, in case the dataset needs to be linked to other sources.

The analytic dataset layout may appear simple and straightforward; however, a large number of processing tasks may be required to convert the data into this format and transform the variables to be ready for analysis. The following activities are likely to be carried out, starting with designing the ADS.

Figure 3.3   Example data matrix layout

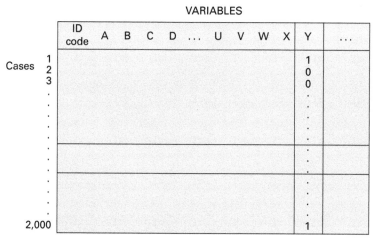

VARIABLES

Notes
1. Target variable is Y, taking values 0 or 1.
2. Candidate predictors are A, B, C ... X.
3. First column contains identifier code for linking
   to other data.

Design ADS

The combined understanding of the business problem and available data should be jointly applied in order to define the analytic dataset. As the ADS will drive the modelling and evaluate the outcome, careful planning should go into its design, which will include the following elements:

- Precise definition of the units on which the ADS and the model will be based. While we generally refer to customers, the actual units could, for example, be accounts, subscribers or shopping baskets.

- Definition of the model universe – the population on which the model will be based – identifying any specific subsets to be excluded, for example inactive and unmarketable customers, VIPs and company staff. The model universe generally corresponds to the customer base that is eligible to receive your marketing communications.

- Specification for selecting the cases to be included in the ADS, by sampling from the model universe.

- The time period(s) on which the data items will be based – timelines should be carefully planned for the development and deployment of the model. These timelines are important, as they determine the data that will be required when constructing the ADS. The timelines used in predictive models are discussed in Chapter 6.

- If the model is predictive – definition of the target variable (the outcome to be predicted) and the potential predictor variables (that may be used in the model). It is important that the predictor and target variables are based upon separate observation and outcome periods, respectively – see Chapter 6 for a discussion of the issues.

- If the model is descriptive (eg segmentation) – definition of the segmentation criteria (used to create segments) and segment descriptors (used to describe segments).

- Specifications for restructuring and merging together data sources – if some of the sources are held at a more disaggregated level, eg individual transactions, and need to be aggregated up to customer level.

- Specifications of derived variables to be created from the existing data. For example, the dataset may include a field containing the customer's date of birth; however, it may be more useful to derive customer age (in years). Similarly, from 'date of first purchase', the more useful variable 'length of relationship' may be derived.

- Requirements for handling cases containing missing or null values.

Build ADS

By 'build ADS' we mean all data-processing tasks such as aggregation, restructuring and merging datasets, in order to create a file that follows the format of the data matrix layout shown in Figure 3.3. The actual steps will vary from company to company and model to model, depending upon how data are stored in your company's IT systems and the business objective of the current project. Examples of operations undertaken in this stage include:

- Aggregate by – summarizes records based on a key field such as customer identifier, for example counting numbers of products held by each customer. For some projects, the data may need to be aggregated by time period, or by product, or by channel, and so on.

- Merge or join – matches records from different sources to produce one record per customer containing all variables.

- Insert or append – combine or concatenate data sources that have the same structure but contain different records, eg transactions from online and offline systems.

- Restructure or pivot – aggregate data by values of a particular attribute, generating multiple variables for that attribute, eg summarize purchases by channel to obtain numbers and values of products that the customer has bought via each channel.

Clean and transform data

Various cleaning and transformation operations are applied to the variables in the ADS, according to their types and likely roles in the model. Their purpose is to remove any defects that were identified when checking the data quality and convert the data into a suitable format for analytical modelling. These tasks typically include:

- Amend categorical variables that contain incorrect values: if a frequency analysis (described above) reveals errors in the values of a categorical variable, then these should be examined and rectified. For example, a common problem with title variables, containing text such as 'MR', 'MRS' and so on, is that data entry may be inconsistent over time – producing multiple values such as 'MR', 'Mr', 'MRS', 'Mrs' etc. This situation should be addressed by recoding all versions of each title to one value.

- Recode categorical variables that contain too many values: sometimes, a categorical variable will contain too many values for meaningful analysis – typical examples could be SKU (stock-keeping unit) product codes, geodemographic codes and postcodes. One solution is to group the values into a smaller number of codes, eg high-level product types and geodemographic groups. Other options, for handling postcodes, may be either to aggregate them to regions, or replace them with some measure of small area characteristics, such as geodemographic variables.

- Identify variables that contain missing values, decide whether/how to correct: missing values may occur for different reasons, and unfortunately some modelling tools will exclude cases for which the data are incomplete. Therefore the presence of missing values should be considered and resolved. Some common ways of handling them are as follows:

  - If missing values occur in a small proportion of cases, then they could be replaced by estimates such as an average value for that variable – either overall or by customer type. This approach could be improved on by building a separate model to estimate missing values, if the variable is important and justifies the additional effort required.

- Sometimes, missing values imply that the customer does not possess that attribute – in which case, missing values for that variable may be replaced by zeros. However, in this situation and in the previous case, it may be prudent to create a flag variable to indicate that the value had originally been missing.

- Sometimes, 'missing' indicates that the customer has decided not to supply information, eg to a survey question, and it can make sense to retain this nuance – by recoding each missing value to a different category.

- Where the majority of values are missing, it can be sensible to recode the variable into two values, representing 'value present' or 'value missing'.

- Identify cases containing outliers and decide how to handle – outliers are abnormally high (or low) values for a variable – if not removed, they could distort or bias the modelling results. Outliers may be due to extreme behaviours or caused by data capture problems; either way, the best option may be to discard those cases from the analysis. Another option is to retain the cases but to bin the variable into groups, so that outliers fall into the top (or bottom) bin, but do not distort the analysis.

- Define the target variable – if the model is predictive, the target variable should be inspected more closely, starting from the data quality analyses described above. It may sometimes be necessary to transform or recode the target variable into a suitable format for model development.

- For a binary target variable (eg purchase/non-purchase), just two values should be present in the data, corresponding to the two outcomes. The values may need to be recoded, because some modelling tools require that the target variable is numeric, taking values of 1 (for purchase, say) or 0 (for non-purchase).

- If the target variable is numeric, eg order amount, first check whether there are any extreme purchases and discard cases containing those outliers. The histogram of values should also be examined – if the distribution is highly skewed, then it may be desirable to apply a mathematical transformation such as the logarithm, so that the transformed variable follows a more normal (bell-shaped) distribution. The model would be built using the transformed target, and predicted values obtained by applying a reverse transformation at the end such as the exponential function, in this case.

- Group or bin numeric variables – numeric variables may also need to be recoded, depending on the objectives for the model and whether outliers are present in the data. Two common approaches are:
  - Numeric variables may be binned into ranges manually defined by the analyst, following initial exploration of the data.
  - Numeric variables may be binned into, say, deciles (10 per cent groups) – ranges automatically defined to assign an equal number of cases in each bin.

- If a numeric variable is binned then care needs to be taken to freeze the bin ranges, as they must align with the data used for validating and deploying the model.

- Derive variables that may be useful in the model – with the help of expert knowledge, new variables may be derived that could help to predict the target outcome. Examples of derivable variables include:
  - ratios of existing variables, eg measuring proportion of credit limit used, or share of transactions made through a particular channel;
  - trends over time, in order to measure whether customer activity is increasing or declining;
  - variability over time, as a measure of stability or volatility.

Key point

Derived variables are a way to explore alternative ideas or hypotheses on the behaviours that may be driving the outcome being predicted. They are an essential part of the analytical process, so that the analyst extracts maximum explanatory power from the data. If an important derived variable gets missed early on, it can still be included by means of further data preparation – prior to the point of determining the final model.

Derived variables may include the outputs of other models that have been deployed on the same customers. For example, in financial services, credit scores could be useful derived variables.

Balancing the sample

For some predictive models, the outcome groups may be highly unbalanced. For example, suppose that your organization requires a model to identify a rare kind of fraud that is only carried out by 0.5 per cent of customers. The rarity of the fraudulent group may mean that the modelling tool has insufficient examples from which to identify a useful set of variables that discriminate between fraudulent and non-fraudulent cases. In this situation, it may be beneficial to boost the incidence of fraudulent examples in the dataset, and reduce the proportion of non-fraudulent, by resampling the data.

This can be achieved by selecting cases for the model development sample at different rates from the two outcome groups, fraudulent and non–fraudulent, in order to produce equal numbers of these groups in the sample (or get closer to equal-sized groups).

Alternatively, if the modelling tool allows cases to be assigned weighting factors, the importance of non-fraudulent cases could be down-weighted in comparison with fraudulent cases. A weighting factor would be calculated for each group in the sample, so that the total weight across fraudulent cases equals the total weight across non-fraudulent cases.

Conclusion

In this chapter, we have seen that:

✔ The most valuable data for predictive analytics will be the information you hold on your past, present and future customers.

✔ External sources are essential to fill in the gaps and for companies such as manufacturers, which do not hold consumer data.

✔ The main deliverable from the data preparation phase is an analytic dataset that will drive your model development. This phase typically takes 60–70 per cent of the work effort in a data-mining project.

✔ It is essential to maximize the potentially useful information in the analytic dataset, by thorough data preparation – including thoughtful creation of derived variables – in order to drive maximum performance from your model.

The analytical   04
modelling toolkit

Introduction

The analytical modelling toolkit is a collection of predictive and descriptive techniques, implemented in a host of software solutions that are designed to meet the needs of different types of users. This chapter discusses how these techniques work – their concepts and principles, and the kinds of problems to which they are best suited.

The main aims of this chapter are to:

- Overview the most widely used predictive and descriptive modelling techniques and the business problems for which they are best suited.

- Demonstrate, by means of a case study, how different predictive approaches may be compared.

- Introduce the Bayesian approach for updating your beliefs about an outcome.

- Discuss which is the right technique to choose and situations where a combination of techniques may be the best way forward.

Before any of these techniques should be applied to your data, it is important to have carried out the data preparation tasks described in Chapter 3 and created a 'clean' analytic dataset ready for model building. Modelling techniques are generally sensitive to missing values and outliers, and so any such issues need to be resolved first. Likewise, derived variables should have been included by this stage, although it is always possible to create new or refined variables suggested from your analysis.

Types of techniques

The analytical modelling toolkit has two main compartments – one containing predictive models where there is a target variable that needs to be

Table 4.1 Examples of widely used analytical modelling techniques

Predictive models	Descriptive models
Decision tree analysis	Factor analysis and principal components analysis
	Cluster analysis
Regression analysis	Latent class analysis
Supervised neural network	Self-organizing map
	Association analysis

predicted from other data, and the other comprising descriptive techniques for identifying patterns or segments. Our main focus will be on methods that are widely used and have proven benefits, rather than on evolving technologies. Our toolkit contents list, shown in Table 4.1, is split into predictive descriptive approaches and forms the agenda for the two sections that follow.

In the next section, we focus on widely used predictive methods. A vast body of textbooks and documentation are available covering detailed methodology and application – sources of further information are included below.

Widely used predictive models

Decision tree analysis

Decision tree analysis is usually a good start point when building a predictive model, and may also be the end point for many users – particularly where the priorities are clarity and ease of deployment.

The decision tree approach

Decision trees are usually employed for situations where the target variable has two possible outcomes, such as 'purchase' and 'non-purchase' or 'good risk' and 'bad risk', although some tree techniques are designed to handle multiple outcomes and quantitative target variables.

The approach is illustrated in Figure 4.1, for a model to predict customer credit rating – 'good' or 'bad'. The top box represents a sample of customers; as we see, half of them are 'good' and half are 'bad'.

The decision tree software examines each of the available predictors in turn, to see the good/bad proportions that would result if the sample were

split into subsets based on that variable. The most useful splitter is identified that produces the greatest differences in good/bad proportions between
subsets. In this example, that split variable is income, because a three-way
split by income produces 'good' proportions of 70 per cent, 45 per cent
and 40 per cent for the high-, medium- and low-income groups respectively.
Therefore, at step 1, the dataset is split on income.

The process is repeated starting from each subset produced by step 1,
searching the remaining variables for the most useful discriminator on
good/bad credit rating. For example, within the medium-income subset, the
best discriminator is found to be age of customer – older versus younger.
Therefore, at step 2 this subset is split by age. Among medium-income older
customers, the 'good' proportion is now 60 per cent.

No further splits are shown in Figure 4.1, however the process continues from each subset in the decision tree, and only stops when no further
discriminatory variables are found or the number of sample cases becomes
too small to warrant further splitting.

Decision tree analysis has a jargon of its own – each subset shown as a
box in the tree is known as a *node* and each *end node* is sometimes termed
a *leaf*. Having created the decision tree, in this example, it may be applied
to predict the credit rating for a new customer. Suppose, for simplicity, that
Figure 4.1 shows the final tree that was built, ie no further splits were made.
The income and age of the new customer are 'presented' to the tree in order
to classify them. For example, if their income is high, then leaf 1 would

Figure 4.1   The decision tree approach – hypothetical example

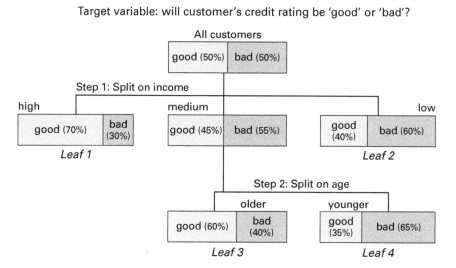

classify them as 'good' with 70 per cent probability. Similarly, if they are low income, leaf 2 would classify them as 'bad'. If their income is medium, then their age would also be used – if older, then leaf 3 would classify them as 'good'; if younger, leaf 4 would classify them as 'bad'.

Key point

The 50/50 split between 'good' and 'bad' customers, in the above example, was not chosen by accident. If the aim of the decision tree is to predict an outcome ('good' or 'bad') for each customer, then having equal-sized groups means that the tree will not be biased to one outcome or the other. If the groups were represented in their true proportions, eg 99 per cent 'good', 1 per cent 'bad', then every leaf would predict 'good' and so the tree would be of no use in identifying likely 'bad' customers.

On the other hand, if the objective of the tree were to predict the *probability* of a customer being 'good', or the *risk* of being 'bad', then equal-sized groups would not be required.

Types of decision trees

There are two main decision tree approaches:

- Rule induction trees come from the world of machine learning, and include various algorithms that decide in different ways which nodes to split. Some methods draw on information theory, a branch of computer science using approaches such as entropy reduction or information gain, to select which node to split into less disorganized subsets. Examples include the C4.5 and C5.0 programs developed by Ross Quinlan (1993, 2015). Another splitting criterion, known as Gini, uses a simple measure of diversity within each node. Other approaches, CART (classification and regression tree) and QUEST (quick, unbiased and efficient statistical tree), have been devised to create trees for quantitative target variables – see Breiman et al (1984). Rule induction methods tend to include a pruning stage, in order to cut the tree back, as the initial tree is liable to contain too many nodes and leafs.

- CHAID (chi square automatic interaction detector) carries out chi square tests, from the world of statistics, to select its splits. The splitting process will automatically stop when no further splits are significant, therefore this approach does not require a tree-pruning stage. CHAID is available in a number of software packages and is widely used in database analysis and market research, due to its automatic operation and its statistical underpinnings.

Strengths of decision trees

Decision tree is the best predictive technique for new users and is also the most straightforward to implement. Customers may be classified to the leafs in the tree by applying sets of rules corresponding to the various end nodes. For instance, in the example of Figure 4.1, four rules would be required, such as: 'If income = medium and age = older, then Leaf = 3', and so on.

Weaknesses of decision trees

A decision tree model is likely to be less discriminatory than other techniques, in which contributions of predictor variables are weighted according to their importance. Decision tree models tend to work best when the development sample is quite large – ideally, greater than 10,000 cases – as repeated splitting can result in small sample sizes deeper in the tree. Finally, validation of the model is highly recommended using a separate sample held out from building the tree.

Applications of decision tree analysis

Decision trees are helpful when you want to visualize the different 'niche' subsets within the data, which can sometimes reveal new insights.

As a decision tree produces rule-based segments, it can be a useful method to select records from a prospect database. A tree analysis would be produced using data from a recent campaign, employing the available selection criteria as candidate predictors and recruitment outcome as the target variable. The analysis would reveal the most successful segments for recruiting customers, and then the corresponding prospects could be selected and targeted.

When there are interactions between predictor variables, such that a particular combination of predictors disproportionately impacts on the target variable, decision tree analysis will identify the situation and reflect it. In fact, the very first decision tree tool, *automatic interaction detector*, was devised purely to identify interactions.

Decision tree is an excellent way to explore data and build a preliminary model. It is often used in combination with other methods, such as regression analysis.

Random forests

Random forests, developed by Breiman and Cutter, is an extension of the decision tree approach. In random forests, many trees are generated automatically from the data – hence the term 'forest' rather than 'tree'. When each tree is produced, around one-third of the cases are excluded from the sample and are used to calculate classification accuracy rates for that tree. In order to apply the forest to a new case, its data values are presented to each tree, which gives a classification or 'vote'. The overall classification is then the outcome that receives the most votes out of all the trees in the forest. The random forests algorithm is highly accurate but more difficult to analyse. For further details, see Breiman (2004).

Regression analysis

Regression analysis is a statistical process for analysing relationships between variables, specifically to predict a target variable from one or more explanatory variables. There are many different regression techniques for modelling different types of data and relationships. Two methods are used particularly widely in predictive analytics – multiple linear regression and logistic regression.

The regression approach

Multiple regression is often employed when the target variable is a quantitative measurement such as customer future value. Explanatory variables are identified, which jointly predict the target variable, using an equation of the following form:

$$Y = b_0 + b_1X_1 + b_2X_2 + b_3X_3 + \ldots + b_nX_n$$

– where:

Y is the predicted value of target variable, eg future customer value.

$X_1, X_2, X_3, \ldots X_n$ are predictor variables, eg historic value, customer age, income and so on.

b_0 is a regression constant.

$b_1, b_2, b_3, \ldots b_n$ are regression coefficients applied to the predictor variables.

b_1X_1 represents coefficient b_1 multiplied by predictor variable X_1 and so on.

This equation is known as a *linear model* because it combines the effects of the predictors (X variables) in a linear way, with each variable multiplied by a regression coefficient and the prediction obtained by summing those terms.

A different approach, logistic regression, may be used when the target variable is a '1/0' or *binary* outcome, such as purchase/non-purchase. Again, predictor variables are identified, which jointly predict the probability that the target variable equals 1, using an equation of the form:

$$ln\left(\frac{P}{1-P}\right) = b_0 + b_1 X_1 + b_2 X_2 + b_3 X_3 + \dots + b_n X_n$$

– where:

P is the probability that target variable equals 1, eg probability of making a purchase.

ln denotes natural logarithm (logarithm to base e).

X_1, X_2, X_3, ... X_n are predictor variables, eg number of past purchases, time since last purchase.

b_0 is a *regression* constant.

b_1, b_2, b_3, ... b_n are regression coefficients that are applied to the predictor variables.

$b_1 X_1$ represents coefficient b_1 multiplied by predictor variable X_1 and so on.

In this model equation $\left(\frac{P}{1-P}\right)$ represents the odds on a positive outcome, and therefore the target variable for logistic regression is the log odds.

All regression methods operate from an analytic dataset (see Chapter 3) containing a sample of cases with values for the target variable and predictors (X variables). The regression software analyses this dataset, discovers a possible model, and outputs values for the regression constant (b_0) and coefficients (b_1, b_2, b_3, ... b_n). At the same time, the software tests the statistical significance of the regression coefficients, under certain assumptions, and outputs various diagnostics to indicate how well the model explains the data.

Regression software usually permits a model to be built in a stepwise manner, adding in one variable at a time, subject to significance criteria set by the user. Stepwise regression is a helpful procedure when there are a large number of possible predictors, in order to search for the subset that gives the most useful model containing the smallest number of variables.

The use of logistic regression is fully discussed by Hosmer et al (2013). Multiple regression is included in many statistics text books; for example, see Fox (2015) for a complete perspective on regression methods and applications.

Strengths of regression analysis

The great attraction of regression analysis is that it should be straightforward to apply the model to make predictions for further customers, based on their corresponding values of the predictor variables.

Weaknesses of regression analysis

The main drawback is that regression models are more time-consuming to develop than other techniques and require an understanding of statistical technicalities. The data may contain a large number of *potential* predictor variables that *could* be included in the model; however, only those that are statistically significant and make business sense *should* be included. There may be a huge number of possible models, in terms of combinations of potential predictors. While the software may include stepwise functionality for selecting which potential predictors should be used, the final model will need to be checked for acceptability and business sense.

Applications of regression analysis

Logistic regression is used to predict a binary target variable, such as which customers are likely to take up a particular service, or which customers are likely to churn or attrite. Alternatively, it can be used to predict *risk*, eg which mortgage customers have a high risk of getting into arrears? The technique is widely used for response modelling – it should be more accurate than a decision tree, at the expense of more effort in building the model. Therefore a logistic model is generally preferred either for large customer databases, where the investment in performance will be worthwhile, or for situations where prediction accuracy is most important.

Multiple regression is used for quantitative target variables, such as customer future value. Subject to statistical assumptions about the target variable, regression will quantify the significance of each predictor in the model. Therefore the analysis can be used to identify important factors that have most impact on future value.

Supervised neural network

While regression analysis entails selecting a model to predict the target variable, the unique selling point (USP) of a supervised neural network is that it can achieve an equivalent result on a more automated basis without specifying a structure or relationship. In the context of machine learning, neural networks are often now referred to as 'deep learning'.

The approach

A supervised neural network consists of a number of *neurons* organized in layers, shown as the grey circles in the example of Figure 4.2. This example represents a simple neural network to predict customer lifetime value using three predictor variables – income, age and whether married.

Another type of neural network is *unsupervised*, in the sense that it does not predict a target variable. This network, also known as a self-organizing map, is a useful descriptive modelling technique and is outlined later in this chapter.

On the left side of Figure 4.2 there is an input column or *layer* of neurons comprising one neuron for each predictor variable – this represents each input to the network. On the right side, there is a single output neuron representing the output variable, the predicted lifetime value. A single neural network may have one or more output neurons, and therefore may predict multiple target variables.

Between the input and output layers, there is a hidden layer of neurons used for network processing. The values that enter at the input nodes are weighted, using numeric weights, and are combined together to calculate the hidden layer values. As Figure 4.2 shows, there are pathways between all the input and hidden layer nodes – the network uses a separate weight value for each pathway. Then the hidden layer values are weighted and combined

Figure 4.2   Example of a supervised neural network – for predicting customer lifetime value – hypothetical example

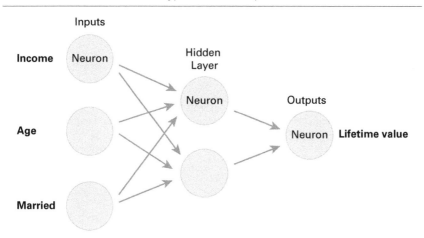

together to calculate the output value. Therefore this example network uses eight weights, corresponding to the eight connections shown in Figure 4.2. The hidden layer neurons involve non-linear computations and this is one of the reasons why neural networks have the power that they do.

Before the network can make predictions, the neural network software must first calculate the weight values – a process known as training. This is achieved by an estimation phase, using known example cases that contain values for both the predictor and target variables. For fitting the network, the example cases are split into training and testing subsets. An initial set of weight values is automatically set, and then the training cases are processed by the network to produce outputs that are compared with the true values of the target variable. The errors in the predictions are measured, and are applied back through the network to update the weights. This process is repeated using the new weights, to obtain new output values, new prediction errors, updated weights and so on.

The separate testing sample is employed at each cycle to calculate an overall measure of network accuracy, keep track of performance and decide when the training process should stop. This mitigates the risk of overfitting, which means estimating a set of weights that predict perfectly for the training cases, but perform badly on other data.

Although the numbers of input and output neurons are predetermined by the problem and available predictors, the number of hidden layers and neurons are flexible and are chosen to give the most accurate predictions while avoiding overfitting the network. At the same time there are various types of predictive neural network techniques and different options for the calculations performed by each neuron, when combining inputs from other neurons.

Strengths of neural networks

Neural networks can handle a wide range of problems – target variables may be numeric or binary, and a single network may have more than one output. The neural network may be a good solution when the relationship between target and predictor variables is non-linear and has no known formula – in other words, when the linear model equations widely used in regression analysis do not work well. Network training and testing is an automatic process and may be carried out repeatedly, so that the network can learn from recent cases.

Weaknesses of neural networks

Neural nets are 'black box' in the sense that there is no way to understand why a case receives a particular prediction from the network. There are usually far too many weight values and hidden nodes to permit interpretation; therefore, visualization of the solution becomes important and is often provided by the neural network software.

Without careful management, the network may converge to an inferior solution or may overfit the data. Neural networks tend to work poorly with very large numbers of input variables, implying that a preliminary analysis should be carried out first, in order to select the most useful variables for inclusion in the network. Finally, neural network algorithms can be highly complex to implement, unless there is a way to pass the complete algorithm across from the development phase to the deployment phase.

Applications of supervised neural networks

Neural networks are a good solution when the relationship between the target variable and predictors is complex and unknown, and may be 'learnt' from the data – and where individual predictions made by the network do not need to be understood or explained.

Widely used descriptive methods

In this section we look at some widely used descriptive methods, where there is no specific target outcome.

Factor analysis and principal components analysis

Factor analysis and principal components analysis (PCA) are two closely related techniques designed for exploring multivariate data containing many correlated variables and extracting useful new measures that summarize the information in an efficient way.

The amount of information in a dataset may be expressed by its total variance – the variance is a measure of spread of values for each variable. Both factor analysis and PCA aim to explore the variance and help to explain it, but they operate in slightly different ways.

The PCA approach

The main purpose of PCA is to explore the total variance present in a set of data and derive a set of measures that explain as much of it as possible using a smaller number of new variables – these new variables are known as principal components. If the original variables are highly correlated with one another, then this may be achieved with little loss of information. On the

Figure 4.3   Geometric interpretation of principal components analysis – hypothetical example

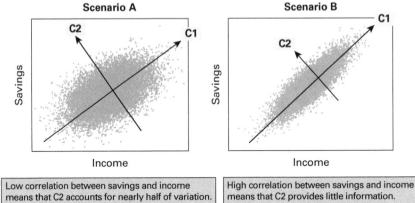

Suppose that there are two input variables – Savings and Income – in each scenario
Principal components analysis has produced components C1 and C2 in each case

Scenario A	Scenario B
Low correlation between savings and income means that C2 accounts for nearly half of variation. Decision: Retain both C1 and C2 for analysis.	High correlation between savings and income means that C2 provides little information. Decision: Only retain C1 for analysis.

other hand, if the variables are uncorrelated, then it may be necessary to use a larger number of components or work with the original variables.

To illustrate this, two situations – scenario A and scenario B – are shown in Figure 4.3 for principal components analyses on two input variables, savings and income. The cloud of points for each scenario represents a plot of people on their savings and income values. Each PCA has produced two new components – these are shown as diagonal lines on each graph, and are labelled C1 and C2. By definition in PCA, component 1 (C1) runs through the longest part of the cloud and has maximum variance; the C2 axis runs perpendicular to C1 and accounts for the remaining variance in savings and income.

In scenario A the cloud is a fat ellipse shape, indicating a low correlation between savings and income. Correspondingly, the spread of points along the C2 axis is almost as great as the spread along C1, implying that C2 is accounting for nearly half of the total variation. Therefore, to avoid losing the information conveyed in C2, the analyst might decide to retain both the C1 and C2 components.

In scenario B, the plot is a narrow 'cigar' shape, indicating a strong correlation between savings and income. For example, if a person's income is low, then their level of savings is likely to be low. In this case, the spread of points along the C2 axis is much smaller than the spread along C1, implying that there would be little loss if the data were represented solely by C1. Therefore the analyst might justifiably decide to retain just C1, and represent the two initial variables by a single component score.

When there are many variables, PCA can effectively 'group' the variables into dimensions or themes that are present but less obvious in the data. Furthermore, the analysis always extracts components in order of size, so that component 1 has highest variance, and so is of greatest importance, component 2 has second-highest variance, and so on.

The factor analysis approach

The approach taken by factor analysis is similar to PCA, however the goal is to explain *shared variation* that is common between input variables. For this reason, the technique is sometimes more properly known as *common factor analysis*. The aim of the technique is to help understand the relationships between variables or the structure in the data.

Common issues in the two approaches

The most important issue is that both analyses are driven by the correlations between input variables, therefore the meanings of the components or factors should be carefully interpreted – they should only be used for further analysis if they are understandable and make business sense.

The analysis software is able to transform or rotate the axes in order to derive alternative solutions. The user should explore the results from rotated and unrotated analyses in order to look for the clearest and most meaningful results. A rotation known as *Varimax* often works better than an unrotated solution, in grouping the input variables into distinct sets that produce the resultant components.

Lastly, there is sometimes confusion between the two approaches – in some software tools 'factor analysis' is used as a name for both techniques, and the new derived scores are called 'factors'. Therefore, when discussing factor analysis with colleagues, it is important to be clear about which method is really meant – PCA for data reduction, or common factor analysis for explaining shared variation.

Strengths of the techniques

These techniques are able to extract *dimensions* or themes that underpin or help explain a large set of multivariate data. Those dimensions can be used as new variables in their own right. When some of the original variables are highly correlated, and therefore giving the same message as each other, these will be replaced by a new variable that delivers the same message.

The new dimensions may have some statistical advantages such as being closer to normally distributed than the original variables and also being uncorrelated with one another (or weakly correlated).

Weaknesses of the techniques

The analysis will always extract components or factors, even when the input variables have low correlations. Therefore, the user must interpret the output and only accept the solution if it seems sufficiently successful and makes business sense.

The analyst must decide how many components or factors to retain, with the aid of outputs and charts from the analysis. When using PCA to reduce the number of variables, the analyst will usually aim to retain the first N components that account for more than 50 per cent of the total variation in the input data.

Applications

PCA is often applied in customer segmentation projects, in order to summarize customer behaviour across many different variables, in terms of a smaller set of components. This can be a first stage before going on to cluster customers into segments, using the component scores. Some widely used clustering techniques are described below.

One of the domains where this approach has been applied is geodemographics, the analysis of people by where they live. PCA is a highly effective way of extracting the underlying dimensions from large numbers of census variables (and other statistics) measured at neighbourhood level. For further information, see Leventhal (2016).

Factor analysis is more likely to be used in attitude research to identify latent or underlying dimensions that cause an outcome. For example, the data could be a set of consumer ratings of the importance of different attributes in choosing a motor car. The analysis would identify a smaller number of underlying dimensions to be considered.

Cluster analysis

Cluster analysis is a general term for a number of different techniques for assigning customers to groups or clusters. The goal is to identify groups such that the members of each group are more similar to one another than to members of other groups. When the clustering is applied to business problems, the groups also need to be understandable, make business sense and be suitable for their intended use.

The cluster analysis approach

Cluster analysis relies on the ability to measure the similarity or *distance* between any customers. Two customers who are close together are more likely to be placed in the same group, whereas two that are far apart should be assigned to different clusters.

Once the clustering variables have been decided, on which similarity will be based, there are various measures that can be applied to calculate the similarity between any two customers. For quantitative clustering variables a measure of distance may be used, such as the Euclidean or 'straight line' distance between their two sets of values. For categorical variables, a measure of match rate or association may be used, which views individuals as similar if they have common characteristics.

Having selected the clustering variables and an appropriate measure of similarity, the next decision is which method of cluster formation to employ. There are two widely used types of clustering – hierarchical techniques and partitioning techniques.

Hierarchical techniques are designed to create a tree or hierarchy of clusters, from which a preferred solution may be chosen. They work in two alternative ways – either by successively combining cases into clusters or by successively splitting the data into smaller clusters. These two approaches are known as:

- Agglomerative methods – each case starts off as its own cluster, the two most similar are combined into a new cluster, then the next two most similar are combined, and so on. Eventually, one single cluster is formed containing all cases. One popular approach is Ward's method, in which clusters are combined that give smallest loss of information (in terms of variances within clusters).

- Divisive methods – the start is a single cluster containing all cases. This cluster is split into two groups, based on the distances between cases. Then each group is examined in turn and one of these gets split into two further groups, and so on.

One particular feature of hierarchical techniques is that the 'combine' or 'split' decisions are irrevocable – once two cases have been combined into the same cluster, they will never be moved into different clusters. Likewise,

Figure 4.4   Example of a clustering dendogram

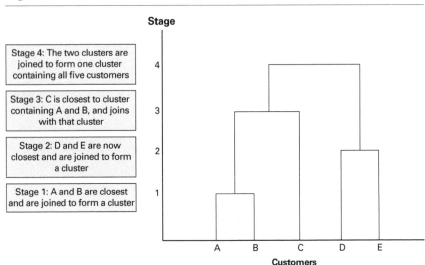

On the left side of the figure:

Stage 4: The two clusters are joined to form one cluster containing all five customers

Stage 3: C is closest to cluster containing A and B, and joins with that cluster

Stage 2: D and E are now closest and are joined to form a cluster

Stage 1: A and B are closest and are joined to form a cluster

once cases have been split into separate clusters, they will never be recombined. All hierarchical techniques employ some measure of clustering success in order to decide where to stop the combining or splitting process.

The output is often summarized using a tree diagram known as a dendogram, which displays the results of the process – an example dendogram, and the clustering steps that produced it, are shown in Figure 4.4.

On the other hand, partitioning techniques work in an iterative way – they repeatedly cycle through the data – and do not make irrevocable clustering decisions. They operate by partitioning all the cases into a set of initial clusters based on a predefined optimization criterion that measures cluster consistency or homogeneity. Then the clusters are automatically reviewed and a case will be reassigned to a different cluster, in order to improve the allocation. This process gets repeated many times, until the degree of improvement becomes negligible.

The most widely used partitioning technique is K-means cluster analysis. K-means aims to minimize the distances between cases and their cluster centroids – effectively, the centroid is the centre of gravity, or average point, within each cluster. Although K-means is an efficient method and works well with large datasets, it suffers from the weakness that the eventual solution can be highly dependent on the initial values of the centroids used at the start. Different software packages employ various methods for selecting the initial values; however, the user should employ K-means with caution, eg by randomly splitting the dataset and seeing whether the same clusters are produced for each part.

Most partitioning techniques, including K-means, require that the desired number of clusters has been decided in advance. To overcome this limitation, the user would need to apply the technique repeatedly to produce alternative solutions containing different numbers of clusters over some acceptable range, eg between 5 and 10 clusters. Each solution would then be examined in some detail in order to select the most useful set.

Strengths of cluster analysis

Cluster analysis can be a powerful way to summarize data containing multiple measurements on each customer. It can identify new, interesting and potentially useful groups.

Weaknesses of cluster analysis

The clustering algorithm will always create a set of groups, but cannot know whether they will be of use to you – or even whether they are statistically significant. Therefore, cluster analysis needs to be backed up by validation, to check whether similar groups occur in other data, and by examining the profile of each cluster and interpreting its characteristics.

Applications

Cluster analysis is often used when developing a segmentation solution that may be used to manage customers or market to them on a segmented basis – ie applying different strategies, treatments or communication styles to different segments. The approach is applied widely in market research, for segmenting markets on criteria such as attitudes and lifestyles in order to identify interesting target audiences. Likewise it can be applied to customer data, for identifying behavioural segments – for example, different types of mobile phone users for which tailored products and services would be appropriate. The same analytical techniques are also employed in the geodemographic industry for building area classifications – see Leventhal (2016). The process of customer segmentation, drawing on cluster analysis, is discussed in Chapter 8.

Latent class analysis (LCA)

In passing, we shall introduce latent class analysis (LCA) as a potential alternative approach to cluster analysis for developing a segmentation. LCA is mainly applied to survey data, in fields such as market and social research, or medical diagnosis; however, it could also be used for customer analysis.

The LCA technique is similar to principal components or factor analysis, in the sense of discovering underlying themes; however, it is mainly used to discover unseen or *latent* categories, or classes, rather than numeric scores.

In order to decide how many latent classes that are required, a series of statistical models are estimated, with increasing numbers of classes, using a method known as expectation maximization (EM). Essentially the EM approach finds the set of classes with maximum likelihood of explaining the data. Each EM model is assessed in terms of statistical criteria and the usefulness of the discovered latent classes, until the best number of classes is found. Muthén (2001) discusses latent class analysis and other types of models involving latent variables.

Self-organizing map

A self-organizing map (SOM) – also known as a Kohonen network, after its inventor – is a type of unsupervised neural network, used for undirected data-mining tasks such as clustering data. The SOM is an alternative approach to cluster analysis and is an option particularly in situations where the clustering process needs to be automated.

The SOM approach

Like the supervised neural network discussed earlier in this chapter, a SOM consists of an interconnected set of neurons; however, the network architecture is very different, as shown in Figure 4.5. There is an input layer of neurons, one for each input variable, and these are directly connected to an output layer. In a SOM, the output neurons are arranged in a grid, such as the '3 × 3' array shown in Figure 4.5. In this example, mobile phone customers are being segmented on their usage.

All of the input neurons are connected to all of the output neurons, and each connection has a weight value as for the supervised network. The network is trained, or in other words the set of weights is calculated, by an iterative process. Each case is presented to the network, its weighted value is calculated, and the output nodes 'compete' to win it. The output node with the highest value 'wins' the case and the weights on that node are updated. At the same time, the weights on neighbouring output nodes are adjusted to increase their scores on that set of input values. This introduces an element of 'neighbourliness' into the output layer.

After training is complete, the output nodes will correspond to clusters; because of the neighbourliness element, several nodes can jointly represent

Figure 4.5   Example of a self-organizing map for segmenting mobile phone customers

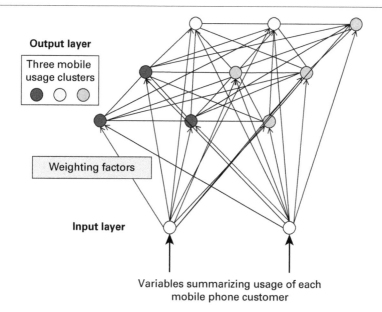

a single cluster. At the same time, similar clusters will have nodes that are closer together in the output layer. The distribution of clusters across output nodes is often visualized using a coloured map – Figure 4.5 shows the clusters as three shades of grey across the output layer nodes. Having created the network, new cases may be input and will be assigned to clusters – therefore a set of network computations is required in order to classify each new case.

Strengths of a SOM

The desired number of clusters does not need to be chosen in advance, although the number of output nodes must be decided. There will usually be a smaller number of final clusters than output nodes. The network can continue to learn, ie update its weights, as new cases are presented to it.

Weaknesses of a SOM

The SOM is a black box solution, so while a SOM can identify clusters, it gives no indication as to what the clusters mean or why a case has been assigned to a particular cluster. Profiling by the input variables is required in order to interpret each cluster. Depending upon your data-mining architecture, a neural network may be a more complex solution to implement.

Applications

A self-organizing map may be a useful technique in situations where automated clustering and updating are required, particularly for markets that are constantly changing.

Association analysis

In a retail environment, such as a store or online, purchases of selected products are sometimes linked or associated, as a result of their usage. Well-known examples are shampoo and conditioner, or shaving foam and razor blades; however, not all associations are so obvious. The purpose of association analysis is to discover those products and services that customers are likely to purchase together, either in the same transaction or over time. Associations are sometimes a first step towards data mining – they can provide useful insights and also be employed in predictive analytics projects, such as price optimization (see Chapter 10).

The approach

The technique works by calculating affinities between pairs of products, based upon the numbers of customers buying each product and the number buying both. This is illustrated in Figure 4.6, which looks at low-affinity and high-affinity situations. In Figure 4.6a, the oval shapes for products X and Y represent the groups of customers buying each of these products. Only a small number bought both X and Y, therefore the overlap between X and Y is small – a low-affinity situation. In Figure 4.6b, the overlap between products A and B is much greater – if a customer bought product A, then they are likely to have also bought product B. This high affinity is summarized as an association rule: A → B.

The software tools for association analysis will examine relationships between all pairs of products and will calculate various metrics summarizing the strengths of affinities. The user can then identify which affinities are most helpful and are worth extracting as association rules.

A variation of the technique, sequence analysis, identifies associations between purchases or events that occur in *time order* – for example, it might identify that a new customer of a bank starts off with a current account, next acquires a credit account and this is followed by a loan, and so on.

Figure 4.6 Examples of association analysis for low-affinity and high-affinity products

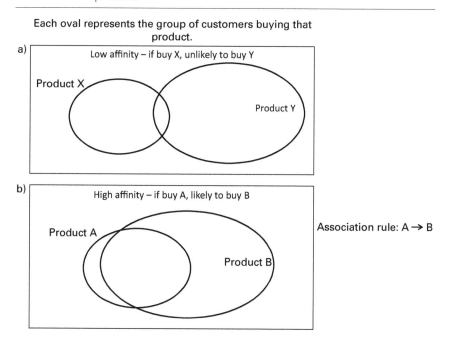

Each oval represents the group of customers buying that product.

a) Low affinity – if buy X, unlikely to buy Y

Product X

Product Y

b) High affinity – if buy A, likely to buy B

Product A

Product B

Association rule: A → B

Strengths of association analysis

The technique identifies association rules that should be intuitive and accurate, and are unlikely to be discovered from other analyses.

Weaknesses of association analysis

The analysis may require significant processing time, for example if it is being run for all items sold by a large supermarket. Some experimentation and focusing may be needed in order to obtain useful results. For example, in a supermarket application, an item such as milk may be identified as associated with all manner of unrelated products, simply because milk is a common additional purchase in many shopping baskets.

Applications

The technique is used widely in the retail sector to help with merchandise ranging and offer design. In the case of supermarket retailers, it may be applied to identify substitute products that a customer would purchase if an intended item were out of stock. For example, an online supermarket might use this to suggest a possible substitute if the customer choice is unavailable.

If the retailer operates a loyalty card, then associations may be obtained at customer level, based on all purchases over a period of time, and compared with corresponding results at basket level. Substitute products will tend to have associations that are high at customer level and low at basket level.

DiY (do-it-yourself) retailers can use sequence analysis to help understand the sequence of projects that customers carry out around the home. In the telco sector, association analysis can be used to identify which combinations of phone services and features tend to be purchased together.

CASE STUDY

Comparison of techniques

Some years ago, the DMA Statistics in Direct Marketing Group carried out a study to compare the effectiveness of four analytical modelling techniques – cluster analysis, regression, decision tree and neural networks. The purpose of the exercise was to show how different techniques could be applied and provide insights into the various methods, rather than to identify the most powerful approach. The study was arranged and documented by Mark Patron (1994).

The techniques were applied by four analysis agencies to a sample of data from CMT's National Shoppers' Survey (NSS), a large-scale lifestyle database based on surveys completed by millions of consumers. The NSS contained 179 variables on demographics, product purchasing, hobbies and interests, totalling 407 answer categories. Each analyst was provided with samples of 42,000 questionnaires for model development and 28,000 records for validation. The target variable was the survey question on private health insurance – this had an incidence of 8.32 per cent across the total NSS sample.

The analysts applied the following techniques to the development sample:

Cluster analysis

A preliminary analysis identified those variables that showed an association with private health insurance, and these variables were included in the cluster development. An initial partitioning analysis was carried out using *nearest centroid sorting*, which is similar to the K-means method. This gave an initial set of 50 clusters, on which hierarchical clustering by Ward's method was applied to obtain nine final clusters.

Regression

The variables were first screened to find those that were correlated with private health insurance and a regression model was then developed from a subset of those variables.

Decision tree

The Automatic Interaction Detector (AID) programme was used to build a decision tree. This proceeded by first randomly splitting the development sample into two equal subsets, and applying AID to each subset. The set of predictor variables was adjusted until similar results were obtained on both files, from which a solution containing seven segments was selected. The solution was applied to the validation sample as rule sets, in order to measure performance.

Neural network

A supervised neural network known as a *multilayer perceptron*, was applied to the data. This was used with a *back-propagation* learning algorithm for training the weights. The network was trained on the 42,000 development sample, which was split into 75 per cent and 25 per cent subsets for training and testing respectively. The network contained one input node for each answer category in the NSS dataset. The resultant network was applied to the validation file to score each record and measure the results.

Results

Figure 4.7 summarizes the results in gains chart format; this shows, for each technique, the cumulative percentages of healthcare holders identified within the validation sample, at 10 per cent intervals for the top 50 per cent of prospects.

This type of graph, known as a gains chart, summarizes the gains achieved by a targeting model, in terms of the proportion of healthcare insurance holders identified by the model versus the proportion of the population that would need to be targeted. The stronger the model, the greater the gains and therefore the higher the gains curve on the chart. Gains charts are discussed further in Chapter 6.

The regression model produced the best gains, closely followed by the decision tree model. Theoretically, a neural network should be more powerful than other techniques; however, in this study the neural net was not quite as strong.

The cluster solution performed reasonably well; however, clustering is not designed to be a predictive technique and this was borne out by its lower gains curve.

Figure 4.7 Comparison of four predictive analytics techniques

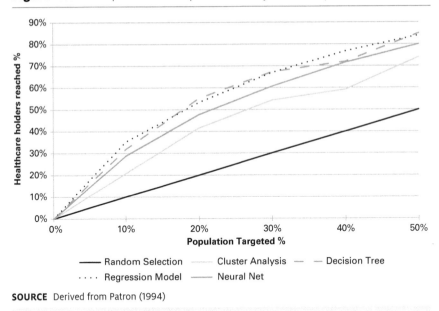

SOURCE Derived from Patron (1994)

The Bayesian approach

The techniques presented earlier in this chapter employ classical statistical methodology, which is sometimes known as the frequentist approach. A different approach started to gain popularity from the 1960s onwards – the Bayesian school.

The Bayesian approach is named after Reverend Thomas Bayes, an English Presbyterian minister who lived from 1702 to 1761. Bayes first formulated the theorem that underpins all Bayesian statistics. Bayes theorem connects posterior beliefs, the beliefs in the probability of an event *after seeing data*, with prior beliefs, the beliefs *prior to seeing data*. The theorem states that:

$$\text{posterior belief} = \frac{\text{prior belief} * \text{probability of data given belief}}{\text{probability of data}}$$

This theorem is effectively a recipe for learning from data, and so is intuitively very appealing. You might start off with little or no knowledge about an unknown event and therefore your prior beliefs will be quite vague, giving equal chance to each possible event outcome. As you start to collect data, the formula allows you to update the situation and calculate posterior beliefs, where the event probabilities are no longer equal. If you continue collecting data, those posterior probabilities would become your new prior beliefs, and you would derive an updated set of posterior beliefs.

As an example, suppose you want to decide which version of a page performs better on your website, and you have two options: page A and page B. At the start, you have no firm belief and so your prior probabilities are 50 per cent for each option. After running an experiment for some time, showing each page design to site visitors selected at random, Bayes theorem allows you to update your beliefs and conclude, for example, that page A has 80 per cent probability of working better, and page B has 20 per cent chance. A Bayesian approach to online testing is used by Google within its content experiments system – see Chapter 12.

Many types of statistical models may be formulated in a Bayesian framework, as Lee (2012) explains. However, apart from straightforward situations, a large amount of computation is usually required in order to calculate posterior beliefs each time Bayes theorem is applied to real-world data. Largely for this reason, most analytical modelling packages follow the frequentist approach and ignore the Bayesian school.

Bayesian networks (BNs)

One of the most powerful Bayesian techniques is the Bayesian Network (BN), which is overviewed by Fenton and Neil (2007). A BN describes the relationships between causes and effects as a graph containing nodes and arcs. The nodes can represent events; each node has an associated probability table containing the probabilities of the various possible outcomes. The arcs explain the relationships between the nodes. Data can be entered into the network and the probabilities will be updated by applying Bayes theorem.

The earliest uses of BNs, from the late 1980s to the mid-1990s, were mainly for medical diagnosis and fault diagnosis. One of the early users was Microsoft, for diagnosing faults automatically and for user support. In 1996, Bill Gates was reported as saying 'Microsoft's competitive advantage is its expertise in Bayesian networks' (*Los Angeles Times*, 28 October 1996). Fenton and Neil (2012) explain how to use BNs for decision analysis and prediction.

Which is the right technique to use?

The choice of analytical modelling technique generally depends upon several factors:

- Your business problem – exactly what do you need to obtain from the analysis and how will this be used?
- Is the problem predictive or descriptive in nature, and what needs to be predicted or described?
- Your data environment – how are your data stored, are there any particular issues such as large numbers of missing values?
- The ability of your IT system to deploy the model solution – for example, there is no point in building a complex neural network model if your database can only realistically accept rule-based selections.
- Whether key statistical assumptions hold in the data – some techniques, eg multiple regression, make underpinning assumptions in order to quantify the significance of the model.

If you are unsure about the choice of technique, then your analyst or data-mining consultant should be willing to discuss and advise. The choice should depend upon the business problem and not on the sophistication of the technique – so beware being lured by an unnecessarily complicated approach or by a new methodology that your IT colleagues cannot implement.

Finally, it is often the case that a combination of approaches will work best, as we will discuss in the following section.

Combining models together

The techniques reviewed in this chapter, together with the wider armoury of analytical methods, are literally a set of tools that may be applied either separately or in combination – depending upon the data and business problem. Often, the best approach will involve using several methods in combination – there are two reasons why a combined approach can be either desirable or essential.

First, as we have seen, each of the core techniques looks at your data in a different way and so is likely to deliver different insights. While we do not recommend attempting to apply *every* technique to your business problem, examining several is likely to yield increased understanding and help to refine the eventual modelling solution. For example, it is often useful to apply decision tree analysis before building a regression model. The tree will show the most discriminatory variables and any interactions going on between them. These interactions may be included in the regression modelling and should improve the model accuracy. In some cases, the tree can identify important segments of customers for which separate models may be beneficial.

A combined modelling approach can sometimes be essential, due to the requirements of your business problem and the features of your data. For example, when applying cluster analysis to a large dataset, it is often good practice to use both partitioning and hierarchical clustering procedures – partitioning to create low-level 'atomic' clusters and hierarchical to fuse these into a small number of high-level groups.

There are many other situations where a combination of techniques is required in order to address business problems that may not seem complex but actually are! For example, suppose that the problem is to predict customer spend in response to an offer, so that the offer can be targeted in order to maximize revenues. This may sound straightforward, however customer spend depends on two events – responding to the offer and placing an order. Therefore, two models are likely to be needed – such as a logistic regression model to predict response, and a multiple regression model to predict value of spending amongst those predicted to respond.

Conclusion

In this chapter, we have seen that:

✔ Decision trees are a useful way to explore data before going on to build a model. They produce rule-based selection criteria.

✔ Regression is a widely used and powerful family of predictive methods for large customer databases.

✔ Supervised neural networks are potentially more powerful and do not assume an explicit relationship between the target and predictor variables. However, they are also more complex to deploy on a customer database.

✔ Factor analysis and principal component analysis are useful techniques for exploring relationships between variables, and may be applied to reduce data to a smaller number of underlying dimensions.

✓ Cluster analysis methods are often used in segmentation projects for discovering groups containing similar customers.

✓ Self-organizing maps are a particular type of neural network for clustering data; however, they may be complex to deploy.

✓ Association analysis identifies affinity products that customers are more likely to buy together, either in the same purchase or over time.

✓ Bayesian statistics is underpinned by Bayes Theorem, which is effectively a recipe for learning from data. The Bayesian network is a powerful approach for updating the probabilities of events, using a network of relationships between causes and effects.

✓ The choice of technique should depend primarily upon the business problem, the available data, whether the data satisfy any key statistical assumptions, and whether your IT system is able to deploy the solution.

✓ In many projects a combination of approaches is likely to work best.

Software solutions for predictive analytics

05

Introduction

Predictive analytics is an expanding industry and is being applied in a myriad of ways. These have given rise to literally hundreds of software products that cover a host of analytical modelling techniques, for different applications and types of use. At the same time, the rapid growth in volumes of data being generated and stored by companies has necessitated the development of IT architectures and solutions to help manage the data-mining process.

If your company's data-processing environment is 'small scale' and entirely operates on a single computer, then IT architectures and solutions may be of little interest to you. However, as data volumes increase and require separate storage systems, then you are more likely to require a data-mining system that will 'scale up' and run efficiently. In this chapter, we discuss some of the most likely options.

The main aims of this chapter are to:

- Discuss the most frequently encountered IT architectures for data mining.

- Identify the main types of software packages for data analysis and modelling.

- Consider ways for communicating models between their development and deployment phases.

- Pick out systems for storing and managing libraries of models, to aid in their deployment.

- Introduce scaleable analytics in the Cloud, as a route to making large-scale predictive analytics more widely available.

The architecture required for data mining

When we discuss data-mining architectures, we presuppose that your data will be stored in a database that exceeds the capacity of the user's computer. The store could be anything from a Microsoft Access database held on a server, through to a data mart designed for data mining, through to an enterprise-wide data warehouse – all of these can be your source, provided of course that they contain the necessary information!

Two alternative approaches are widely employed for data mining, which we will refer to as 'one tier' and 'two tier' architectures. Each is discussed in turn below.

One-tier architecture

The traditional approach is one-tier – this just means that all data-mining activities take place on the user's computer (which we will refer to as 'local computer'). The database is involved solely to provide data extracts and load results.

Under the one-tier approach illustrated in Figure 5.1, the user first obtains a sample extract of development data from the database, which is exported and loaded into the local computer. Using this development

Figure 5.1   A one-tier data-mining architecture

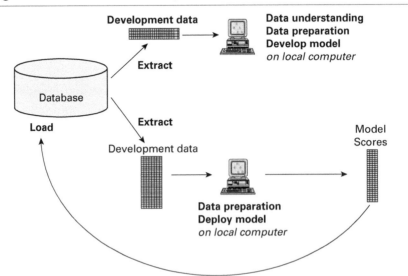

file, all data understanding, preparation and analytical modelling tasks take place on the local machine. Having developed the model, an extract of deployment data is taken – this contains all customers to be scored using the model and the variables required for each customer. The deployment dataset is loaded into the local computer, where data preparation is applied to the predictor variables and the model is applied to score each customer. Finally, the dataset of model scores gets loaded back into the database.

The one-tier approach is straightforward but has a number of drawbacks. First, depending upon computer capacity, the development extract is likely to be a relatively small subset of records, so only a fraction of your database contributes to data mining. In order to avoid biasing or distorting the model, the extract will need to be a random sample that is representative of the customer population for which the model is intended.

Subsequently, in order to deploy the model, a deployment extract is taken containing the required predictor variables for every customer. This can be a huge dataset, which may take many hours to extract from the database and load onto the local computer. After scoring, the file of model scores has to be loaded back into the database, which again takes time. Therefore, under this approach, there are large datasets being moved around and the process is slow and time-consuming. Each time the model needs to be deployed, these steps have to be repeated, which represents a major amount of effort.

Two-tier architecture

In the two-tier architecture, shown in Figure 5.2, data-mining tasks are shared between the database and the local computer. The understanding and preparation phases take place in the database and therefore the analyst has access to a much greater amount of information when creating the development ADS. Model development may either be run in the database or on the local machine. If the latter route is taken, the model algorithm may be input and scored in the database, giving a table of model scores.

The two-tier approach therefore avoids moving huge amounts of data between the two systems, and so is quicker and more efficient. It exploits the processing capacity of the database system and so the local computer does not need to be as powerful. Finally, the deployment ADS may be refreshed and rescored in-database, each time the model needs to be deployed.

Figure 5.2   A two-tier data-mining architecture

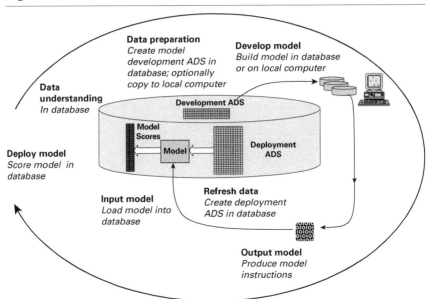

Software for analytical modelling

Literally hundreds of software tools are available for building analytical models. These range from spreadsheet add-in modules through to complete data-mining systems. In this section we discuss the main types of solutions, overview what you can expect from them and identify example products of each type. For a more complete product list, see KDnuggets (2017).

Key point

Analytical modelling requires logical thought processes and an understanding of statistics. No matter how automated the software tool might be, it will always require the analyst to apply it in a thoughtful and meaningful way, and interpret whether the results make sense and are useful.

The software solutions are presented below as four levels, corresponding to the degree of integration that they are likely to achieve with your business systems.

Most of these software products have associated licence fees, or alternatively may be purchased outright. The open-source tools have been designed for free access, which means that they have entry-level versions that are free of charge. They may also have versions designed for larger applications that incur licensing costs and so help to fund product development. Further details on licensing arrangements may be obtained from the vendors' websites, which are listed in Table 5.1, 5.2 and 5.3 below.

Level 1: analytical modelling in spreadsheets

In Level 1, analytical modelling takes place in a spreadsheet, such as Excel; this enables you to use modelling for your business planning, but makes it difficult to deploy those models across your customer base.

A collection of data analysis functions, known as the Analysis ToolPak, is available as an add-in for Microsoft Excel. The add-in is free to download, for installations of MS Office or MS Excel, however it is unavailable for older versions of Excel for Apple Mac – alternative tools may be used instead, such as StatPlus:mac LE.

The Excel function is designed to fit a linear regression model using a known set of predictor variables. It is not well suited to discovering the best subset of predictors from a much longer list. The model can be applied to score cases within the spreadsheet; however, to deploy it elsewhere, eg in your marketing database, the regression equation would need to be copied and programmed to run scoring on a different system – this would take time and be prone to errors.

The Excel add-in could be a helpful way to start exploring some of the analytical techniques, before moving on to a statistical package. Alternatively, if your data are stored and analysed in Excel, then the add-in may provide useful enhancements.

In most circumstances, we would recommend employing a bespoke statistics package, data-mining system or other analytical software, as approaches that are better geared to building models that can be applied to your customers.

Level 2: statistics packages

Statistics packages are standalone software products primarily designed for statistical users. We term them 'Level 2' – although they are capable of creating models that can be deployed across your customers, model-building is likely to be a manual process. Therefore, they are less likely to be used in situations where large numbers of models need to be built, deployed and managed, which may limit the business benefits that you gain from them. These products offer all or most of the following functionality:

- Options for reading data from different sources, including spreadsheets and relational databases, and creating analytic datasets.

- A range of data exploration and preparation functions, such as those discussed in Chapter 3.
- A toolkit of analytical modelling techniques, such as decision trees, regression and cluster analysis (see Chapter 4), for developing and deploying models.
- Graphing and visualization tools that enable the user to explore data such as predicted values.

Table 5.1 provides some examples of statistics packages, together with websites that will give information about them.

Table 5.1 Some examples of statistics packages

Products	Supplier	Website	Notes
Anaconda	Continuum Analytics	https://www.continuum.io/	Open source platform powered by the Python programming language
IBM SPSS Statistics	IBM	http://www-03.ibm.com/software/products/en/spss-statistics	Formerly SPSS Statistics
MATLAB	Mathworks	http://uk.mathworks.com/products/matlab/	Language for technical computing
Minitab	Minitab	https://www.minitab.com/en-us/products/minitab/	
R	Free Software Foundation	https://www.r-project.org/foundation/	Open-source language for statistical computing
Rstudio	Rstudio	https://www.rstudio.com/	Open-source environment for R
SAS Analytics Pro	SAS Institute	http://www.sas.com/en_gb/software/analytics/analytics-pro.html#	
Spotfire S+	TIBCO Software	http://spotfire.tibco.com/discover-spotfire/who-uses-spotfire/by-role/statisticians	Language for data analysis and graphics
Stata	StataCorp	http://www.stata.com/	

(continued)

Table 5.1 *(Continued)*

Products	Supplier	Website	Notes
Statistica	Statistica	http://www.statsoft.com/Products/STATISTICA/Product-Index	Statistica was acquired by TIBCO in June 2017
SYSTAT	Systat Software	https://systatsoftware.com/products/systat/	

Note Websites accessed on 7 January 2017.

Level 3: data-mining products

Data-mining products, such as those listed in Table 5.2, offer similar functions to statistics packages but are designed to operate on a greater scale – analysing vast customer databases and/or building and maintaining large numbers of models. For this reason, we term them 'Level 3' – the benefits of predictive analytics may be more fully exploited, provided that systems are available for deploying many models across your customers. Their users are typically

Table 5.2 Some examples of data-mining products

Products	Supplier	Website	Notes
FICO Model Builder	FICO	http://www.fico.com/en/products/fico-model-builder#overview	
IBM Smart Analytics System	IBM	http://www-03.ibm.com/software/products/en/ibm-smart-analytics-system	For use with IBM databases
IBM SPSS Modeler	IBM(SPSS)	http://www-03.ibm.com/software/products/en/spss-modeler	Formerly SPSS Clementine
KNIME Analytics Platform	KNIME	https://www.knime.org/knime-analytics-platform	Open source
Knowledge STUDIO	Angoss	http://www.angoss.com/predictive-analytics-software/software/knowledgestudio/	
SAP InfiniteInsight	SAP	https://help.sap.com/ii65?current=ii	Formerly KXEN Analytic Framework

(continued)

Table 5.2   *(Continued)*

Products	Supplier	Website	Notes
Oracle Data Mining	Oracle	http://www.oracle.com/ technetwork/database/options/ advanced-analytics/odm/ overview/index.html	For use with Oracle databases
Spectrum Miner	Pitney Bowes	http://www.pitneybowes. com/uk/customer-information- management/customer-analytics/ spectrum-miner.html	
RapidMiner	RapidMiner Inc.	https://rapidminer.com/	Open source
SAS Enterprise Miner	SAS Institute	http://www.sas.com/en_us/ software/analytics/enterprise- miner.html	
SQL Server Analysis Services	Microsoft	https://msdn.microsoft.com/en- us/library/bb522607.aspx	
Statistica	Statistica	http://statistica.io/	Statistica was acquired by TIBCO in June 2017
Teradata Warehouse Miner	Teradata	http://www.teradata.co.uk/ products-and-services/teradata- warehouse-miner/?LangType=205 7&LangSelect=true	For use with Teradata databases
TIBCO Spotfire Miner	TIBCO Software	https://docs.tibco.com/products/ tibco-spotfire-miner-8-2	

Note Websites accessed 7 January 2017.

database analysts and data scientists with a good understanding of statistics. These products often include additional functionality for:

- Automating the tasks in a data-mining project, eg by setting up a work-flow of steps that can be executed as a sequence, or scheduled to run at a future time.

- Saving model algorithms and maintaining a library of models available to be deployed – this model management function is discussed later on in this chapter.

Level 4: embedded analytical models

At level 4, model building is embedded directly into your own business systems so that the results may be leveraged with maximum speed and greatest benefit. Your company is likely to face significant development implications and costs to achieve this level of integration, and so it mainly gets applied in situations where the business need greatly outweighs the costs. For example, in the retail sector, supply chain management requires accurate forecasts of consumer demand, so analytical modelling may be embedded in a retailer's supply chain system.

A number of commercial solution providers have capabilities for embedded advanced analytics, including Alteryx, BeyondCore, Pentaho, SAS and TIBCO Software.

Alternatively, embedded modelling may be achieved in-house by your own developers, with the help of pre-written mathematical and statistical algorithms called from your business systems. There are several suppliers of algorithm libraries that can provide functions for building and deploying different types of models – see Table 5.3 for further details.

Communicating models between development and deployment

As we saw in Chapter 2, analytical models are developed and deployed in two separate phases of the data-mining process. This implies that each model, and the analytic dataset it requires, must be communicated precisely between those two phases. Unfortunately, this communication of data and models represents one of the greatest technical challenges to continuous widespread use of predictive analytics.

Table 5.3 Examples of algorithm libraries for embedded modelling

Products	Supplier	Website
IMSL Numerical Libraries	Rogue Wave Software	http://www.roguewave. com/products-services/ imsl-numerical-libraries
MATLAB Statistics and Machine Learning Toolbox	MathWorks	http://uk.mathworks.com/ products/statistics/
NAG Library	NAG Software	https://www.nag.co.uk/ content/nag-library

Note Websites accessed 7 January 2017.

In the early days of data mining, communication of models was undertaken by manually documenting the specifications of variables and model algorithm, and carefully coding those definitions for the deployment phase. This sometimes led to catastrophic errors occurring when models were employed for segmenting and targeting customers. In one company alone (many years ago), nine out of ten models were found to have been incorrectly implemented, when transferred manually between the analyst team and the IT department.

Nowadays, it is still common for specifications to be communicated manually, even though this is not ideal.

Key point

If the model specification has to be communicated manually, then the analyst should also supply a file of test cases together with their model scores. The implementer should ensure that their results, from programming the data transformations and model algorithm, produce identical model scores for all records.

A preferable approach is obviously to automate the communications in order to remove this reliance on manual specifications and coding, speed up the process and reduce the risk of implementation errors. Analytics software suppliers have introduced several solutions that aim to achieve this automation – we identify four approaches below.

Use the same software

If the same software package can be employed for developing and deploying a model, then there is a good likelihood that the model can be saved as an executable program, and run or applied in a separate step. Also, transformations of variables should be repeatable in order to create the dataset for deployment.

Export SQL programs

An option available in some packages is to output the data creation and model scoring, from the development phase, as code – using a programming language such as Structured Query Language (SQL). The SQL programs can then be used for model deployment – they may require modifying for a different data environment, however the amendments are likely to be minor.

Predictive Model Markup Language

In the late 1990s, Predictive Model Markup Language (PMML) was devised as a method of communicating models between packages. PMML uses Extensible Markup Language (XML) to specify a model as a series of elements, including a data dictionary, data transformations, model algorithm type and list of variables. PMML is maintained by the Data Mining Group (2017) and has gone through progressive enhancements through to version 4.3 released in August 2016.

For PMML to be a useful solution, the version that is output when a model is developed – the PMML 'producer' – must be compatible with the version of the PMML 'consumer' in the software to be used for deployment. This restriction is liable to limit the combinations of packages that can be connected using PMML. For example, when a new model type is agreed upon, it results in a new version of PMML, requiring the different software vendors to update their packages in order to support it.

In order to get round this limitation, a standard known as the Portable Format for Analytics (PFA) was launched by the Data Mining Group in 2015. PFA is a mini language for defining mathematical calculations and is intended to be an alternative standard for communicating analytic workflows between processing environments.

Scoring Accelerator product

A fourth approach, taken by the Scoring Accelerator product from SAS, is to publish the model-scoring algorithm as a user function, when models are built using tools such as SAS Enterprise Miner and SAS/STAT. The user function may then be run by partner data environments. If your company uses SAS together with one of the supported data environments, then this could be a highly efficient way to deploy your models.

Model management

In order to maximize the return from predictive analytics, advanced users will employ models wherever possible – eg for all products, relationship stages (recruitment, cross-sales, retention), channels (offline, online) and sales territories. Handling all combinations of these factors implies building and maintaining literally hundreds of models, together with programs for refreshing their corresponding ADSs.

The term 'modelling factory' has been coined for such large-scale use of models. A modelling-factory environment demands a systematic method for storing model algorithms and ADS creation programs so that they can be executed, or scheduled to be run, as required. This type of system is known as model management and is available in combination with some of the data-mining products listed in Table 5.2. Suppliers of model management solutions include IBM (SPSS), SAP (KXEN), SAS and Teradata.

A model management system will typically carry out the following tasks:

- Storing and documenting model algorithms.

- Storing the SQL programs required to create analytic datasets (in order to apply those models).

- Running ADS creation and/or model algorithms when required, or scheduling jobs to execute those steps automatically.

- Monitoring the results of deploying each model, checking whether they meet prior expectations and sending an e-mail notification if a problem is encountered, such as scores not agreeing with a prior profile.

Your use of analytical models does not need to reach the scale of a modelling factory for model management to be a helpful part of your data-mining system. If your analytics team is regularly deploying a set of analytical models, then model management is a 'best practice' approach that is worthy of consideration.

Scalable analytics in the Cloud

Throughout this book, we have been assuming that your data are stored, and your analytics are carried out, on your own in-house system. It could be operated on your behalf by an external agency – we do not mind, as we have been carefully avoiding discussion of system and technology issues. However, the single 'game changer' that has caused predictive analytics to become available on a large scale, or on big data, is of course the Cloud.

We have all witnessed the impact of the Cloud on our everyday lives, for example enabling data to be shared between our computers, tablets and smartphones. It has no lesser impact on the way that analytical processes can be implemented.

All the components of the data-mining process may be implemented in the Cloud, including data storage, preliminary analysis, analytical modelling, model scoring and storage of results – any of these elements, delivered through a cloud, has become known as cloud analytics, which naturally leads to a certain amount of confusion!

Cloud analytics services and applications are typically available from a *public cloud* on a pay-per-use or subscription basis. This enables smaller organizations to scale-up their analytics when they need to, or pre-process big data and extract small data for integration with their in-house systems. For example, applications could include:

- Carry out text analysis of e-mails and comments received from customers to identify key indicators such as complaints that could lead to churn.

- Analyse social media data in order to extract new attributes about your customers.

- Analyse your customers' web logs to identify products that they may be interested in purchasing.

All these applications are likely to require preliminary screening of vast amounts of data, leading to a small set of results for each customer, and so are ideally suited to analysis in the Cloud. However, when planning to use the Cloud for processing personal customer information, you should also consider whether there are data protection issues, such as security, that need to be managed (see Chapter 1).

For a larger organization a public cloud can be uneconomic, therefore the answer can be to set up a *private cloud* as an in-house resource. This enables big data to be shared internally, while avoiding issues such as data protection. To obtain the best of both worlds, there are hybrid solutions that make use of public *and* private clouds for different parts of the analytics process.

The Cloud implies that data are automatically distributed and stored across many processors, which means that different system architectures, software products and resources are involved for cloud analytics. For example, important toolsets for cloud processing include Hadoop, Python and R – all of which are available as open-source products. And the user of these tools is likely to be a data scientist, whose role is discussed further in Chapter 2.

Conclusion

In this chapter, we have seen that:

- ✔ A two-tier data-mining architecture that exploits the power of your database system is faster and more efficient than the simpler one-tier approach.

- ✔ Four types of modelling software solutions are available, geared to meet your business needs for predictive analytics.

- ✔ When planning data-mining activities, careful thought is required on how the variables and model will be communicated between development and deployment phases.

- ✔ Model management is a useful tool for organizing and automating deployment, particularly if large numbers of models are in operation.

- ✔ The Cloud makes large-scale predictive analytics available to a greater number of organizations than could be achieved using traditional in-house solutions.

Predicting customer behaviour using analytical models

06

Introduction

Earlier chapters have discussed the process, data, techniques and tools for predictive analytics. From this chapter onwards, we examine how these resources are applied in various industries and domains. The most common application is for predicting customer behaviour, which is the main focus of this chapter.

The main aims of this chapter are to:

- Consider the use of predictive models for helping to manage the customer journey.

- Review critical elements that need to be designed when planning a new model that will deliver value for your business.

- Walk through all the steps required for building and implementing predictive models.

- Show how model performance can be evaluated using lift and gains charts.

Overview – building and deploying predictive models

The use of predictive models goes back to the early days of direct marketing, when companies started to record customers' responses and transactions, and used the data to target their marketing campaigns.

The data-mining process, reviewed in Chapter 2, translates into a series of main steps for building and deploying targeting models. These steps are summarized in Figure 6.1 and are discussed in the sections that follow.

Managing the customer journey

The *customer journey* is the series of interactions that each customer makes with your business, from becoming aware of your products or services, through to making a first purchase and eventually to leaving. This journey is liable to be long and complex, and will be different for each individual. Many companies find it helpful to map the steps in the journey, in order to help identify how to improve their customer-facing processes. This, in turn, should lead to more satisfied customers, who will stay with your company for longer, purchase more and be more profitable.

Predictive models can help to target resources for managing key stages of the customer journey – for example:

- *Customer recruitment* may be targeted, in order to maximize your return on investment. This applies irrespective of how your company recruits customers; so, for example, targeting may be used for direct marketing, online ads and newspaper advertising.

- Once a customer has been recruited, ie purchased an initial product or service from your company, you will want to strengthen the relationship and grow their value by selling them further products or add-ons. *Cross-sales and up-sales models* may be used to identify the best prospects for these offers.

Figure 6.1   How targeting models are built and deployed

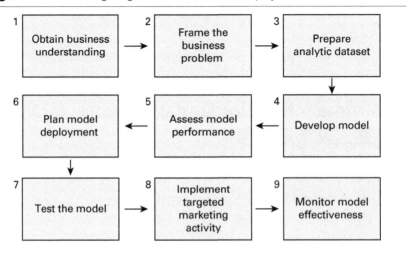

- After customers have been with you for some time, they may become vulnerable to leave and switch to a competitor. *Retention models* are used in sectors that experience high attrition rates in order to identify those at risk. For example, mobile phone companies employ *churn models* to target likely switchers and make offers designed to retain them.

- *Win-back models* are sometimes employed to target lapsed customers, and regain those who are likely to be susceptible to an attractive offer and return to you – provided, of course, that those customers are likely to be profitable and worth having back!

Defining the business requirements

You may have decided that a predictive model is required to support a particular stage in the customer journey, such as growing customer value by cross-selling further products or services. Before starting to specify the model, you will need to research and understand the business requirements completely (Figure 6.1, step 1). The requirements will define what the model needs to deliver, how its output will be applied and how this will integrate with your existing processes. This set of business requirements is essential, since the benefits from the model are delivered when it gets implemented, and it will never be implemented if your system cannot apply it.

Your business requirements will answer questions such as:

- Which of your company's products (or services) are to be cross-sold and targeted? Is a separate model required for each distinct product, or for each product category? If large numbers of separate products are to be targeted, then this will have profound implications for the number of models that will need to be built, and the choice of a viable technique.

- How will cross-sell offers be delivered to customers? For example, will you be employing cross-sell campaigns, via direct mail or e-mail? Or will 'next best product' suggestions be made by your call centre, when customers phone in? Or will product recommendations be made online, when a customer visits your website?

- Which customers are eligible for cross-selling? Campaigns usually have exclusions, such as non-marketable customers, VIPs and staff.

- Does your existing cross-sale system apply any selections or deselections, eg to exclude customers who are unlikely to purchase? If so, should these selections be maintained or removed when the model is implemented?

- What format is required for the model's outputs, eg probabilities or 'yes/no' predictions?
- How will the model outputs be used by your cross-sales system in order to produce a targeted selection for the campaign?
- Is the cross-sales activity repeated on a regular basis? If so, how often and should the model be applied prior to each selection in order to generate up-to-date prospects? And how should previously selected customers be treated?

Your detailed requirements will supply the business understanding needed by your analyst in order to plan how they will employ data mining on your behalf. This should result in a dialogue between you, to understand how your analyst intends to approach the project and satisfy your requirements.

Framing the business problem

The final element of the business requirements is to define the target variable for the model, or, in other words, the activity that the model will be designed to predict. At the same time, you will be defining the audience that the model will operate within, for example a group of prospects, existing customers or past customers (Figure 6.1 step 2).

Let us assume that your goal is to recruit customers from a population of prospects and that the 'product' is a financial service that comes with an attractive opening offer. Four alternative levels of targets might be considered:

1 Which prospects are most likely to respond to your offer?

2 Which prospects are most likely to respond and purchase?

3 Which prospects are most likely to respond, purchase and use the product?

4 Which prospects are most likely to respond, purchase, use the product and remain loyal?

Of these alternatives, target 1 will be the largest group; however, a proportion of them will not go on to purchase your product. Target 2 will identify better prospects who are more likely to purchase; however, they will not necessarily use the product. Target 3 may use the product for a short time, but may be easily attracted to a competitor's offer. Finally, target 4 may represent your ideal customers that you would most want to recruit.

The 'catch' here is that target 4 may represent your ideal kind of customers; however, the number of examples available for analysis will progressively diminish, as we move from 1 to 4, which will reduce the accuracy of the model. By the time we reach target 4, there may be insufficient data to build a model.

Key points

Framing the business problem is an 'art'

The 'art' of framing the business problem is to select the level that will achieve an ideal balance between business value and model accuracy.

Keep to the full modelling population

Having decided on the audience or modelling population you should never 'break the rules' by restricting the model to an arbitrary subset of this population. For example, you might believe that some prospects are unlikely to purchase and that those people should be excluded from the model. But if you do that from the outset, then you will never learn whether there is a niche group of buyers within those unlikely prospects. The model will identify for itself whether those unlikely prospects have low purchase propensities and, if so, the end result will be the same.

The timelines for model development and deployment

Predictive models employ past events that can be observed, such as customer behaviour, to predict outcomes in the future. In order to prepare the analytic dataset for a model (Figure 6.1 step 3), we first need to plan the timelines for these past events and future outcomes.

It is essential to plan two timelines, as shown in Figure 6.2 – the development timeline for building the model, and the timeline for its deployment. The actual timelines that you construct will include date ranges for each of the observation and outcome periods. An example is shown in Figure 9.1 for the financial services case study presented in Chapter 9.

Model development timeline – Figure 6.2a

As we have seen in earlier chapters, the model development dataset includes example cases containing outcomes for the target variable, so that your

Figure 6.2   Timelines for predictive model development and deployment

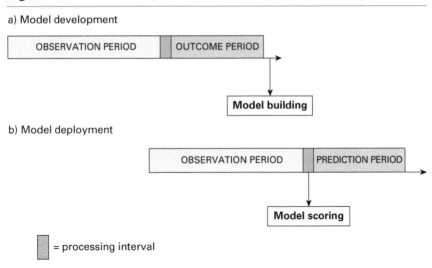

a) Model development

OBSERVATION PERIOD | OUTCOME PERIOD

Model building

b) Model deployment

OBSERVATION PERIOD | PREDICTION PERIOD

Model scoring

■ = processing interval

modelling software can be trained to be predict it. The *outcome period* is therefore a recent-past time span over which the target variable can be measured – this period needs to be sufficiently long to capture a representative number of instances of the target event, but also needs to accord with your marketing actions that will be applied to predicted target customers. A typical outcome period is usually somewhere between one month and one year.

The *observation period* is the timeframe over which consumer behaviour will be observed, in order to obtain predictor variables and construct the model. This period must, by definition, precede the outcome period and will typically be a longer time span. Its length will mainly depend upon how much history is available for each customer and the amount of seasonality inherent in your market. An observation period of one to two years is often used, which controls for seasonal variation and is sufficiently long to measure behavioural change. If the period is much longer, this would mean that more recently recruited customers would have incomplete histories and so would need to be excluded from the model. At the same time, it is valid to include variables that summarize how each customer was initially recruited, even though this may precede the start of the observation period; indeed attributes such as recruitment channel – online or offline – and length of relationship (from recruitment to end of observation period) can sometimes be useful predictors.

It is essential that the timeline is followed strictly, in terms of the time periods on which the variables are based. All variables for the observation period *must* precede the outcome period. Failure to maintain this time ordering could lead to a situation where a potential predictor variable is 'tainted' or affected by the target variable, producing a spurious correlation between the two. The modelling software will detect this relationship, will assume that it is real and predictive, and will include the predictor variable in the model. The resultant model will appear to be very strong, but will fail to deliver when it gets deployed.

As an example of this situation, suppose that a bank is building a model to cross-sell mortgages to existing customers and accidentally allows the observation and outcome periods to overlap. Since new mortgage customers often take out personal loans in order to fund the balance of their deposits, the bank discovers that holding a loan is highly predictive of mortgage take-up. This could result in a model that primarily picks out holders of personal loans, most of whom have no intention of acquiring a mortgage.

Model deployment timeline – Figure 6.2b

At the same time as planning the development timeline, you should think about the corresponding time periods for your first deployment of the model; this serves as a check that the time periods will work in practice. For subsequent deployments, the periods should simply roll forward, and so should not require separate timeline plans.

For the deployment timeline, the observation period should be the same length as for model development, but rolled forward to the most recent period for which the model's predictor variables may be obtained. Likewise, the outcome period is replaced by the corresponding future prediction period.

Between the observation and outcome periods, there is an interval that allows for the processing time to deploy the model, ie the time taken to extract the required data, score the model, decide marketing actions and deliver those treatments to your targeted customers. Ideally, you would want this interval to be as short as possible, so that predictions can be based upon the most recent customer behaviour. However, if the speed of your systems means that it takes up to one month (say) to carry out all these processes, then a one-month processing interval should be included.

The corresponding processing interval, ie one month, should be included in the development timeline (Figure 6.2a) to ensure that the model will predict in exactly the same way when it gets deployed.

The sample size required

The question of *'what sample size is needed for model development?'* is frequently asked by new users – however, often there is no simple answer. This is one of those 'how long is a piece of string?' questions!

The numbers of cases available in your database will depend upon how you have framed the business problem and the timeline that you are planning to use for model development. So if achieving an adequate sample size is likely to be an issue, then start by applying a set of ideal requirements and checking the numbers of eligible records that would be delivered – for 'positives' (eg responders) and 'negatives' (non-responders). If insufficient cases are available – see below – then you might need to consider reframing the business problem and/or shortening the observation period.

In the early days of predictive analytics, when targeting models were first being used for applications such as cross-selling, your author's regular answer to the sample size question was '*as a rule of thumb, around 1,500 positives and a similar-size sample of negatives*'. This order of size allowed around two-thirds of the sample to be used for building a sound model and one-third held aside for validation. Within these groups, the sample sizes supported gains and lift charts at decile level – ie 10 equal subsets – to evaluate the model and plan its use (described in this chapter).

The requirement for a sample of 1,500 known responders was sometimes a challenge, and occasionally smaller volumes had to be used. This had the consequence that resultant models employed smaller numbers of predictor variables and categories, and were less predictive.

Key point

The balance between numbers of sample positives and negatives is dependent upon the objective of your model:

- If the model is being built to classify future cases as 'positive' or 'negative', then the development sample should contain equal numbers of each outcome. (However, the need to have equal numbers depends to some extent on the method and software tool being used, as some tools allow differential weighting of the sample cases.)

- If the objective is to predict the probability that a case will be positive, then the two outcomes should be present in their naturally occurring proportions. However, if the positive outcome (say) occurs in a very small proportion of cases, then this could lead to a massive sample size.

In the latter situation, a useful strategy is to build the model using a disproportionate sample containing 100 per cent of positives and a representative sample of negatives, eg 10 per cent. The sample should then be weighted back to the correct population proportions in order to assess the benefit of the model.

Now that we are in the era of large-scale marketing databases and big data, achieving 1,500 responders is less often a challenge. Indeed, the opposite problem is more likely to arise – you may have access to vast numbers of records, so how many of them should you use?

The general answer is 'the more the better', as a larger sample size will support a more detailed model that gives more accurate predictions. Studies have shown that model accuracy improves *at a decreasing rate*, as the sample size is increased – for example, see James Morgan et al (2003) who looked at this relationship for decision tree data-mining tools. The researchers concluded that, in order to locate the optimal size, models should be built using progressively increasing sample sizes and a curve fitted to assess the point at which model error is minimized.

A simpler strategy is to build an initial model, measure its accuracy, and then repeat the process using double the sample size. If this produces a noticeably more accurate model, then continue to repeat using double the sample, until a stable accuracy rate is obtained.

Such experiments are only normally necessary in early use of predictive models, if your analyst wants to explore statistically robust sample sizes. After that, users often settle on a fixed data extract size, in order to err on the safe side for each model.

Key point

It is more important to use a smaller development sample that is representative of your modelling population, rather than a much larger sample that is known to be incomplete or biased.

Modelling software cannot detect sampling biases, nor can it identify groups or behaviours that are missing from your data. It can only accept your data at face value.

Preparing the analytic dataset

The tasks involved in constructing the analytic dataset (ADS) were discussed in Chapter 3. For building a predictive model, the ADS will correspond to the model development timeline shown in Figure 6.2a, and will include the following:

- Demographics of each customer, such as their age at the end of the observation period, marital status, presence of children, income and so on.
- Recruitment attributes such as channel and length of relationship.

- Existing and previous product holdings based on the observation period.

- Summary transaction behaviour by product and channel, for the observation period.

- Other behavioural variables that can be measured for the same observation period.

- The target variable to be used for model development and assessment, based on the outcome period.

The equivalent information – with the exception of the target variable – will need to be available when you come to the deployment phase, but only for those variables that have been identified as useful predictors and included in the final model. Any variables that would be unavailable for deployment should be excluded from the model development ADS, unless there is a special reason to include them. For example, you might wish to identify predictive supplementary questions to ask customers and use the modelling project to explore data captured in a recent customer survey. This is fine, provided that the final model excludes survey information – until such time as the predictive survey variables are available for all customers.

Bear in mind that, when it comes to future deployment, the model's predictor variables will need to be defined and calculated exactly as they were for the initial development – but for a future observation period, as in Figure 6.2b. Therefore, all fields in the development ADS should be well documented, at the very least, and ideally there should be a mechanism to select the final predictor variables and roll their creation forward to the next observation period; some of the model management systems mentioned in Chapter 5 include this capability.

Building the model

At the heart of the project we arrive at developing the model, using one or more of the predictive algorithms described in Chapter 4. Having carefully framed the business problem and constructed the analytic dataset, one might naturally imagine that the modelling software will take over and automatically deliver a great model. However, this is rarely the case, even with automated data-mining tools. A number of problems can potentially arise – in this section, we identify the most common ones and discuss how to overcome them, as frequently occurring issues and answers.

Frequently occurring issues

Issue 1: how should the performance of the model be assessed?

Answer 1: prior to analysing the ADS and developing the model, the dataset should be split in separate subsets for model development and validation. Depending upon the available sample size, 70 per cent of cases are typically assigned to the development group (A) and 30 per cent to validation (B). The splitting should be carried out by a random or pseudo-random process, such as pre-sorting the file and then assigning the first seven records to group A, the next three to group B, the next seven to group A, and so on. The process should ensure that the two groups are well matched; the model development takes place solely using group A, while assessment compares the two groups – see below.

Issue 2: the analytic dataset contains too many predictor variables for the modelling tool to handle.

Answer 2: before starting to build models, many analysts carry out a preliminary analysis in order to screen the available variables and identify a set of candidate predictors. In this phase, sometimes known as a characteristics analysis, cross-tabs and measures of association are produced, which look at the relationships between the target variable and each available predictor. Variables that prove to be either missing, constant, or very sparsely populated, should be removed. Those that show no sign of a useful relationship with the target variable are also discarded.

Issue 3: some of the potential predictor variables are very similar to one another – for example, gross income and net income both discriminate strongly but are highly correlated. Can they both be included in the model?

Answer 3: the situation of highly correlated variables is known as multi-collinearity – there is no set definition of when this occurs; however, most analysts would regard a correlation of 0.95 or more, between two variables, as evidence of the condition. Keeping both highly correlated variables in the model is likely to produce instability, effectively because the modelling software will find it difficult to estimate the regression coefficients for those two variables. Therefore, most analysts will check for multi-collinearity, often by examining the correlations between pairs of candidate predictors. Once the condition is discovered, then a common solution is to retain one of the highly correlated variables and discard the other – preferring to keep the version that has a stronger relationship with the target variable.

Sometimes it might be appropriate to pre-process the data using principal component analysis (see Chapter 4) if there is a large amount of multi-collinearity, and discard the least relevant components. This approach enables all the highly correlated variables to be used; however, its drawback is that it will require a pre-processing stage to calculate the required components, each time the model is deployed.

If two variables are perfectly correlated – in other words, one is a copy of the other – then one of those variables will need to be excluded for regression-based methods to be able to fit a model.

Issue 4: the sample size is so large that all available predictors appear to be significant variables in the model.

Answer 4: regression modelling techniques will quantify the statistical significance of each predictor variable, and of the model as a whole. These techniques assume that the dataset is a relatively small sample from a much larger population. Therefore, if the model is being built on a vast sample, the amount of sampling variation will be tiny and every predictor variable will seem to be significant. The solution is to carry out an initial analysis on a much smaller sample (selected at random to be representative of the full sample), and use this to select the useful predictors and build an initial model. The final model can be fitted to the same variables, using the full sample in order to obtain accurate estimates of the regression coefficients.

Stepwise regression models can be helpful here, by setting very tight criteria for inclusion and exclusion of variables, or by restricting the number of steps.

Issue 5: a model has been developed, but it discriminates too weakly to be any use.

Answer 5: first of all, do not abandon the model without testing its benefits – for some applications even weak models can be useful. However, if the model really doesn't perform well, then try to reframe the problem in a way that would still give useful results, and see whether this delivers a stronger outcome.

Issue 6: is the model going to target people who would purchase anyway? If so, then what is the solution?

Answer 6: the solution, known as uplift modelling, is to model the effect of receiving the marketing treatment. The approach measures the effect of receiving the treatment, compared with a control group who do not receive the treatment. Using the results of a test campaign, involving a treatment group and a control, the treatment uplift effect is predicted for each individual. Best prospects can then be selected, for whom the treatment will have greatest predicted benefit. The approach is discussed more fully by Nicholas Radcliffe (2007).

Issue 7: some customer events occur infrequently but are likely to result in a positive outcome. Can such events be included in the model?

Answer 7: events of this type are known as triggers and can be highly predictive. For example, a sharp decrease in mobile phone usage may indicate that the customer is switching their telephone provider, and so is a strong churn indicator. Trigger events may be included in models; however, a better strategy is to monitor separately for those behaviours and take rapid action when they occur. If triggers were included in a model then the resultant marketing action would be taken too late to influence the customer.

Issue 8: what is the shelf life of the model? When will it need to be redeveloped?

Answer 8: if consumer behaviour in your market does not undergo significant change, then the model shelf-life is likely to be at least two to three years. However, should a predictive new data source become available, then you should consider redeveloping the model in order to benefit from it. After the model has been implemented, its effectiveness should be monitored continuously – the results will tell you when the model is no longer so discriminatory and needs to be replaced.

Assessing model performance

Traditional statistical measures

When it comes to assessing model performance (step 5 in Figure 6.1) traditional statistical methods tend not to be very helpful. Statistical techniques employ measures such as the R^2 statistic, which expresses the amount of variation in the target outcome that is explained by the model. In scientific disciplines, statisticians may expect the R^2 value to exceed 50 per cent, meaning that the model explains the most of the variation. However, marketing analysts often achieve R^2 values of less than 10 per cent in their models, because they are aiming to predict a customer's future behaviour or decisions, using largely past behaviour as a clue.

An R^2 value, whether high or low, provides no information about whether a model would be useful if implemented, nor does it indicate how much benefit the model would deliver. And a model with a low R^2 can still be a worthwhile targeting tool. Partly, this is because marketers are primarily interested in the targeting success rate, which depends on R, whereas statistical goodness-of-fit uses the square of R. For example, an R value of 25 per cent, which might be regarded as helpful, converts to an R^2 of 6.25 per cent, which might not appear to be sufficiently useful.

Assessment using gains and lift charts

A more practical and effective way to assess and demonstrate model accuracy is via gains and/or lift charts. Both of these graphs may be derived from a gains analysis, which may be produced once the model has been built and applied to score the development and validation samples.

A gains analysis shows numbers of customers, by positive and negative outcomes, analysed by model score bands. Depending on the total sample size available, the analysis will typically split the predicted model scores into from 10 to 25 bands containing equal numbers of cases.

Separate gains analyses should be produced for the development and validation samples recommended in the previous section. The model will invariably appear to be more predictive for the development group, since by definition it was based on those cases – this characteristic is known as optimistic bias. The validation group ought to be unbiased, and so will give a better idea of how the model is likely to perform in the future. However, a live test, discussed later in this chapter, is really the best way to prove the benefits of the model (step 7 in Figure 6.1).

Example gains analyses are shown in Table 6.1 for the development and validation samples from a targeting model project. From these analyses we can see that the model predicts positives particularly well across the top three score bands.

By comparing the development and validation gains, we can assess how well the model predicts and whether overfitting is likely to have occurred. Overfitting implies that too many variables were included in the model, therefore it performs well for the development sample, but not when applied to other data.

The gains results are generally presented in two types of graphs that help in assessing model performance by score bands – these are the gains chart and the lift chart.

Gains chart

The gains chart indicates how well the model identifies positives within the best score bands. It plots the cumulative proportion of all positives that are identified in each score band, starting with band 1, then bands 1+2, 1+2+3, and so on. By definition, this graph will ascend steeply and then

Table 6.1   Example gains analyses

a) Development sample								
	Positives		Negatives		Total development sample			
Model score band	% of positives	Cum. % of positives	% of negatives	Cum. % of negatives	% of sample	Cum. % of sample	Cum. positives rate	Cum. index
1 (highest)	21.1%	21.1%	3.1%	3.1%	3.9%	3.9%	25.0%	539.4
2	15.9%	36.9%	2.9%	6.0%	3.5%	7.4%	23.1%	499.5
3	16.4%	53.3%	4.0%	9.9%	4.5%	11.9%	20.7%	447.2
4	6.7%	60.0%	3.5%	13.5%	3.7%	15.6%	17.8%	384.3
5	5.3%	65.3%	4.0%	17.4%	4.0%	19.7%	15.4%	332.4
6	5.1%	70.4%	4.3%	21.8%	4.4%	24.0%	13.6%	293.4
7	4.3%	74.7%	3.9%	25.6%	3.9%	27.9%	12.4%	267.9
8	4.6%	79.3%	4.1%	29.7%	4.1%	32.0%	11.5%	247.9
9	2.8%	82.0%	4.1%	33.7%	4.0%	36.0%	10.5%	228.0
10	3.4%	85.5%	3.7%	37.5%	3.7%	39.7%	10.0%	215.2
11	1.7%	87.1%	3.3%	40.8%	3.2%	42.9%	9.4%	203.1
12	1.6%	88.7%	5.3%	46.1%	5.2%	48.1%	8.5%	184.6
13	0.8%	89.5%	4.1%	50.2%	3.9%	52.0%	8.0%	172.1
14	0.3%	89.7%	0.4%	50.6%	0.4%	52.4%	7.9%	171.1
15	1.9%	91.6%	7.7%	58.4%	7.5%	59.9%	7.1%	153.0
16	1.8%	93.4%	4.2%	62.5%	4.0%	63.9%	6.8%	146.1
17	0.8%	94.2%	2.3%	64.8%	2.2%	66.1%	6.6%	142.5
18	1.4%	95.7%	5.5%	70.3%	5.3%	71.5%	6.2%	133.8
19	1.3%	96.9%	4.6%	74.9%	4.4%	75.9%	5.9%	127.6
20	0.7%	97.6%	4.2%	79.1%	4.0%	80.0%	5.6%	122.0
21	0.8%	98.4%	3.3%	82.4%	3.2%	83.1%	5.5%	118.4
22	0.3%	98.7%	5.0%	87.4%	4.8%	88.0%	5.2%	112.3
23	0.3%	99.1%	3.2%	90.6%	3.0%	91.0%	5.0%	108.9
24	0.3%	99.3%	4.7%	95.3%	4.5%	95.5%	4.8%	104.0
25 (lowest)	0.7%	100.0%	4.7%	100.0%	4.5%	100.0%	4.6%	100.0
Total	100.0%		100.0%		100.0%		4.6%	

(continued)

Table 6.1   *(Continued)*

b) Validation sample								
	Positives		**Negatives**		**Total development sample**			
Model score band	% of positives	Cum. % of positives	% of negatives	Cum. % of negatives	% of sample	Cum. % of sample	Cum. positives rate	Cum. index
1 (highest)	18.1%	18.1%	2.8%	2.8%	3.5%	3.5%	22.7%	517.8
2	16.3%	34.4%	3.5%	6.3%	4.1%	7.6%	19.9%	453.8
3	14.4%	48.8%	3.8%	10.2%	4.3%	11.9%	18.1%	411.0
4	6.6%	55.3%	4.0%	14.1%	4.1%	15.9%	15.3%	347.4
5	6.4%	61.7%	3.9%	18.0%	4.0%	19.9%	13.6%	309.5
6	6.0%	67.7%	3.8%	21.8%	3.8%	23.8%	12.5%	284.5
7	4.5%	72.2%	4.1%	25.9%	4.1%	27.9%	11.4%	258.7
8	5.3%	77.6%	4.3%	30.2%	4.3%	32.3%	10.6%	240.5
9	2.3%	79.8%	3.7%	33.9%	3.6%	35.9%	9.8%	222.5
10	2.1%	81.9%	4.1%	38.0%	4.0%	39.9%	9.0%	205.2
11	1.9%	83.7%	4.2%	42.1%	4.1%	44.0%	8.4%	190.4
12	1.2%	85.0%	4.5%	46.7%	4.4%	48.3%	7.7%	175.8
13	1.9%	86.8%	3.4%	50.1%	3.4%	51.7%	7.4%	167.9
14	0.0%	86.8%	4.2%	54.3%	4.0%	55.8%	6.8%	155.7
15	2.7%	89.5%	4.6%	58.9%	4.5%	60.3%	6.5%	148.5
16	1.9%	91.4%	4.0%	62.9%	3.9%	64.2%	6.3%	142.3
17	0.6%	92.0%	2.9%	65.8%	2.8%	67.0%	6.0%	137.3
18	3.1%	95.1%	5.0%	70.8%	4.9%	71.9%	5.8%	132.2
19	1.6%	96.7%	4.1%	74.9%	4.0%	75.9%	5.6%	127.4
20	0.8%	97.5%	4.1%	79.1%	4.0%	79.9%	5.4%	122.1
21	0.4%	97.9%	2.0%	81.1%	1.9%	81.8%	5.3%	119.7
22	1.0%	99.0%	6.3%	87.3%	6.0%	87.9%	4.9%	112.7
23	0.4%	99.4%	3.2%	90.5%	3.1%	90.9%	4.8%	109.3
24	0.4%	99.8%	5.0%	95.5%	4.8%	95.7%	4.6%	104.3
25 (lowest)	0.2%	100.0%	4.5%	100.0%	4.3%	100.0%	4.4%	100.0
Total	100.0%		100.0%		100.0%		4.4%	

start to level off, reaching 100 per cent by the final score band. For reference, the chart includes a diagonal line representing a model that produces completely random results. The extent to which the actual model rises above the diagonal line, giving a 'bow shaped area' between the two lines, indicates the discriminatory power of the model.

Figure 6.3 Example gains chart for development and validation samples

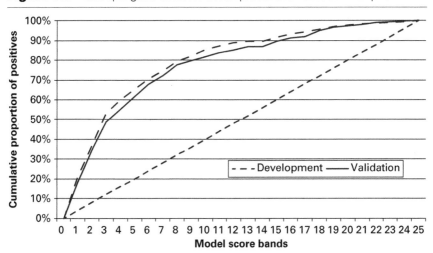

It is most useful to compare the model gains for the development and validation samples in one gains chart – as illustrated in Figure 6.3, which corresponds to the gains analyses in Table 6.1. This example shows that model gains based on the development samples are, as expected, higher than those on the validation sample. However, the two gains curves are consistently close together, suggesting that the model discriminates well across the validation file and that overfitting is unlikely to be an issue.

The gains chart is equivalent to another diagnostic chart, known as a receiver operating characteristic (ROC) curve, which is explained by Vuk and Curk (2006).

Lift chart

Lift charts are an alternative way of presenting the gains analysis results, in terms of improvement against a random selection; a lift chart displays the cumulative index by cumulative model score bands. This index is simply the proportion of positives identified by each score band, indexed on the proportion of positives across the total sample. Score band 1 should have the highest index; the index will decrease as further bands are added, reaching 100 by the last score band. Although the lift and gains charts produce directly equivalent results, the lift chart version tends to show performance differences more clearly for the top score bands.

Again the lift chart is used to compare performance for the development and validation samples, as illustrated in Figure 6.4, which again is based upon the same data as above. Now we see more clearly a difference in lift for the top-five score bands, after which the two curves start to converge.

Figure 6.4   Example lift chart for development and validation samples

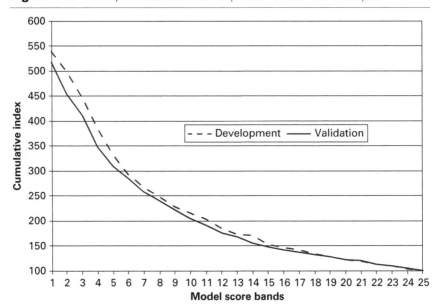

Planning model deployment

If there is a known cost of promoting to each individual, for example the cost of printing and posting a pack in a direct mail campaign, then the gains analysis can be used to compare the promotion costs for the top score bands against the corresponding costs that would be incurred to reach the same number of responders without the aid of a model. This is where we can see the financial pay-off from using a targeting model.

For example, referring to Table 6.1 for the validation sample, if the company wanted to reach 80 per cent of positives, it could achieve this by selecting the 36 per cent of customers in score bands 1 to 9. Without the model (or another method of targeting), it would have to contact 80 per cent of customers to reach that many positives. Therefore, the model halves the number of contacts that need to be made and so saves significant costs.

Key point

This single example demonstrates why predictive analytics makes excellent business sense. It means that a model does not need to predict perfectly for it to be useful. As long as the model delivers a small but consistent gain it can potentially save your company from making large numbers of unnecessary contacts.

If the average profitability contribution of each positive response can be estimated, then a total profit or loss can be calculated for each score band in the gains analysis. The notional profitability can be used to determine which score bands should be targeted in future campaigns, in order to achieve your business objectives. For example, your business might wish to send its materials to the largest number of people and break even overall, or it might wish to limit the campaign to profitable score bands only, or maximize the profitability of this campaign. Therefore, the gains analysis can be a very useful tool for helping marketers to plan campaigns.

Continuing the above example, suppose that the cost per contact is 1 unit (eg £1 or $1), and the expected value of reaching each positive is 15 units. Then, using Table 6.1 we can estimate the cumulative profitability of a direct campaign – see Figure 6.5. We see that, by contacting customers in the top 15 bands, the campaign will just about break even overall. From Table 6.1b, we see that this would involve contacting 60 per cent of customers and would reach 90 per cent of positives. Alternatively, in order to maximize cumulative profitability, only the first six bands would be targeted, which would result in contacting 24 per cent of customers and would reach 68 per cent of positives. A third option is to limit the campaign to bands delivering the greatest returns – namely the first three bands. Just 12 per cent of customers would be contacted, reaching 49 per cent of positives. Note that all such calculations should be performed using the gains analysis for the validation (or evaluation) sample, which has not been involved in building the model.

Figure 6.5   Predicted campaign profitability by model score bands

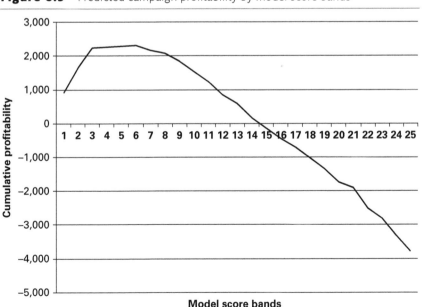

From testing to implementation

Steps 7, 8 and 9 of the targeting model process (Figure 6.1) cover the operational stages of putting the model into practice.

Testing the model (step 7) implies conducting a live test in order to prove that the model is effective and to quantify its effects when put into operation. This test is essential, no matter how well the model appears to discriminate or how strong its assessment results seem; the 'acid test' is whether it continues to work for a different time period and delivers benefits in practice. Market conditions are likely to change over time, or there may be seasonal differences, and so it is important to see that the model generalizes to be useful for more than just its development period.

In order to measure the effect, the test should compare two groups of customers – a group targeted using the model versus a control group. In order to minimize the risk to your business, the targeted group should be relatively small – just sufficiently large to be able to measure a difference in response rate with a required level of confidence. How to achieve this is discussed in Chapter 12, on testing the benefits of predictive analytics.

Implementing the targeted marketing activity (step 8) is, of course, where actual value should be delivered, in terms of either cost savings or revenue increases. By this stage, the model effectiveness has been proven, therefore the majority of contacts should be targeted using the model.

Finally, it is best practice to keep aside some customers as a control group, in order to **monitor model effectiveness** (step 9); however, now the control group will be relatively small – so that the financial benefits gained from the targeting are as large as possible.

Key point

A control group should continue to be included, even after the model has been proven effective, because this enables any change in performance to be identified.

Conclusion

In this chapter, we have seen that:

✔ Framing the business problem to be modelled is an art, which can have a major impact upon the success of your project. Redefining the problem may significantly improve your results.

- ✓ When building a model, all predictors must be based on behaviours or attributes defined *prior* to the outcome period. The outcome must not be allowed to affect or taint any of the predictors.

- ✓ It is better to use a smaller development sample that is properly representative of your model population, than employ a much larger dataset that is biased or omits a key group.

- ✓ Traditional statistical methods of model assessment, such as R^2 values, are not very useful for targeting models. Gains and lift charts are widely employed and can help to plan model deployment.

- ✓ A model will always predict best on its build data, due to *optimistic bias*. To assess its performance more accurately, use a validation sample containing cases held back from the model's development.

- ✓ No matter how well the model appears to predict on its development and validation data, a live test should be conducted that deploys the model and uses a control group to measure its performance.

- ✓ A control group should continue to be used, each time the model is deployed, in order to monitor its effectiveness and help identify any issues.

Predicting lifetimes

07

From customers to machines

Introduction

A key dimension that is easy to overlook is *time* – how do events take place over time and when is a future event likely to occur? This chapter discusses the analysis of time – such as intervals between purchases or the time remaining before a customer lapses or churns. Similarly, we could be looking at machinery maintenance and incidents such as equipment failures or warranty claims. All these events can be examined using a branch of statistics known as survival analysis – we shall focus on its main principles and applications in various industries.

The main aims of this chapter are to:

- Introduce the concepts of survival analysis.
- Discuss the use of survival analysis for describing time durations.
- Overview the use of survival analysis models to predict time paths for individual customers.
- Consider the main differences between survival analysis and churn prediction.
- Identify business applications of survival analysis for customer management.
- Show how the same techniques may be applied to managing the maintenance cycles of assets such as motor cars and machinery.

Importance of the customer lifecycle

In many consumer markets, products have lifecycles that depend upon the ages of customers or the life stages that they go through. For example, the financial services that are likely to be of interest to an individual will depend on whether they are:

- 'just starting out' – such as a bank account or loan;
- 'forming a family' – such as a mortgage or life insurance;
- 'moving up the ladder' – such as investments and retirement plans;
- 'in their golden years' – such as pensions and annuities.

Similarly, the mobile phone and services that people use are often age-related. For example, children and young people are likely to be more interested in messaging, while the elderly are likely to prefer straightforward handsets and access to emergency services. Although we can all think of exceptions to such generalizations, these broad trends are often true.

This lifecycle effect suggests that a customer's mobile phone, say, is unlikely to be kept forever. As a person becomes older and their needs change, so their requirements for a device and services will change also – leaving aside the new models and technological advances that will appear on the way.

For these reasons, marketers need to track the customer lifecycle and identify the right time to offer the next product or upgrade. Unless they do this, the customer is likely to be attracted by a competitor's product that now meets their needs. Survival analysis techniques can help to track the lifecycle and identify when to make those marketing interventions.

Survival analysis applications

Survival analysis has applications in a great variety of industries and for many different business problems, including:

- Telecommunications – predicting customer lifetimes and lifetime values (LTVs).
- Insurance – time until lapsing on a policy.
- Mortgages – time until mortgage redemption.
- Mail-order catalogues – time until next purchase.
- Public sector – time to a critical event, eg length of time in employment or unemployed.
- Manufacturing – lifetime of a machine component or piece of equipment.
- Car industry – time until warranty claim.

Key concepts of this technique

Survival analysis is essentially the analysis of time. The approach was first developed in medical statistics for examining how long patients would be likely to survive; however, it is now being used in less morbid fields, including marketing and asset management. As we have seen for other techniques, survival analysis may be used either descriptively – to understand how survival rates vary between groups – or in a predictive mode, to predict survival times for customers. These applications are discussed in this chapter, together with case study examples.

We shall discuss some of the essential concepts of survival analysis for applications to customer management. A complete introduction to the technique is provided by Hosmer et al (2008). To illustrate the concepts, we focus on its application to customers, to analyse time until churn or attrition. The first concept, unique to survival analysis, is that of censored data.

Censored data

For customers who have already churned, we have complete information; we know their start and end dates, and hence how long they were customers. However, for existing customers, we know their start dates and that they have yet to lapse, but we do not know when that will occur. For this reason, these existing customers are said to be censored cases – their end dates are missing, because they have yet to churn. This situation is illustrated in Figure 7.1 for several churners and current customers.

In survival analysis, censored cases are explicitly allowed for, in order to make use of what we do know about those customers – which is how long they have been with us *up until now*. The danger of analysing only those

Figure 7.1   The concept of censored data

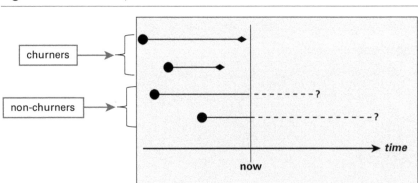

customers with known start and end dates, and excluding the censored cases, is that the true length of relationship will be understated – because churners tend to stay for shorter lengths of time than non-churners.

Terminology used in survival analysis

Survival analysis measures and predicts time-related aspects of churn behaviour, such as the rate at which customers churn over time and the likelihood that they will churn in a future period. Two measures most useful for churn management are the survival function and the hazard function – they are both functions of time (t), which can be measured in whatever units are most appropriate to your business. Typically, for many consumer products this would be either months or years.

Survival function

The survival function or survival curve is the probability that a customer will have a survival time greater than or equal to t. In other words, it is the chance they will be a customer for at least t months (or whatever time units are appropriate). This quantity is usually denoted as S(t) and may be measured either for all customers or any subsets.

By definition, the survival function starts off at 100 per cent at time zero, since all new recruits are customers at the moment that they join you, therefore S(0) is 100 per cent. As t increases, some customers will churn and therefore S(t) decreases from 100 per cent; eventually, S(t) approaches 0 per cent as t becomes large. Two examples of possible survival curves are illustrated in Figure 7.2 – in example (a), the churn rate is initially low

Figure 7.2   Example survival curves

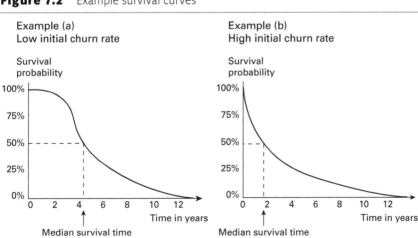

and increases gradually, whereas in example (b) the churn rate starts high and then reduces. Once the survival curve has dropped below 50 per cent, customers are more likely to leave than stay. This median survival time occurs at just over four years in example (a) and close to two years in example (b).

Hazard function

The hazard function, usually denoted by $h(t)$, is the instantaneous churn rate in the next unit time period, given that the customer has survived to time t.

Depending upon the nature of your product or service, the hazard function could increase, decrease or be fairly constant over time, as illustrated by the first three scenarios shown in Figure 7.3. For example, an increasing churn rate, shown in Figure 7.3a, may arise for products that start perfect and wear out after a long period of use. A decreasing churn rate, as in Figure 7.3b, implies higher rates of churn at the outset – perhaps due to new customers changing their minds early on. A constant churn rate, as in Figure 7.3c, is the least likely to apply over the entire life of the product. However, it may hold over the mid-life period, combined with a decreasing churn rate at the start and increasing churn towards the end. This combination is known as a 'bathtub curve' – see Figure 7.3d – and is one of the most widely occurring shapes for the hazard function.

Figure 7.3 Example hazard functions

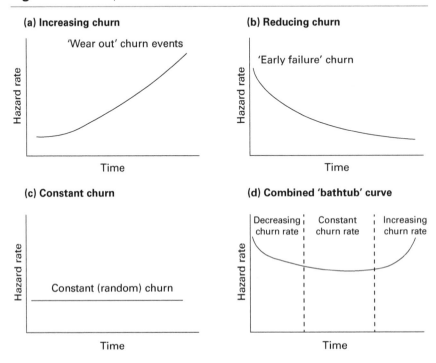

Cumulative hazard function

The cumulative hazard, denoted by H(t), is the sum total of the hazard function h(t), from time 0 through to time t. The cumulative hazard is the 'mirror image' of the survival function – they are related by the equation:

$$H(t) = -\ln(S(t))$$

– where 'ln' represents 'log to base e' and S(t) is expressed as a proportion between 0 and 1.

At time 0, when S(0) is 1, the cumulative hazard will therefore be 0. And as t increases, ln(S(t)) will be negative and decreasing, therefore the cumulative hazard will be positive and increasing.

Benefits from using both survival and hazard functions

Although the survival and cumulative hazard functions are mathematically related, there is benefit to be gained from calculating and looking at both measures. The survival curve shows how likely customers are to stay over time and the points at which they become most likely to churn; furthermore, the area under the curve represents the true average customer lifetime, taking both churners and non-churners into account. This finding comes from a mathematical result that the expected value of t is equal to the area under the survival curve – Hosmer et al (2008) discuss this further.

The hazard function, in measuring churn rates over time, can identify moments at which you are most vulnerable to losing customers. Armed with this knowledge, you may be able to make marketing interventions at the right times, to encourage customers to stay.

As we shall see in this chapter, survival times may be predicted by modelling the hazard function for each individual.

Describing customer lifetimes

The survival and hazard functions may be calculated for your customer base, using survival analysis techniques that are often available in statistics packages such as those listed in Table 5.1. Many packages include the Kaplan-Meier technique for estimating the survival function – the approach is described in detail by Hosmer et al (2008). The method requires, as its input, start and end dates for each customer, together with a flag to indicate whether the customer has churned – to identify censored cases (non-churners). Additional attributes may be supplied for each customer, in order to compare groups of interest.

Descriptive survival analysis allows you to compare survival curves between different groups of customers, for example demographic groups, marketing segments, holders of various product types or service plans, and recruits via the available sales channels. By seeing the differences for dimensions such as these, you are able to identify key factors that influence customer longevity for your product.

CASE STUDY

Which types of customers lapse early?

This case study concerns a financial services company that was cross-selling personal accident insurance to its clients, using telemarketing. The company had experienced an increase in monthly lapse rates and a reduction in retention levels. Therefore, it wanted to understand which types of customers were lapsing early and identify an optimal time to make some kind of intervention or offer that might help to reduce lapse rates.

We start by looking at the hazard rates, to see how lapsing varied over time. When each new customer agreed to take the product, their personal accident cover started immediately and they received free cover for the first one to two months. During this period, the company set up their direct debit and their policy became 'converted' after the first payment was received. In Figure 7.4, we see the hazards for all policies that were initiated and for those that were converted.

Figure 7.4   Example hazard functions for personal accident insurance

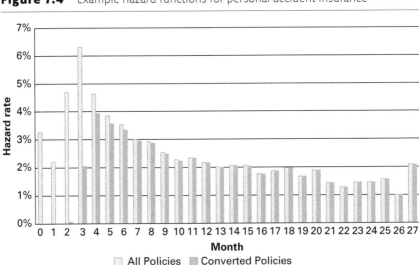

Note: Figures have been disguised.

We can see from Figure 7.4 that the overall lapse rate climbs to a peak at month three and then declines thereafter. At month three, customers most probably noticed the first payment of the policy premium and a proportion of them immediately cancelled. Amongst converted policies, the lapse rate peaks at month four and then reduces steadily. Therefore, once the customer has continued with the policy for one month of payment, they are slightly less likely to lapse in each subsequent month. These results suggest that the company might consider offering an incentive to customers *early on, at month one*, to retain their policies for at least one or two initial payments.

Survival analysis was also used to compare how long different types of customers retained their policies. Survival curves were produced for all available subsets, including splits by age and gender, geodemographic segments and affluence. Figure 7.5 shows the comparison for three affluence groups based on customer postcode. As might be expected, the survival curves are ranked in order on affluence, with the affluent having highest survival probabilities; furthermore, the difference between the affluent and other groups increases over time. The less affluent consistently show higher survival chances than the poor, by a small constant margin.

Figure 7.5   Example survival curves by affluence level

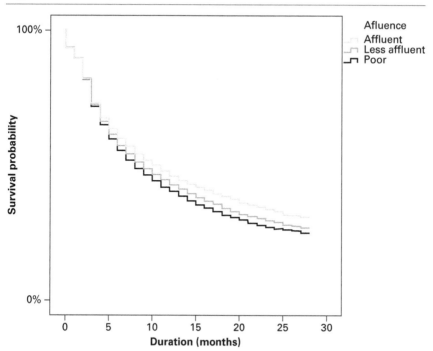

Predicting survival times

While a descriptive analysis can identify which groups are more vulnerable to churn, it does not assess the churn risk for each individual customer or predict their survival over time. The most effective way to achieve this is to apply a special form of regression analysis to model the hazard function for each individual.

A hazards model predicts the hazard function for each customer, as the product of a baseline hazard and a customer effect. The baseline hazard describes how the churn rate changes over time across all customers, and may be estimated from the data in the same way as for a descriptive survival analysis. The customer effect predicts how the characteristics of each individual will increase or reduce the hazard rate.

The general equation for a hazard model is the product of the baseline hazard and the customer effect:

$$h(t, x, b) = h_0(t) * r(x, b)$$

– where:

- $h(t, x, b)$ is the predicted hazard at time t for a customer with data value x and regression coefficient b;
- $h_0(t)$ is the baseline hazard across all customers at time t;
- $r(x, b)$ is the customer effect of having data value x and regression coefficient b.

David Cox (1972) proposed the following more specific hazard model:

$$h(t, x, b) = h_0(t) * exp(b * x)$$

– where:

- $exp(\ )$ is the exponential function and $exp(b * x)$ is again the customer effect.

Cox's approach is known as the proportional hazards model, due to the fact that the customer effect is a constant multiplier that does not involve the survival time t. So, for example, suppose that a particular customer had a customer effect of 1.2. For that customer, the predicted hazard function would be the baseline hazard $h_0(t)$ increased by 20 per cent – a proportional increase that is constant over time.

The proportional hazards model is the most widely used predictive technique in survival analysis. It extends to allow many variables (x values) to be included in the model, each with its own regression coefficient (b value). As well as identifying which customer attributes significantly affect survival times, the model enables an individual hazard function to be predicted for each customer, and from this gives their predicted survival curve.

The model makes a major assumption – that the customer effect can be represented by a constant multiplier. Survival analysis packages are able to test how well this assumption holds true and, if necessary, include time-dependent factors in the model.

CASE STUDY

Predicting survival times of mobile phone customers

A mobile phone company wanted to understand better the lifetimes of its pre-pay customers. The pre-pay business accounted for a large share of the company's turnover and also experienced high churn rates – so any reduction in churn that could be achieved would be very valuable.

Data used for project

For pre-pay customers there was no official disconnection date when a customer could be said to have churned. Therefore churn was defined as absence of activity in a 30-day period.

The survival time for each customer was calculated from their date of subscription activation through to:

- churn date, for churners, or

- data extract date, for non-churners (censored cases).

A large number of behavioural and attribute variables were extracted for each customer, including:

- phone-usage variables by types of call, inbound/outbound, in-network/out-of-network, home/roaming calls and abnormal call terminations;

- top-up payments by frequency and value;

- customer attributes such as age and gender.

Project description

An exploratory analysis was carried out to identify characteristics that could help in predicting time till churn. A number of new variables were derived such as recency, frequency and value of top-up payments, together with trend and variability of phone usage.

A survival-time model was developed using the Cox proportional hazards technique. Predictor variables were included in the model using a stepwise procedure.

The predictors in the model were examined to determine how they affected customer longevity. For example, if the average number of text messages per week increases by 'x', expected longevity increases by 'y' days.

Example results

The final model contained a range of customer attributes and behavioural variables that tend to increase or reduce survival times. These included:

● age and gender;

● recency and value of top-up payments;

● calling patterns for voice and text messages;

● service quality issues (dropped calls);

● geodemographic segments.

The model was used to predict the survival function for each customer – the curves for three hypothetical customers are shown in Figure 7.6.

Figure 7.6   Predicted survival curves for three customers

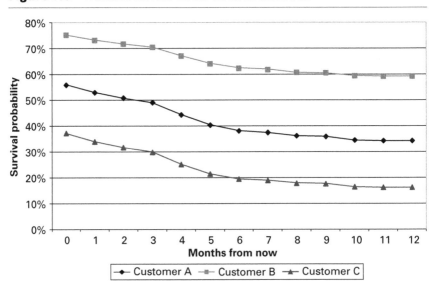

As we can see, Customer B starts off with a survival probability of around 75 per cent, which is predicted to decline at a gradual rate – reaching around 60 per cent in 12 months' time. Therefore, 'B' appears likely to remain a customer for at least another 12 months and so has a relatively low risk of churn.

On the other hand, Customer C begins with less than 40 per cent survival probability, which is predicted to fall below 20 per cent by six months from now. Therefore 'C' is a likely churner who is probably too far advanced to be 'saved'.

The third customer, 'A', has about 55 per cent survival probability at the outset, which is likely to decrease to below 50 per cent in three months' time, and continue declining to under 40 per cent thereafter. It may be that, by making a marketing intervention in the next month or two, 'A' might be saved – that is, if 'A' is sufficiently profitable to justify their retention.

Applications to customer management

Survival analysis has a number of applications for businesses with large numbers of customers to manage. For example:

- Monitoring and acting on predicted customer survival rates – continuing the last case study example, suppose that Customer A has been identified as 'becoming at risk', as their survival probability is expected to drop below 50 per cent in three months' time. By considering the behavioural predictors in the model, we can forecast an alternative survival curve for Customer A, if a key behaviour could be permanently changed. We can therefore select the best marketing offer for 'A', which raises their survival probabilities and produces the greatest increase in the revenues expected from them.

- Business planning – the model may be used to predict future numbers of lapses and monitor current lapse rates.

- Lifetime value prediction – the expected lifetime of each customer may be derived from their predicted survival curve. By combining this with their monthly revenue, a measure of lifetime value may be derived.

- Identifying active versus inactive customers – in a retail context, the time to each customer's next purchase may be predicted. This may be used to identify those customers who are likely to have become inactive, in the sense of not making a purchase within their expected timeframe.

- Campaign evaluation – monitoring the effects of marketing campaigns on customer longevity.

Differences between survival and churn models

In Chapter 6 we discussed the use of predictive models for business applications such as identifying future churners. Therefore the reader might reasonably ask how that approach differs from survival analysis.

Churn modelling examines a predefined outcome period, such as the next three months, and predicts the likelihood of a customer to churn during that timeframe. It provides no information about the subsequent risk of churn amongst customers who are 'safe' during the outcome period. Churn models are often used to identify likely imminent churners, so that retention offers may be sent to them.

Survival analysis does not employ a set outcome period during which customers may or may not churn. It examines how churn takes place over time and identifies key times at which the churn rate is likely to change – thus helping business users to plan the customer lifecycle.

Applications to asset management

The same mathematical techniques may be employed by manufacturers or operators of car fleets or other assets to manage their maintenance cycles. Rather than looking at customers and when they will churn, asset management looks at machinery and examines when it will fail. How is this relevant to marketers? By tracking failures of products such as motor vehicles, the manufacturer can identify and rectify problems earlier. For example, over the last few years there has been rapid development in the use of warranty analytics to identify early 'teething problems' in new cars, by applying survival analysis to warranty claims.

The following article by Dr Atai Winkler discusses the asset management application, drawing on the concepts of survival analysis introduced earlier in this chapter. Dr Winkler is a consultant mathematician with many years' experience in helping companies to solve their business problems. He has developed a set of analytical solutions for predictive asset management.

PREDICTIVE ANALYTICS APPLIED TO ASSET MANAGEMENT

Dr Atai Winkler

Introduction

The relentless march of technology is omnipresent, partly fuelled by the ever-increasing amount of data. Furthermore, the rate at which the amount of data is increasing is itself increasing. The technology required to process all this data has to advance at the same rate just 'to stand still'. Predictive analytics can be used to analyse and model this data to gain business advantage.

We are all aware of the advance of technology and the increasing amount of data collected about us and for us in our everyday lives. But what about those aspects of modern life that are essential and we take for granted without ever thinking about or even being aware of? Two examples are the uninterrupted supply of electricity and water. How can predictive analytics be used by the providers of these essential services to improve their service to the public? This article describes how assets in the water industry are currently maintained and why this policy is not optimal.

Results from the water industry are presented. They show how predictive analytics can be used to optimize asset management by minimizing asset maintenance and replacement costs at the operational, tactical and strategic levels, and to improve understanding of asset failure. Even though the results presented here are from the water industry, the analysis is applicable to all asset-rich sectors where the core requirement is the uninterrupted supply of the service. This requires the continuous operation of critical assets with no adverse side-effects.

Availability of asset and maintenance data, past and present

This article is concerned with assets such as pumps and valves in water treatment works and pumping stations. Traditionally, and still today but to a slightly lesser extent, assets have been maintained according to the regular service schedules specified by the manufacturers. Assets that fail between the scheduled maintenance periods are repaired but the asset owners do not, in general, consider the reasons for the failures. Before technology to collect and store real-time asset performance data was available, the extent to which asset owners could use predictive analytics to optimize the performance of their assets was limited. They serviced their assets according to the schedules specified by the manufacturers – they did what they were told to do, so as not to invalidate the manufacturers' warranties. Unfortunately, this minimal approach to asset management is still all too common.

This approach to asset management is far from optimal with respect to minimizing the assets' maintenance and replacement costs or maximizing their availability. It can lead to assets not being maintained when they need maintenance and assets being maintained when they do not need maintenance. Furthermore, it does not take advantage of all the available data and the results that can be obtained from applying predictive analytics to the data, and so does not allow asset owners to understand and gain insight into the causes of asset failure and then develop asset management policies that are close to optimal.

The amount of data collected from assets in the water industry and other utilities increased very significantly with the advent of new technologies such as telemetry and sensors. This data allowed assets to be monitored in real time, so allowing predictive analytics to be used to a much greater extent than had been the case up to then. The use of predictive analytics was also motivated by a number of social and environmental factors, including:

- movement of people from rural areas to urban areas, particularly in the developing world, with a corresponding increase in the demand for clean water and the associated need for more water treatment facilities;
- stricter environmental regulations and much higher penalties for not meeting them;
- ageing infrastructure and assets, more demanding operating conditions and higher throughputs;
- the public's increasing awareness of and care for the environment;
- shifting economic and political power balances;
- investors' attitudes to risk and how it can be controlled or preferably reduced.

Asset management policies based on predictive analytics have a much greater element of proactive maintenance than current maintenance policies that are based exclusively or almost exclusively on reactive maintenance. Reactive maintenance will always be required, as assets fail unexpectedly, but the aim of applying predictive analytics to asset management is to minimize the risk of asset failure. The minimization is invariably subject to constraints, for example the organization's capacity to carry out all the required maintenance work and its attitude to the risk of asset failure, ie to what extent it is prepared to accept the consequences of asset failure, for example flooding, pollution and service interruption, which can incur very high fines.

Application to asset management

Cox's proportional hazards model, discussed earlier in this chapter, can be applied to asset management to get an insight into the factors that cause asset failure. The inputs are the times to failure and the available asset data; the latter are the predictor variables in Cox's (1972) hazard model equation shown on page 128. They describe the assets' specifications, for example the manufacturer and power consumption, and external data such as weather (rainfall, temperature), location (rural, residential or industrial) and holidays/seasonality. In addition, this equation can also include asset maintenance data.

As with all types of regression model, the Cox proportional hazards model has two outputs: the values of the target variable predicted by the model and the model itself. Two sets of target variable values are provided in the detailed output from the models – the predicted cumulative hazard and the predicted survival probability.

The model output is very similar to the equivalent output from other types of regression analysis but there are a few additional columns. For example, Table 7.1 shows the output from a Cox proportional hazards model for modelling pump failure. Here, the target variable is the hazard rate and the predictor variables are the number of failures (num_failures), salinity of the water (salinity) and the power rating of the pump (power).

In Table 7.1, Coeff is the model coefficient for each variable and Exp(Coeff) is the exponential of Coeff. Exp(Coeff) represents the change in predicted hazard rate for a one-unit increase in the variable. Negative values of Coeff are associated with values of Exp(Coeff) smaller than one (implying a reduced predicted hazard) and positive values of Coeff are associated with values of Exp(Coeff) greater than one (increased predicted hazard). For example, the coefficient of num_failures is 0.352 and Exp(0.352) is 1.422; so if num_failures increases by 1, the predicted hazard rate is increased by 1.422 times, and therefore the probability of the asset failing has increased. Significance is the statistical significance of each variable in the model – a value of less than 0.05 is regarded as significant. Significance represents

Table 7.1 Extract of output from a Cox proportional hazards model

Variable	Coeff	Significance	Exp(Coeff)
num_failures	0.352	0.027	1.422
salinity	0.035	0.045	1.036
power	− 0.145	0.034	0.865

the chance that the variable actually has no effect on hazard rate, so the smaller its value the more certain we can be that the variable has a real effect.

The model can be used at the operational and strategic levels to improve asset management.

Operational asset optimization

Operational asset optimization identifies assets at greatest risk of imminent failure so that proactive maintenance can be carried out on them before they fail, rather than having to carry out reactive maintenance on them after they fail. The assets at greatest risk of failure have the highest cumulative hazards. It is quite common for a small proportion of the assets to account for a disproportionate amount of the maintenance time and cost – a more skewed version of Pareto's 80/20 rule is not uncommon. The reasons for this high degree of skewness depend on many factors. Most likely causes are how well suited are the specifications of the assets to their operating environment and the assets' maintenance histories.

Figure 7.7 shows the distribution of the cumulative hazard for a group of 8,500 assets when they are ranked by their cumulative hazard. The distribution has a highly skewed shape – a very steep decrease followed by a long tail. Figure 7.7 clearly shows the assets in greatest need of immediate proactive maintenance.

Figure 7.7   Ranked distribution of cumulative hazards for 8,500 assets

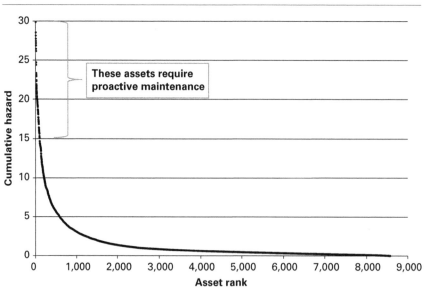

Table 7.2 Cumulative hazard of worst 500 assets

Asset rank	Cumulative hazard
1–100	14.4–29.9
101–200	10.0–14.3
201–300	7.8–9.9
301–400	6.4–7.7
401–500	5.5–6.3

Table 7.2 summarizes the cumulative hazards of the worst-performing 500 out of the 8,500 assets. The maximum cumulative hazard is 29.9 and the lowest cumulative hazard is very small (tending to 0 across all assets). The range of the 100 largest cumulative hazards is 15.5. This is half the range of the total cumulative hazard but is accounted for by only 1.17 per cent of the assets, thus showing again the highly skewed distribution of the cumulative hazards.

Strategic asset optimization

Strategic asset optimization involves combining the Cox proportional hazards model with discrete event simulation, which is a way to simulate a process, involving chance events, at discrete points in time. Peter Furness (2011) discusses the benefits of simulation and presents a number of case studies on various applications. In this case, the outcome is a 'risk-cost' simulation where risk is the risk of repeated asset failure and the cost represents the assets' maintenance and replacement costs. Repeated asset failure will ultimately lead to asset replacement, and the aim of the simulation is to find the maintenance policy that minimizes the cost. The simulation calculates the state of the system at regular periods in the future as a result of the scenario specified in the input. The state of the system at time t depends on the state of the system at all previous times.

The input data to the simulation describes the assets' costs and the organization's maintenance policies and attitude to risk. The optimization works by simulating a large number of scenarios and then identifying the scenario that meets the business and performance objectives of the organization.

Risk tolerance is the maximum acceptable level of repeated asset failure. It is measured on a five-point scale ranging from risk averse to risk tolerant. Even though risk-tolerant maintenance policies result in lower asset maintenance and replacement costs than risk-averse maintenance policies, they are much more likely to result in higher-consequence costs than risk-averse maintenance policies, and so these costs must be considered when working out the optimal asset management policy.

Use of descriptive analysis for asset management

Descriptive analysis of survival curves (discussed earlier in this chapter) can be used for tactical asset optimization. It can help asset managers compare the reliability of, for example, different manufacturers as the assets age. They show how the survival probability and cumulative hazard change during the assets' lifetimes. Curves can be produced both for single factors, eg manufacturer, and for stratified factors, eg manufacturer stratified by functional site.

Figure 7.8 shows the survival curves for different manufacturers. Manufacturer D has the lowest survival probability and manufacturer A has the highest survival probability at all times to failure.

An equivalent graph for the cumulative hazard can be drawn, as shown in Figure 7.9. Figures 7.8 and 7.9 are mirror images of one another and they yield the same results and conclusions because high cumulative hazards are associated with low survival probabilities, and vice versa.

Implementation

The benefits of applying predictive analytics to modelling asset failure depend on the number of assets, with direct proportionality between the cost saving and

Figure 7.8   Survival curves for different manufacturers

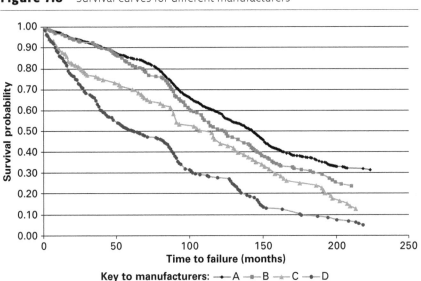

Key to manufacturers: A B C D

Figure 7.9   Cumulative hazards for different manufacturers

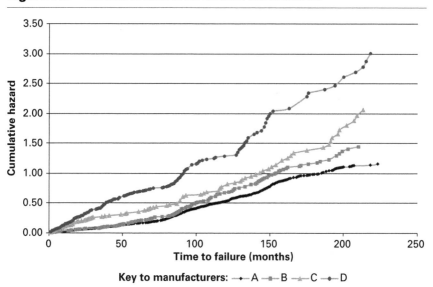

Key to manufacturers: ──◆── A ──■── B ──▲── C ──◆── D

the number of assets. Furthermore, the savings in dirty water are much greater than the savings in clean water because dirty water is a much more aggressive environment than clean water. Even in the dirty-water process cycle, some types of asset, for example pumping stations, have higher failure rates than other types of asset. Initial results from applying the methods described in this contribution suggest that savings of about £1 million over five years are possible, for a small to medium-size water company.

In summary

This contribution has shown how predictive analytics can be used to analyse and model historical failure data and use the resulting models to predict the likelihood of asset failure at each future time period.

Conclusion

In this chapter, we have seen that:

✔ Survival analysis focuses on analysing events that occur over time, such as customer attrition or churn.

✔ The technique allows for churners, whose lifetimes are known, and non-churners who have survived up to the current time point. The latter are termed 'censored cases' as their end dates have yet to occur. Censored cases tend to have longer lifetimes than churners and survival analysis properly reflects this difference.

- ✔ Descriptive techniques show how survival probabilities change over time. These methods can identify which factors, such as attributes and behaviour patterns, have greatest influence on customer longevity.

- ✔ Predictive survival analysis calculates an individual survival curve for each customer, quantifying how their churn risk changes over time.

- ✔ Survival analysis applications range from business planning, eg predicting future churn levels across the customer base, through to individual customer management, eg acting on a customer's predicted survival probabilities.

- ✔ Similar techniques may be employed by firms such as utility companies to manage the maintenance cycles for their assets, in order to move towards optimizing their operations and minimizing repair costs.

How to build a customer segmentation

08

Introduction

Segmentation is a well-established marketing tool for businesses to gain a better understanding of their customers, and then tailor communications and offers to the needs of each segment. A variety of techniques and criteria are available – the 'art' of segmentation is to select a suitable approach that meets your company's objectives and create segments that are useful when put into practice.

Having created a segmentation, success is achieved by applying it throughout your business and for relevant interactions with your customers.

The main aims of this chapter are to:

- Introduce the main principles of customer segmentation.
- Review the steps involved in order to develop and implement a segmentation system.
- Identify criteria on which segments are commonly based.
- Compare two main routes for creating the solution – segmenting on customer data and on external surveys.

This chapter focuses on strategic rather than tactical segmentation. Strategic segments are used for planning and implementing marketing strategy and then measuring market success among their audiences. Tactical segments are employed for specific purposes, such as cross-sell, up-sell and retention – these generally involve a different set of approaches, such as the predictive modelling techniques discussed in Chapter 6.

Principles of segmentation

The idea of segmentation is to divide your customers into a number of groups that differ from one another in a way that is relevant to your business. By understanding the types of people in each group, you are able to market to each group more effectively, using an appropriate channel, tone and message, and offering the products and services that are most likely to be of interest. Segmentation is vital to a successful marketing strategy because it allows you to start looking at customers more as individuals, rather than as one mass of people.

There are numerous ways to define customer segments; however, there are some common guiding principles to follow. As Dillon and Mukherjee (2006) advise, for the segments to be useful, they must be relevant to your business and have some immediate and obvious effects on how your company will market its products and services in the future.

There are three basic requirements for a good segmentation – segments must be:

1 *Identifiable* – members of each segment must have specific attributes that enable them to be identified.

2 *Viable* – there must be an adequate number of customers in each segment for it to be valuable and justifiable.

3 *Distinctive* – there must be characteristics for each segment that make it unique and differentiate it from the other segments.

Potential business applications

Segmentation may be applied to many aspects of your business – in summary, there are three broad levels of applications: strategic, tactical and operational:

- Strategic applications include different types of planning such as corporate development, marketing and advertising strategy.

- Tactical applications include communications selection and campaign targeting.

- Operational applications include customer management, providing tiered servicing to customers, and differentiating web pages or content between segments.

Figure 8.1   Segmentation applications and customers segmented

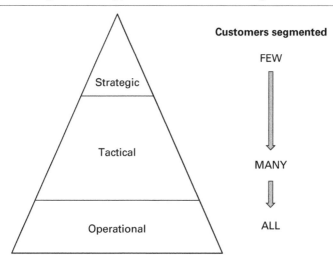

These broad applications may be thought of as a pyramid, as shown in Figure 8.1, in terms of the numbers of customers who are directly impacted and so need to be assigned to segments.

Steps in developing and implementing customer segmentation

The overall approach to customer segmentation may be summarized in seven steps – these parallel the phases in a data-mining project, discussed in Chapter 2.

> **Key point**
>
> When developing any segmentation it is essential to make a realistic plan of the entire journey, through to step 7, before setting out. Inadequate planning may lead to an apparently good segmentation, but no way to assign your customers to the segments.

The seven steps are as follows, each is then discussed in turn below.

Step 1: assess business needs and available data.

Step 2: define segmentation criteria.

Step 3: identify data for developing segments.

Step 4: plan segmentation development approach.

Step 5: create the segments.

Step 6: evaluate the segmentation.

Step 7: implement the segmentation.

These steps should not be seen as a simple linear flow – there can be a high level of iteration between them, in order to arrive at a successful solution. For example, the business might ideally desire a particular segmentation criterion at step 1; however, step 3 might discover a vital gap in the data required to support it. In that case, it would become necessary to revisit steps 1 and 2, in order to arrive at an alternative criterion that is both acceptable and viable. In the following sections, we discuss each of the steps in turn, ignoring their iterative nature.

Step 1: assess business needs and available data

If your company has decided to invest the time and resources to devise a new segmentation, then it is likely to have some idea of what the segments should look like, and how they are going to be used. For this reason, it is essential for the developers to understand fully the requirements and prior expectations of your business leaders and your colleagues who will be the owners, stakeholders and users of the new system. If the business has yet to define or align on its needs, then the first step should be to explore the views of senior managers to identify and summarize what they expect of the segments.

This step requires answering a series of questions that will enable the developers to plan the appropriate approach and ultimately answer the big question – why is this segmentation required? It is far better to identify just one or two definite uses, rather than a vague list of 10 or 20 potential applications.

There are some further detailed questions to consider, which will help to guide the approach, including:

- For which purpose(s) will the segmentation be used – strategic, tactical or operational, and for what specific applications within each?
- Is there a single segmentation criterion, or dimension, that will support all uses – if so, what is this and how should it be defined?
- Or does the segmentation need to be based upon multiple criteria – if so, what are these criteria, and how should they be combined together?

- Which internal and external data sources are available for creating and describing the segments?

- What are the actual units to be segmented, eg customers, events or transactions?

- Do all customers need to be assigned to segments? If so, how should recent recruits be handled, on whom little is known at the outset?

- Does each customer's segment assignment need to be kept up to date, as their behaviour changes over time? How frequently does segment membership need to be updated?

- Does the segmentation need to be assigned to prospects as well as customers, so that it can play a part in the recruitment process?

- How much complexity can the users tolerate? For example, is there an upper limit to the number of segments that your managers can handle? And is your IT system capable of running bespoke programs for assigning customers to segments, or does the assignment process need to be kept simple?

- If your business operates in more than one country, is a single global segmentation required, or separate local solutions?

It is critical to ensure that the development satisfies all stated business requirements as failure to do so can be costly. For example, the board of a credit-card company once specified that its customer segmentation had to define no more than five segments, which was considered the largest number that a manager would be able to remember! However, the analytics team ignored this limit and instead delivered 10 segments. Despite the merits of their solution, considerable further time and effort had to be expended in order to reduce the number of segments down to five.

If conducted well, the business requirements step can also help in obtaining buy-in from business users, identify the most senior owner or stakeholder for the segmentation and start to manage the expectations of users on what will be delivered.

Step 2: define segmentation criteria

The segmentation criteria, or dimensions, define how the segments will differ from one another and what the segmentation is measuring. Selecting the right criteria is critical to meeting the business objectives. Here are some examples of commonly used measures:

- Standard demographics – such as age, sex and region.
- Social grade – the 'ABC1' classification employed widely in advertising, marketing and market research.
- Life stage – this measures the phase in their lives that people have reached, using attributes such as age, marital and working status, and presence of children.
- Psychographics – measuring people's attitudes, lifestyles and behaviours, and applied mainly by advertising agencies.
- Ethnic origins – people's ethnic and cultural origins, classified using first and last names.
- Geodemographic segmentation systems – these analyse people according to where they live; for further information, see Leventhal (2016).
- Behavioural segmentation – classifies customers based on their purchasing or product usage patterns – discussed further in this chapter.
- Recency, frequency and monetary value – a specific example of behavioural segmentation, also known as RFM; see later in this chapter.
- Customer value – either current value based on recent expenditure and/ or predicted future value.
- Market-wide behaviour – segmenting on the products and services that each individual uses across the entire marketplace, rather than just with your company.
- Share of wallet – customer value with your company as a share of predicted value across all suppliers in your market.

The choice of segmentation criteria should come from the assessment made in step 1. Your business may decide on a single dimension such as purchasing behaviour – in which case, the input variables used to define the segments would summarize each customer's purchase patterns. Alternatively, multiple criteria may be required – for example, Hinshaw and Kasanoff (2012) advocate that customers should be segmented by two separate criteria: 1) needs – what customers actually need or expect; and 2) value – what customers are worth – currently and/or in the future.

By employing these criteria in combination, the segmentation identifies which customers to serve and how to serve them, in order to deliver the experience and products that they need.

> **Key point**
>
> A two-dimensional segmentation offers more flexibility and is likely to discriminate better than a single criterion. When the dimensions are interlaced they will give rise to a large number of cells, which are typically too small to be segments in their own right. However, if a third, overriding, criterion can be identified, this may be used to combine the cells and form a third segmentation dimension. This approach was taken when developing the FRuitS segmentation of the financial services market, which is discussed later in this chapter.

Step 3: identify data for developing segments

Identifying the appropriate data is largely driven by the choice of segmentation criteria made at step 2, supplemented by additional information that will be used to understand the segments and plan out their use.

For example, if segmenting on purchasing behaviour, transactional data would be required; however, demographics, lifestyles and media consumption are likely to be valuable in order to understand the kinds of customers assigned to each segment and where to find more people like them.

Alternatively, segmentation on needs or attitudes would require information that is not usually known, and so may have to be captured by carrying out a survey on a sample of customers. While this would take time and resource to conduct, it would enable valuable descriptive characteristics to be collected at the same time.

It is important to consider how the segmentation is going to be used and determine whether the end objective is to assign all customers to segments. If so, does each customer's segment membership need to be updated over time? These requirements are more straightforward to achieve if the segments are defined by behavioural data, such as purchase transactions or product usage, rather than by external variables or survey data.

In practice, the decisions made in steps 1 to 3 are highly interrelated, and the segmentation planning will benefit from an iterative approach that considers all three steps together – until a strategy has been developed that meets the business needs and is feasible to deliver.

Step 4: plan segmentation development approach

The development approach will depend on the segmentation strategy arrived at from steps 1 to 3. Broadly speaking, there are two main alternative routes that we shall term 'customer data segmentation' and 'survey segmentation' – the idea of each is summarized as follows, and is discussed more fully in the latter part of this chapter.

Customer data segmentation

This approach implies that the segments are created using variables that are known for each customer, such as transaction behaviour. Using this method, customers can be assigned to segments, both initially and in the future, with complete accuracy. The main drawback is the lack of in-depth knowledge that will be provided about the segments – depending upon how much other information is held on your customers. Additionally, this route is largely useful for segmenting customers' current behaviour patterns, but may not be robust enough to predict completely different behaviours, such as their likelihood to purchase new products and services.

Survey segmentation

This route entails employing external information from a customer survey or market research source to create the segments. By including survey data in the development, it is possible to go beyond known customer behaviour, into criteria such as attitudes, needs or market-wide behaviour. Survey segmentation offers the benefit of obtaining greater insights into the resulting segments; however, the potential drawback is the risk of not being able to assign customers to segments with such high accuracy.

Step 5: create the segments

Having established the business requirements, defined the approach and identified the available data, creating the segments should be 'merely' an analytical task. Nonetheless, this step is crucial in using the data to understand differences between customers and encapsulate those into useful groups.

A clustering procedure is often employed to measure similarities between customers, and group together those who tend to be more similar to one another – and more different from customers in other groups. A wide variety of analytical techniques are available, both traditional statistical methods and newer techniques such as artificial intelligence and machine learning. One or more descriptive model approaches are likely to be used, such as those discussed in Chapter 4.

The wealth of clustering approaches that are now available can present a challenge to any analyst seeking to select the best technique. Ideally, the analyst should experiment by applying different methods to their data, in order to discover which one delivers the most beneficial results. To help make this choice, Vidden et al (2016) carried out a thorough comparison of clustering methods on a series of simulated datasets. They found that latent class analysis performed best in most cases, both in identifying true cluster members and finding the correct number of clusters. Ensemble methods, which combine multiple cluster solutions, came second. The more traditional method of K-means analysis performed reasonably well with continuous variables.

Key point

When a provisional set of segments has been formed, each one needs to be portrayed and described in a way that can be understood and considered by the business. This is done by producing segment profiles using all available data. Sometimes, this extends to overlaying external data or surveying a sample of customers from each segment, in order to gain a deeper understanding. The most actionable profiles provide a detailed and meaningful picture of the types of customers belonging to each segment and highlights key differences of importance to your business.

The key metrics for measuring segment performance vary from sector to sector. For example, in telecom, the average revenue per user (ARPU) may be important, while in retail it may be the average basket size.

Step 6: evaluate the segmentation

Three separate questions need to be addressed at the evaluation stage, as follows.

Question 1: do the segments discriminate usefully for your business?

By applying the segmentation to relevant datasets – according to the original objectives – and producing profiles of different groups, the goal is to determine whether the segments are useful for the business and to provide evidence towards successful implementation. For example, if the objective had been to segment by customer loyalty, then attrition data should be analysed in order to demonstrate that loyal segments have the lowest churn rates.

Question 2: are the segments stable over time?

Segments must stand the test of time – that is, if customers are assigned to segments in two consecutive time periods, and then the results are compared, a reasonable level of consistency should be observed. If the segmentation were being used to control marketing activities, it would be undesirable if most customers were constantly moving between segments and so receiving different treatments from one month to the next.

For example, a common instance of an unstable segmentation is where the segments are defined by whether customers purchase or not, during a specific time period. As a result, customers can continually switch between 'high' and 'low' value segments, according to whether they happen to purchase in this period compared with the last. Instead, a customer's long-term value may be a more relevant and useful basis.

Question 3: are the segments acceptable to the business?

The final test is for the business to evaluate the segmentation and decide whether it is likely to be useful and should be tested further. Answering this question usually involves presenting the following information back to the business:

- the criteria that were used to identify the segments;
- the size, value, behaviour and composition of each segment;
- examples showing how the segments discriminate on data from the business;
- proposed business projects on which the segments should initially be tested or deployed;
- the estimated benefits of implementing the segments and any major cost implications such as process change, technology requirements and user training.

Step 7: implement the segmentation

Communication is critical in order for a segmentation to be successful. The first task in introducing a new segmentation should be to communicate it clearly throughout your business, that is, brief business users and produce readily accessible descriptions and profiles of each segment.

When deployed, one or two initial business projects should be selected – prioritizing 'quick wins' over 'long-term changes' – for testing the segmentation, in comparison with control groups where possible.

At the same time, the process of updating each customer's segment membership needs to be set up and carried out as a regular task. Previous segment assignments should be saved in your company database, so that, in time, it becomes possible to identify customers who are moving up or down the segmentation 'ladder' and take appropriate marketing actions.

In order to become more *data-driven* it is helpful to share success stories, interesting findings and applications of the segmentation. This can lead to further projects and wider adoption across your business.

Key point

There are many ways to create a useful segmentation. Segmentation is an actionable tool rather than a theoretical solution, and should be developed using the data and techniques at your disposal, in order to meet your business requirements.

Some useful segmentation approaches

In this section we discuss different approaches to segmentation, covering both the 'customer data' and 'survey' routes identified in step 4 above.

RFM segmentation

RFM is a straightforward way to segment your customers on their purchasing behaviour. It is non-statistical and can be developed by any analyst with access to descriptive tools such as a spreadsheet. RFM is widely applied for targeting campaigns in the retail sector, and as a tool for aiding management understanding.

A specific issue with RFM is that it is designed for customers who have purchased at least once from your company. Non-purchasers are excluded from the segmentation; if non-buyers need to be targeted, then other approaches may be employed for them, such as predictive models or geodemographics.

RFM involves describing each customer in terms of three dimensions:

- Recency (R) – the length of time since the last purchase that the customer makes, measured through to the latest update of your database. In many retail sectors, the more recent the last purchase, the greater the recency and the more likely the customer is to purchase again.

- Frequency (F) – the number of transactions made by the customer.
- Monetary value (M) – the value of all purchases made, either in total or on average per purchase occasion.

A typical approach to developing RFM segmentation is as follows:

1 Calculate the recency, frequency and monetary values for each customer – either over their lifetime with your company, or for a fixed period such as the latest year.

2 Exclude non-buyers, outliers with extreme values, fraudulent cases, marketing opt-outs, other suppressions and employees.

3 Rank customers on each of the three dimensions, and divide each ranking into a maximum of five groups, representing lowest to highest values. Within each ranking, the groups should be defined to contain approximately equal numbers of customers.

4 Assign all customers to their recency, frequency and monetary value groups, and examine the cells defined by all possible combinations of groups – there will be up to 125 cells, if five groups have been used for each dimension.

These interlaced recency-frequency-monetary value cells typically form the RFM segments, as illustrated in Figure 8.2. In addition, you should examine the importance of each cell – eg number of customers, campaign response rates, average sales value and so on.

Figure 8.2   The concept of RFM segmentation

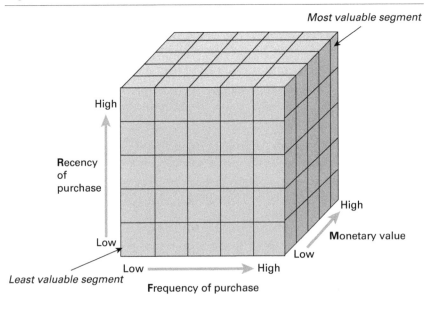

One drawback of RFM segmentation is that 125 segments can be too many for statistical confidence or for users to handle. To overcome this issue, Bauer (1988) proposed an extension of the method, in which a single continuous RFM score is calculated for each customer. Bauer suggested a simple RFM score, which is calculated as:

$$(1/R) * F * \sqrt{M}$$

– where:

R is recency in months since last transaction;

F is number of transactions made;

M is total monetary value.

Looking at this formula, recency has the greatest impact on the RFM score, through the 1/R factor – as the months since last transaction increases, the RFM score will be reduced, by a 50 per cent factor at two months, 33 per cent at three months, and so on. Also, we see that the monetary value component is damped down, by using the square root of M. This is designed to avoid the RFM score being dominated by customers with high monetary values.

Having applied this formula to calculate an RFM score for each customer, and checked the results, your database may be ranked on this score. Customers may then be divided into deciles (10 equal subsets), or however many groups are required.

RFM segmentation has some important key strengths and weaknesses, as follows.

Strengths

- RFM segments may be developed by non-statisticians – taking care that the data and results make good business sense.

- The segmentation is simple for management to understand, provided that the number of cells is not too large. Alternatively, results on the three dimensions may be presented separately.

- The process is straightforward to recalculate from time to time, in order to keep the segmentation up to date.

Weaknesses

- RFM provides little information about the type of customer in each segment.

- Predictive models will perform more strongly than RFM segments, for targeting campaigns. However, RFM is a good substitute in situations where a model is not feasible.

- RFM segmentation is more relevant in sectors where recency, frequency and monetary value all vary between customers. Typically it works best in the retail sector, eg for mail order and online retailers.

Behavioural segmentation

Behavioural segmentation creates segments driven by customer behaviour, such as purchasing, usage or web browsing – depending on the sector in which your business operates.

According to your business needs, segments may be developed for all customers or within existing subsets. This situation applies in the following example case from the mobile phone sector. Further examples of behavioural segmentation are included in Chapter 9 – one for business mobile phone subscribers and others on customers of a supermarket chain.

CASE STUDY

Example A: segmentation of high-value pre-pay customers

High-value customers are always of interest to marketers – in this case, a segmentation of top subscribers was developed by a pre-pay mobile phone operator, in order to understand the types of behaviour patterns within this valuable group.

A set of usage variables was first extracted for each customer, including measures such as the numbers of inbound and outbound voice calls and text messages, and similarly the total durations of voice calls.

The segmentation was developed using cluster analysis, which subdivided high-value customers into five distinct groups. The groups were profiled by the available variables and interpreted to understand the characteristics of each. This resulted in five interesting segments, labelled according to their main features – with names such as 'outbound voice sociables' and 'quick chatters'.

Based on the behaviour patterns of each segment, a clear marketing strategy was devised in order to address its needs.

Survey segmentation

The survey segmentation approach is summarized in Figure 8.3 and overviewed below. At the cost of the additional time and effort required to conduct a customer survey, it creates a rich information base for gaining a deeper understanding of your customers.

The process shown in Figure 8.3 starts by extracting a representative sample of customers together with their internal transaction data and other known attributes. A sample survey is designed and carried out to collect additional variables required in order to develop and describe the required customer segmentation. The survey may be administered either online, if e-mail addresses are held for all customers, or by post or telephone. Several points about the survey are important, irrespective of the data collection method:

- The preamble to the survey should explain that the purpose is to enable your company to understand its customers better, and that the results will not be used to directly send out marketing communications. By including this statement, and also keeping the survey length as short as possible, response will be maximized – which is essential for ensuring that the survey results are representative of your customer base and to give you a sufficiently large responding sample. The responding sample forms the

Figure 8.3 The survey segmentation approach

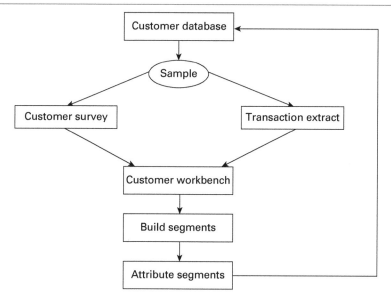

base for the customer workbench, which is used for segment development and attribution, therefore its size needs to be planned with care.
Before sending out a large-scale customer survey, it is advisable to run
a small pilot survey to give you an idea of the response rate and also to
check how well the questions are answered.

- The return questionnaire should contain a unique identifier for each
  customer, and the same identifier should be present in the transaction
  extract. Therefore it will be possible to join together the final dataset of
  survey information and the internal data extract, at individual level. This
  combined dataset is known as a customer workbench.

The customer workbench is used to describe your customer base – by bringing together survey and transactional information into a single dataset, many
different business questions may be answered for the first time, eg how do
revenue and profitability vary by demographics and attitudes? The workbench could therefore be a valuable data resource for use in understanding
your customers. Using the workbench, segments are developed, profiled and
interpreted; having approved the segmentation, segmented marketing strategies may also be planned.

The final stage is to employ the workbench to attribute the segments
back onto the customer database. This entails building a series of attribution models to predict segment memberships using transaction and other
customer variables. Predictive modelling techniques such as decision tree or
logistic regression are typically employed for these models (see Chapter 4).
Once customers on the database have been assigned to segments, the results
may be used for applying different marketing strategies and managing the
groups separately.

CASE STUDY

Example B: survey segmentation for share-of-wallet analysis

An investment company wished to understand better the share of wallet that
it was gaining amongst its customers – that is, the total amount invested with
the company as a share of each customer's total portfolio of investments
market-wide.

Two segmentation criteria were identified by the business stakeholders:
1) each customer's current investment activity with the company; and 2) their
market-wide assets across all providers.

A customer survey was carried out that included questions to capture market-wide assets, demographics and satisfaction with the company. The two segmentation criteria, market-wide wealth and investment activity, were each created using the resultant customer workbench, and were then interlaced to form a matrix of cells. Finally the cells were grouped into high-level segments.

Within each cell and segment, the company's share of wallet was measured – reassuringly, the cells with stronger wallet share corresponded to higher levels of customer satisfaction. Finally, attribution models were developed to assign all customers to segments.

The segmentation was used to develop a marketing strategy for each segment, for example retaining high-value customers, growing low-value customers with investment potential, and maintaining other low-value customers.

Finally, segment memberships were attributed onto the customer database, so that the customers belonging to each group could be managed and tracked separately.

Using 'off-the-shelf' survey data for segmentation

In some sectors, market research data may already exist and could potentially be used for survey segmentation – in two alternative ways: as a 'ready-made' customer survey, and as a data source for market-wide segmentation.

The 'ready-made' customer survey

One of the drawbacks of the survey segmentation process, discussed in the last section, is that it takes time and effort to carry out a bespoke customer survey. Therefore, if a market research database already exists that collects the right information for your segmentation project, then it may be attractive to employ this source as if it were a ready-made survey. However, the main difference is that, in order to achieve this result, the research responders would need to be merged with your customer base, at individual name and address level. Having merged the two sources, a workbench would be created containing the matched customers together with their survey and transaction data.

Since this matching involves processing personal data, there are data protection and research ethics considerations that would need to be satisfied. First the process would need to satisfy the data protection legislation applicable in your country – see Chapter 1. Covering the field of survey research, the MRS Code of Conduct (2014) sets out to protect the anonymity of respondents, as one of its fundamental principles. However it permits survey and customer data to be merged under certain conditions – more information is given by MRS (2017).

The ready-made customer survey may seem like an ideal approach, however its uses are limited due to the small sample size that would often be achieved. Consider the size of workbench that could be produced if the research data could be matched to your customer base at individual level. Taking the UK as an example, the population contains around 54 million adults (as at 2016). Suppose that your company has 1 per cent penetration of this market – then your customer base would be around 540,000. Now suppose that the market research sample size is 5,000 adults – that is around 0.01 per cent of the adult population. Matching this sample against your customers, you would expect around 0.01 per cent of your customers to be present in the research database, resulting in a workbench size of about 50 customers (at best – ignoring non-matches and address changes). While appending the research might provide interesting facts about these 50 customers, the sample size is far too small for quantitative analysis.

In the UK, it would take a customer base of millions and a research database of tens of thousands to generate a sufficiently large workbench sample; this therefore limits the approach to large companies and industry-wide market research surveys. Andy Brown and Catherine Haire (1998) provide a case study example on how the Barclaycard Customer Database was merged with the Target Group Index (TGI) survey that was operated by BMRB (now Kantar Media). Their paper includes a discussion of the merge process and the associated ethical and data protection issues; their case study gives several analysis examples of using the merged dataset for segment profiling and predictive modelling.

Market-wide segmentation

Existing market research data can be a valuable resource for creating a market-wide segmentation that summarizes all consumer activity – rather than only seeing the customer's product holdings with your company. Taking a market-wide view will, of course, give a different outcome from customer segmentation. If you can compare the two perspectives at individual level, then you can identify gaps and opportunities, such as products that are likely to be of interest to each customer, even though they have not been purchased from your company before. For example, a financial services company could see which of its insurance customers also hold savings and investment products, albeit with other providers.

CASE STUDY

Example C: market-wide segmentation in financial services

An off-the-shelf segmentation of the UK consumer financial services market was developed using a large-scale market research database, the Financial Research Survey (FRS) carried out by NOP Market Research (now GfK). The segmentation was named 'FRuitS' (pronounced 'fruits') and was widely used by financial services providers during the late 1990s.

The FRuitS segmentation was based on three dimensions of known importance in consumer financial services:

- Life stage – as an individual's needs for financial products typically varies by age, marital status, presence of children, employment status and so on.

- Wealth – as measured by household income and total savings/investments, which determines an individual's ability to satisfy their needs and acquire products.

- Product portfolio – the range of financial products that each individual holds, via any provider and channel.

The survey included variables that measured these dimensions, and therefore a multidimensional segmentation could be developed from the survey data – this resulted in eight FRuitS segments, which were then profiled and described using the FRS data. Continuing the fruits theme, the segments were named 'plums', 'pears' and so on.

The segmentation was attributed onto company databases through a matching process that maintained confidentiality of both the FRS and customer data. This produced a workbench dataset for each client company, from which segment attribution models were built, and those models were then applied onto the customer database. In a similar way, the segments were assigned to all individuals held in the UK Electoral Roll, operated by Equifax, and used for direct marketing. For a description of the segmentation and the matching process for segment attribution, see Leventhal (1997).

Although this example goes back 20 years, the approach remains valid today and the corresponding segmentation nowadays is 'Fresco' from CACI, which again was developed using GfK's Financial Research Survey.

The segment names used in FRuitS prompt a final key point (see overleaf), which applies to all types of segmentation systems.

> ## Key point
>
> ### Segment names
>
> When finalizing any segmentation, the choice of segment names can
> be more crucial than all of the work that has gone into developing the
> segments. It is invariably best to devise a name that encapsulates
> the essential characteristics of each segment, such as 'high income
> professionals' or 'home-owning families' rather than a meaningless
> label such as 'plum' or 'pear'. Also, ensure that all segment names are
> professional and objective, and so would not cause offence to potential
> users. This advice comes from the author's personal experience!

Use of lifestyle data in segmentation

Lifestyle databases could be another useful source for building, describing
or attributing segmentation systems. These databases contain vast banks
of individual responses to lifestyle surveys conducted for direct marketing
purposes. Therefore, unlike market research surveys, lifestyle data are subject
to a number of potential statistical concerns – biases due to the self-selecting
sample, population coverage issues and accuracy issues due to the varying
recency of the responses and the opportunity for inaccurate survey completion.

If you are considering using a set of lifestyle data as the source for building a survey segmentation, then we would advise first examining the data
quality and how well the source represents the required population. The
data may allow you to construct a much larger workbench sample than
could be obtained using market research; however, this workbench could be
highly biased and unrepresentative of your customer base.

Lifestyle data may be a useful way to profile each segment on a wide
range of demographics, hobbies and interests – as discussed earlier in this
chapter – in order to help gain a deeper understanding of 'what makes each
segment tick'. Any biases present in the data would matter less, as the main
segment features should come through.

If each individual's demographics are needed, in order to assign them to a
segment, then lifestyle data may provide the required attributes – we would
advise testing the attribution accuracy on a sample of customers before
adopting this approach, and comparing the results with alternative options.

If the segmentation needs to be applied to prospects, as well as customers,
then it could be useful to model the segments onto a prospect database built
from lifestyle data.

Conclusion

In this chapter, we have seen that:

✓ Segmentation should be an actionable tool rather than a theoretical solution. It should be developed to make best use of the data and techniques at your disposal, in order to satisfy your business requirements.

✓ When planning a segmentation project, it is essential to plan how all steps will be undertaken; identify any major risks and how they can be mitigated.

✓ A multidimensional segmentation offers more flexibility and is likely to discriminate better than a single criterion.

✓ Segmenting on internal data allows customers to be accurately assigned to segments, but gives a less in-depth picture of each group.

✓ Segmenting on external survey data gives a richer picture and deeper insights, but increases the risk of not being able to assign customers to segments with sufficiently high accuracy.

✓ The naming process can be more crucial than all of the work that has gone into developing the segments. It is invariably best to devise names that encapsulate objectively the essential characteristics of the segments.

Accounts, baskets, citizens or businesses

09

Applying predictive analytics in various sectors

Introduction

Having reviewed some of the main predictive analytics techniques, in this chapter we discuss how they are applied in several significant sectors. The main aims of the chapter are to:

- Discuss some of the applications in retail banking, and illustrate with a case study example on cross-sales modelling.
- Consider the use of subscriber data in the mobile telecoms sector.
- Identify ways of defining 'customer' in the retail sector and demonstrate how they are likely to result in different segmentation solutions.
- Review the use of advanced analytics for helping to manage citizens in the public sector.
- Discuss key differences that exist in the business-to-business (B2B) sector and demonstrate analytical applications with the help of a case study on segmentation.

Applications in retail banking

Retail banking – which provides financial services to domestic consumers – was one of the first sectors that harnessed predictive analytics to support customer management. Its use goes back to the early days of direct marketing from centralized databases, which started in the UK from the 1970s onwards.

Banks that operate current accounts have a definite advantage over their competitors when it comes to applying advanced analytics. Customers differ from one another in terms of the frequencies, values and types of transactions they make. Their transaction data are often summarized monthly in terms of deposits and withdrawals, channels used (eg online, ATM or branch) and so provide a continuous information source on recent financial behaviour.

In addition to this valuable structured data, sources of unstructured textual information can help banks to learn more about their customers. For example, direct debit descriptions can reveal customers' interests and product holdings such as mortgages, loans and credit cards. And communications such as e-mails, call centre interactions, social media posts, and so on, can potentially generate additional insights, eg positive or negative comments, reactions or sentiments about the bank.

Banks typically use predictive analytics for applications such as:

- Cross-sales and up-sales models – prioritizing which customers are the best prospects for other available financial services, or for increasing their holdings in existing products.

- Attrition models – identifying those customers who are most likely to close their accounts.

- Future profitability and lifetime value prediction – by modelling profitability, the most valuable customers can be identified. High-value clients may justify additional resources to manage and retain their business, such as personal account managers and priority phone lines to the call centre.

- Analysis of delinquent accounts – predicting which customers are likely to go into arrears, in order to take appropriate actions to minimize risks.

- Fraud detection – the growth in use of electronic payments over recent years has led to an increase in the incidence of fraud. Predictive analytics techniques are being used to discover repeating circumstances that are likely to result in fraudulent activity.

The following case study describes how a retail bank developed a set of cross-sales models for helping its call centre operators to suggest financial products to customers.

CASE STUDY

Retail bank development of cross-sell models

Business requirements

A retail bank wished to obtain quick wins from its investment in a new data warehouse system. The agreed area of focus was to increase cross-sales amongst current-account customers; therefore, a series of models was developed to predict the propensity that a customer would take up additional products. Six products were selected as 'core' to bank business and natural follow-ons to a current account – these products were:

- personal loans;
- motor loans;
- credit cards;
- mortgages;
- savings accounts;
- online banking.

The aim of the bank was to promote these products to its existing base of current-account holders. For each product, 'take-up' was defined to mean that an existing current-account customer opened an account during one calendar year, actively used the product during the year, and still held the product at the end of the year. The timelines followed for model development and deployment are shown in Figure 9.1.

Figure 9.1   Timelines for financial services cross-sales models

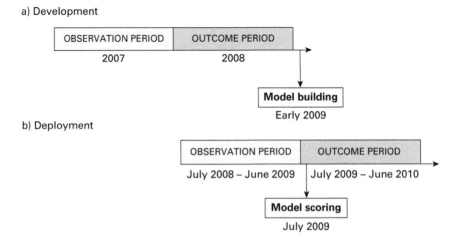

a) Development

OBSERVATION PERIOD | OUTCOME PERIOD
2007 | 2008

Model building
Early 2009

b) Deployment

OBSERVATION PERIOD | OUTCOME PERIOD
July 2008 – June 2009 | July 2009 – June 2010

Model scoring
July 2009

For developing each model, the outcome period was 2008 – this was the take-up year for each product. The observation period for customer attributes and current-account behaviour was 2007.

Certain types of customers were excluded from the modelling population – the models were designed to be applied to personal current-account holders aged 18+, who could be contacted and were not bad credit risks.

Data

The bank extracted three files on all eligible customers, for each of the six products:

- Customer file – containing customer demographics such as date of birth, income and segment code.

- Account file – containing account details such as product type, opening and closing dates.

- Profitability file – containing current-account income and profitability for quarterly periods during the observation period.

Each file was coded with a flag to indicate whether the customer had taken up that particular product during the outcome period. For each product, the data contained an approximate 50/50 split of those who did and did not take it up. This was achieved by extracting all acquirers (who took up the product, as defined above) and an equal number of non-acquirers as a random sample of all those who did not take up the product. The 50/50 split was appropriate as each model was designed to classify whether or not a current-account customer was a prospect for that product (see key point on sample balance in Chapter 6).

Data preparation

The customer and account files were cleaned so that any activity occurring during the outcome period was removed. For example, current accounts closed during 2008 were set to open, and age was calculated as at the end of 2007. In this way, the 'clock was wound back' to the end of the observation period.

The cleaned files were used to derive candidate predictor variables. Predictors could only be selected for model building if they were collected in a consistent way across all customers and would continue to be collected in the same way in the future.

Model development

Prior to building each model, one-third of the sample data was set aside for validation purposes and the remainder was used for model development.

The models were built using the CHAID decision tree technique (see Chapter 4). Gains analyses and charts were produced for each model, comparing the development and validation samples.

Six highly discriminatory models were developed to predict take-up of bank products. The models were tested and successfully implemented on the bank's customer base. The models were used by the bank's call centre to recommend the next best product for each customer to consider. Of the six models, five performed well in practice and continued to be used for some years.

Key point

Arguably there are further areas of opportunity for using advanced analytics in financial services generally, and retail banking in particular. For example, one relatively untapped area lies in helping customers to manage their savings and investments, and select the best products that will meet their needs.

Analytics in mobile telecoms

The mobile telecoms sector is highly competitive, particularly in mature markets such as the UK. According to Ofcom, the UK's communications regulator, there were 91.5 million mobile subscriptions in 2015, of which 33.5 million were pre-pay and 58 million were post-pay (Ofcom, 2016a). This compares strongly against the UK population – estimated at 53.4 million adults in mid-2015 (see JICPOPS, 2017). Ofcom also reported (2016b) that, in 2016, 93 per cent of consumers aged 16 and over had a mobile phone, while 86 per cent had a fixed-line phone.

Therefore, mobile service providers in the UK place high importance on maintaining customer loyalty and taking marketing actions to retain their business and minimize switching. According to Mobile Today (2017) 11 million customers changed networks in 2015, of which 49 per cent switched due to a better deal.

Mobile operators are heavy users of predictive analytics in order to understand customers' needs and preferences, and identify those at risk of churn. Typical projects include:

- Churn prediction – identifying which customers are most likely to switch providers. Amongst those who are likely to churn, the most valuable users can then be identified and targeted with offers to maintain their loyalty.

- Event detection – identifying a significant decline in usage, suggesting that the customer is about to churn, so that a 'save offer' can be made.

- Customer segmentation – identifying different types of users in order to develop tailored marketing strategies and products for them.

Fortunately for the telecoms analyst, every phone call, text message and data use generates a record, known as a call detail record (CDR). CDRs are stored in the operator's data warehouse and form the basis for reporting, describing subscriber behaviour and for analytics projects such as those above.

CDRs also record 'who called who' and so may be analysed to determine the extent of each subscriber's calling circle, and their pattern of relationships. This application of *social network analysis* is described more fully in Chapter 11.

Mobile customers subdivide naturally into major market segments, according to their type of contract. Residential or domestic consumers form a separate customer base from business customers, and each is then segmented further:

- The domestic consumer base splits into post-pay subscribers who have mobile phone contracts and are billed on a monthly basis, and pre-pay customers who do not have contracts and who purchase phone credits in advance of their usage. These two groups tend to be analysed and managed separately, due to their differences in data and contractual relationship with the operator.

- Business customers are generally first segmented according to customer size, for example into corporate accounts, small and medium-sized enterprises, small offices and home offices.

We discuss segmentation and analysis of businesses later in this chapter and present a case study on creating micro-segments of subscribers within a mobile operator's business customer base.

Customer analysis in retail

Retailers are heavy users of analytics for managing all sides of their businesses. In this section, we consider applications for managing customers and growing their value; in Chapter 10, we focus on approaches for pricing products and forecasting demand.

The primary source of transaction data in retail typically comes from the electronic point of sale (EPOS) system linked to the checkout till, and so is known as EPOS data. If you examine a supermarket till receipt you will see the amount of detail captured for each transaction – this is likely to include:

- the store, date and time;
- a list of items purchased, their quantity and cost;
- the total transaction value and number of items purchased;
- the value of any discount given, number of loyalty points earned;
- the method of payment and credit card details.

Equivalent data are captured by internet retailers, except of course that the store is 'online'.

This transaction information supports a whole raft of descriptive analyses, which are collectively known as *basket analysis*. For example, they quantify the sales performance of each store and format (grouping stores by size and type), and how this varies by time of day, day of week, and so on. Products are grouped into categories or departments, and stores are then profiled by the types of goods sold. Affinities may be calculated between products that were bought together, using association analysis (see Chapter 4).

Maintaining customer loyalty is crucially important to retailers – to help achieve this objective, many of them operate loyalty schemes. The customer registers in order to join the scheme, receives a loyalty card and has it scanned when making each purchase. This earns loyalty points, which accumulate over time, and then the customer receives benefits such as rewards and special-offer coupons.

Retailers benefit from loyalty schemes in a number of ways, but primarily in helping them to retain existing customers and acquire new customers. Retail analysts benefit also – in the sense that the card identifies the customer who purchased each basket, in terms of the identifier number and attributes collected at the registration stage. Repeat purchases may therefore be linked together, assuming that the same card has been presented each time, enabling analysis of loyalty, long-term customer value and product affinities over time.

Below are some example applications of advanced customer analytics in retail; further examples, for product management, are included in Chapter 10:

- Basket segmentation – classifying baskets into segments that identify each *shopping mission*: the apparent reason a customer had for visiting the store.

- Customer segmentation – grouping together loyalty card holders, or online shoppers, into segments that contain similar characteristics. The results help in gaining a better understanding of the shoppers using each store or channel, and may be used for targeted marketing.

- Store segmentation – grouping stores together based upon their sales patterns. The results identify stores that perform in a similar way, irrespective of their geographic locations. Applications include prioritizing store refurbishment programmes and selecting representative stores for new product testing.

The following case study describes a project in which the above three segmentation approaches were developed in combination.

CASE STUDY

Segmentation development by an Asian supermarket retailer

A supermarket retailer in Asia, with a chain of 150 stores, developed a suite of segmentation systems as part of an upgrade of its infrastructure for customer relationship management (CRM).

Basket segmentation

All baskets were classified into segments according to the nature of their apparent shopping missions. Three types of segment were identified:

- Convenience – one segment containing small, low-value baskets, which are so-called because the store was probably the most convenient place for the customer to purchase an item such as a bottle of milk or a newspaper.

- Destination – a series of segments containing baskets dominated by a small number of related product groups such as fruits or fresh vegetables. Each destination segment corresponds to a specific shopping mission, eg fill up the fruit bowl.

- Variety – higher-value baskets characterized by a wider variety of products purchased, eg the household's main weekly shopping trip.

Customer segmentation

Loyalty card holders were segmented on two separate dimensions: 1) customer value – recency, frequency and monetary value metrics were analysed to create a set of customer value segments; 2) age groups – card holders were grouped by age, as a measure of their likely needs for the retailer's products and services.

Store segmentation

Stores were segmented on three separate dimensions:

- The sales profile in each store, at product group level.
- The customer segment profiles, by customer value and age groups, as created above.
- The basket segment profile for each store.

The resultant store segmentations were each profiled by additional metrics, including store size, profitability and catchment area data, in order to interpret the three dimensions. Finally, a single set of overarching 'mega' segments was developed, by combining together the customer and basket dimensions. The mega segments identified groups of stores with differing performance on basket value and traffic (numbers of customers).

Use of advanced analytics in the public sector

It would be easy to imagine that analytical techniques could be used by public-sector bodies to manage their citizens. In the contribution below, Wajid Shafiq explains the landscape in the public sector, with a focus on the UK. Wajid has spent the majority of his career delivering citizen management and advanced analytics solutions to organizations in the public sector.

DELIVERY OF SERVICES IN THE AFTERMATH OF THE 2007–08 FINANCIAL CRASH…

Wajid Shafiq

Along with the rest of the economy, the last decade has been very challenging for the public sector. Unfortunately, the next decade does not look very promising either. An ageing population combined with shrinking welfare, health and social care budgets are creating a perfect storm. The system is already in crisis; from policing – where a record number of burglaries remain unsolved – to adult social care where lack of domiciliary services are causing bed shortages in hospitals.

The initial response to these challenges has been to increase 'efficiency' – generally translating into a reduction in the capacity and level of services being offered. Although this has delivered short-term financial objectives it has begun to undermine the sector's ability to effectively manage demand and its ability to deliver core statutory 'duty of care' obligations.

In order to deliver further efficiencies the sector is having to undertake organizational, economic and operational restructuring. This is manifesting itself in several ways, for example: from shared services for back-office functions, closer integration of health and social care and an increasing focus on risk/ reward contracts for the provision of services by third parties. Ultimately, most of these strategies are designed to increase the impact of ever-more limited financial resources and it is in this context that there is a building interest in the role of digital and advanced analytics.

From a technology and analytics perspective, there are two main themes emerging:

- Digital by default: this approach focuses on reducing the need for customer-facing teams by enabling citizens to conduct simpler transactions online – replicating the shift of customers to online banking services. Examples in the public sector include booking GP appointments, paying parking fines and so on.

- Demand management: a somewhat contentious term – in the public sector this refers to the early identification of people and families that are likely to escalate from low-intensity, low-cost interventions to high-intensity, high-cost interventions.

In broad terms the first of these strategies addresses the 80 per cent of transactions representing 20 per cent of total costs and the second addresses the 20 per cent of transactions representing 80 per cent of costs.

Demand management – a comparison between private- and public-sector motivations

Many of our private consumer relationships are already a 'numbers game' played out by servers in the Cloud that, for example, work out when a call centre operator should call you, how they should tune what they say and what offer you are most likely to be interested in. In these interactions humans have already been relegated to the role of 'delivery mechanism' – an alternative to an e-mail or a letter.

The processes and analytical models driving these interactions are designed to maximize demand with minimum cost. These goals are fully aligned to the organization's profits and shareholder value drivers.

In contrast, the public-sector raison d'être is to support and foster a fair, civil society in which the most vulnerable are protected. Consequently, processes and analytical models need to be designed to minimize high-cost demand (represented, for example, by mental health or looked-after children services) at minimum cost.

Often these high-cost services are about achieving some form of behavioural change (for example reducing substance misuse or domestic violence). Clearly, we are not at the stage where complex support relationships (delivered by health and social-work professionals) can be replaced by technology and analytics in the same way they are being replaced in the private sector. However, there are several strategic and operational ways in which analytics can be applied to prevent or delay the need for these complex and costly services.

The sector has been laying the foundations for more sophisticated analytics by deploying CRM, case management and performance management systems. In addition to greater integration of these capabilities and the introduction of new analytics capabilities organizations will need to overcome several additional barriers, a few of which are discussed below.

Lack of a blueprint for implementation

Analytics has the potential to transform a range of business processes, from policy making, strategic commissioning, operational targeting of interventions and even emerging applications of behavioural science (for example to increase timely tax returns, encourage benefits claimants to report changes in circumstances) – all of which need to be underpinned by advanced analytics.

However, applications of advanced analytics are limited in number and scope and the sector has some way to go before analytics are embedded as a matter of course to make processes smarter.

Scepticism

As with all forms of innovation, most organizations are comprised of champions, the curious and the staunchly opposed. Opposition is grounded in sound ethical considerations and reservations around whether these techniques will work in a complex public-sector setting, as well as understandable concerns about the impact of advanced analytics on employees' jobs.

The challenge at present is that, even when advanced analytics can be proven to work and ethical considerations resolved, implementation will result in a significant reshaping of organizations and business processes – with a proportionate impact on job roles and responsibilities.

At present, even the champions of these approaches are not necessarily ready for the potential transformation challenges and risks.

Data challenges

Apart from very specific areas, for example counter-terrorism, the public sector has relatively low volumes of data (in big-data terms), very good 'data variety' (broken across agency/organizational silos) and relatively low 'data velocity' (supported for example by periodic social work or health assessments).

In contrast with the private sector a significant proportion of this data is held as unstructured text/notes in various case management systems. These data are typically derived from episodic interactions that front-line teams have with their clients – with more information collected as people's dependence on the public sector increases.

Transforming this disparate data asset into a meaningful resource for sophisticated analytics is a complex challenge spanning the vested interests of software suppliers, data matching as well as broader security and technology issues.

Skills and technology gap

All significant organizations in the public sector have performance management and business intelligence teams. The main demand on these functions comes from central government (as part of periodic statutory returns) and satisfying ad-hoc reporting requirements generated by local politicians and management functions.

As with all other parts of the public sector, these functions are also capacity constrained and, in general, reporting and intelligence demands have not required the application of advanced analytics. Creating a business case to develop these capabilities is difficult when there are so few examples of successful implementations.

Information governance/data sharing

Although both the public and private sector are subject to the same data protection legislation, the private sector has been less risk averse in its interpretation and application. As consumers, our browsing behaviour is passed from one organization's website to the next (enabled, for example, by Google analytics) so that advertisers can place ads for products at a later point in time.

The ability for private-sector organizations to define a data-sharing purpose (as required by the Data Protection Act) is relatively simple and is often linked to your ability to access a product at the discretion of the provider (for example a mortgage or insurance policy).

This ability to connect 'data silos' generated by different organizations is not easily replicated in the public sector. There are several reasons for this, ranging from ethical considerations (the data collected are often very sensitive); core reputational issues (sharing of sensitive data from one support service with another could result in a loss of trust between service providers and their clients); as well as operational issues (for example data are not easy to extract and are often stored in a third-party software system with its own support contract).

As an illustration of these complexities we can consider data-sharing considerations around domestic violence. In these cases the victim may be in contact with a voluntary specialist support agency (possibly funded by the council). If there are children present the victim is likely to be very sensitive about their data being shared with the council, which could result in social-care involvement. The perpetrator is unlikely to know that the victim is in contact with the support agency and that their data have been shared.

Joining up all the dots in these cases, for example, in order to apply advanced analytics to predict cases that are likely to escalate, requires careful consideration of the rights of all the people involved – in particular any children.

Children's services case study

Children in care cost around £2.5 billion to the public sector per annum and with the number of 0 to 17-year-olds increasing (by 4.9 per cent from 2010 to 2014) this demand is rising (by 5 per cent from 2012 to 2016).

In this context, the need to maximize the impact of interventions designed to support families before they reach crisis is paramount. This need has been brought into even sharper focus as funding for this type of early intervention has reduced by £1 billion since 2010.

The potential benefits offered through the application of advanced analytics are obvious and in 2014 a number of councils in London set up a pilot project to answer the following questions:

- Could we predict which families were most at risk of ending up in statutory care?

- Could we do this far enough in advance that early intervention could work?
- Could we help to further maximize resources by targeting early interventions at families where they were most likely to be successful?

Following desk-based research into risk factors it was clear that, to deliver against this set of objectives, the project would need to collect data from multiple service teams across organizations. This in turn gave rise to several underlying operational barriers that would need to be addressed:

- Would it be possible to resolve information governance challenges?
- Could data from across organizations be integrated to create an accurate single view of households?

- Would data be of sufficient quality to support advanced analytics?
- Would the model generate alerts that would be actionable by social-work teams?

Before the project could get access to any data it was necessary to establish data-sharing agreements for over 20 different sources. This process took nearly 10 months to complete and involved documenting data-sharing purpose, defining legal gateways, providing detail on what data would be collected, how it would be processed, who it would be shared with and under what circumstances this sharing could occur.

As well as defining data-sharing agreements this activity also involved defining an information governance (IG) control process, which ensured that identifiable data were only shared when statistical risk thresholds and predefined data-sharing rules had been met.

The initial element of this IG control process was a process for the pseudonymization of data prior to the application of any analytical processes. Pseudonymization is a procedure by which personal identifiers (eg name, address) are replaced by one or more artificial identifiers, or pseudonyms. The purpose is to make it more difficult to identify the individual to which the rest of the data refer. Critically the process can be reversed if required (making the data identifiable).

This pseudonymized asset was then used to populate a data warehouse that facilitated the analysis of risk factors present at least 12 months prior to a safeguarding intervention. Subsequent analytical processes involved clustering and the application of a number of statistical methods to create a predictive model that identified families at highest risk of safeguarding in the next 12 months.

Operational deployment

Having checked that strategic barriers could be addressed and that the data being collected by various organizations would support the development of a sufficiently accurate predictive model, the project then needed to develop a process for the implementation of the model. Illustrative challenges included:

- Ensuring that the solution augmented social-work practice – alerts were designed to trigger existing risk-assessment-based processes led by social-work professionals.
- Supporting alerts with a range of additional analyses that examined risks from a traditional social-work perspective – for example, exploring concepts such as 'family resilience'.

- Recommending interventions based on the previous responsiveness of the family as well as the responsiveness of similar families to wider sets of interventions.

- Surfacing alerts and supporting analysis to social workers in a digestible form – traditional data visualizations did not facilitate rapid review of alerts and the project needed to supplement these data visualizations with a textual narrative generated using natural language-generation techniques.

Summary

As with the private sector, advanced analytics has an increasingly important role in driving efficiency and efficacy in the public sector. Adoption in the public sector will continue to lag behind the private sector for several reasons, some of which have been outlined.

Addressing these additional complexities will mean that the solutions developed in the public sector will need to be at the cutting edge of 'operationalizing analytics'.

Analysing businesses

As we have seen above in earlier sections, predictive analytics techniques are widely applied to support marketing in the business-to-consumer (B2C) sector. While there are also applications in business-to-business (B2B), they tend to differ in approach and use. Why is this?

A key difference between B2B and B2C is that, in a business environment, purchase decisions are typically made by a decision maker who is not the actual user, but who is empowered to act on behalf of the users. Furthermore, in large companies, the sales process can be long and complex, involving talks and negotiations.

In B2B marketing, data and analytics are mainly employed to support the process of acquiring business customers. External *firmographic* information, at individual level, is required to identify the decision maker, their position and role, together with characteristics of the company, such as its industry sector, turnover, age and number of employees. Analytic applications include prospect modelling and lead scoring in order to target companies and prioritize contacts.

Exactly the same analysis techniques may be applied for B2B marketing as for B2C; however, B2B has yet to make as much use of them. In a study by B2B Marketing (2016), 73 per cent of B2B marketers felt that their companies did not make the most of data, with the weakest skills being in predictive analytics.

Nonetheless, there are numerous potential applications for B2B, including:

- Segmentation of business customers or the users within them – helping to understand the customer and often combined with market research to learn more about the segments.

- Share of wallet analysis – applied in combination with segmentation, the aim is to estimate the share of business won by your company, within its sector, to identify priority segments and accounts with growth opportunities.

- Attrition modelling – identifying which customers are at risk of churn when their contracts expire.

In 2016, there were 5.5 million private-sector businesses in the UK, according to the Department for Business, Energy & Industrial Strategy – see BEIS (2016). These included 3.3 million sole proprietorships, 0.4 million ordinary partnerships and 1.8 million companies. For B2B marketing, the business universe is typically segmented into three groups:

- corporate businesses with 250 or more employees;
- small and medium-sized enterprises (SMEs) with 10–249 employees;
- small offices and home offices (SOHOs) with up to nine employees.

Figure 9.2 shows the split between these segments in the UK, in terms of shares of businesses, employees and turnover, and demonstrates the massive imbalances between them. For example, only 0.1 per cent of businesses are corporate; however, they account for 40 per cent of employees and 53 per cent of total turnover. At the other extreme, 96 per cent of businesses are SOHOs; however, they account for less than 20 per cent of turnover. Further business statistics for the UK may be found in a House of Commons Library briefing paper by Rhodes (2016).

Due to the differences in the corporate decision process and the importance of this sector, B2B marketing sometimes treats corporate customers on a personal basis and takes more of an automated approach with SMEs and SOHOs. In this case, it can make sense to exclude corporate companies from segmentation and targeting projects, or to develop separate models for each of the three business segments.

The following case study summarizes a project carried out by a mobile operator, in order to drill down into smaller segments within this framework.

Figure 9.2   UK businesses by size (as at 2016)

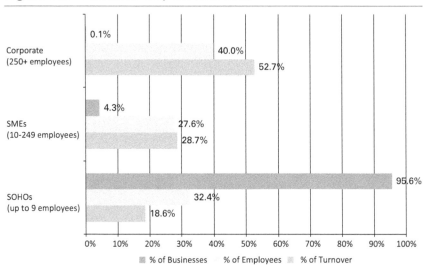

SOURCE Derived from Business Statistics, House of Commons Library Briefing Paper, November 2016. Data relates to the start of 2016

CASE STUDY

Micro-segmentation of business subscribers

A mobile phone operator segmented its business customers into major market segments – corporates, SMEs and SOHOs – these segments primarily determined the way in which customers were managed. However, there was less understanding of the different types of mobile users and their needs. To address this question, the operator decided to create micro-segments of mobile subscribers based on their usage patterns for mobile services.

At the first stage, a segmentation of consumer subscribers was developed. The behaviour pattern of each user was summarized as 100 variables, including usage by time of day and day of week. A set of segments was then developed using a self-organizing map (see Chapter 4).

The company held the view that the same segments would also be found amongst its business users. In order to test this hypothesis, it created the same set of variables for each business subscriber, and ran a clustering program that assigned them to their 'nearest' consumer clusters. The majority of subscribers were sufficiently 'close' to their assigned clusters, and were accepted as 'belonging' to those segments.

Further cluster analyses were conducted for those business subscribers who did not conform to the existing segments. These identified additional user segments within the corporate and SME accounts.

The project enabled all subscribers in the business base to be assigned to a usage segment, and the operator could then view the segment profiles within each business account, industry sector and major market segment.

The final stage was to carry out a customer survey, by telephone interview, in order to understand the types of subscribers who belonged to each micro-segment – the results were highly informative and 'brought the segments to life'. The micro-segmentation had a number of applications to benefit different areas, including sales, channel and customer management, and proposition development.

Conclusion

In this chapter, we have seen that:

✔ Advanced analytics are widely used in retail banking for customer management; potentially, new applications could be developed to advise customers on their use of financial services and the products that would best meet their needs.

✔ Large retailers are heavy users of analytics to help them run all aspects of their operations.

✔ Customer analytics in the mobile telecoms sector mainly focuses on monitoring loyalty and reducing churn, particularly within mature markets with high levels of competition between operators.

✔ Advanced analytics has an increasingly important role in driving efficiency and efficacy in the public sector. Adoption in the public sector will continue to lag behind the private sector for several reasons, including data challenges, a skills and technology gap, and data-sharing issues.

✔ Analytics in the B2B sector has primarily been used to support customer acquisition. However, the same predictive analytics techniques could be applied as for B2C, allowing for the key differences in the ways that business customers are managed.

From people to products   10
Using predictive analytics in retail

Introduction

The applications of predictive analytics extend to any situation where there is a group of items to be managed, for which decisions with cost or revenue implications are being made. One sector that operates in this environment is retail – a retailer selects a merchandise range, decides selling prices, promotes products and has stock to manage. Therefore, large retailers are heavy users of analytical techniques for business operations alone, quite apart from the customer analytics that they need to do.

This chapter looks at analytics in retail, focusing on three business problems that apply to most retailers and in many other sectors as well – price optimization, markdown management and demand forecasting. The main aims of this chapter are to:

- Demonstrate the breadth of analytical applications in retail.
- Discuss the use of predictive analytics for price optimization.
- Consider the application of analytics for managing price markdowns.
- Introduce approaches that retailers use to forecast future base demand.

An overview of retail applications

The wide scope for analytics to support product management is illustrated in Table 10.1, which lists examples of some common business questions faced by retailers and the analytical approaches that can address them.

The retailer's business questions are complex and require, in the main, more than just one analysis to answer them. Rather, the solutions tend to be multi-stage and designed specifically to meeting business objectives.

Table 10.1   Some business questions in retail and approaches designed to address them

Business questions	Analytical approaches
Which products are likely to be bought in combination or as complementary items?	Association analysis
Which products compete or may be substitutes for one another?	Association analysis
Is there a sequence or priority order in which products are bought?	Sequence analysis
How good is the level of product availability in each store?	Availability and lost sales
How many sales have been lost due to gaps in product availability?	Availability and lost sales
Which products may be removed from the retailer's range with least impact?	Item deletion analysis
What is the optimal pricing strategy for a product?	Price optimization
How should products be marked down in price as they reach their sell-by dates?	Markdown pricing
What will the future demand be for a product?	Forecasting techniques

The Table 10.1 exceptions to this rule are association and sequence analysis (discussed in Chapter 4) – these techniques can deliver powerful results in their own right; however, they are also often applied in combination with other methods.

Availability and lost sales analyses are primarily designed for fast-moving consumer goods (FMCG) sold in supermarkets. Maintaining high availability is a constant priority for supermarket chains – business performance is likely to suffer if this goal is not being achieved. The availability analysis identifies periods of zero or low sales of a product in a store, which would be unlikely to have occurred by chance, given the sales rate of the product. Depending on the speed at which the retailer loads transactions into its data warehouse, availability reporting may be used to flag up current issues for immediate resolution, eg 'no milk sales in the last hour in our Milton Keynes store'. More generally, the reporting provides a measure of success in managing product availability and identifies the best- and worst-performing stores.

Linked with this report, the lost sales analysis estimates the sales that were lost due to each occurrence of non-availability. Lost sales reports provide another measure of store performance, out of the total potential sales – lost plus actual – that could have been achieved.

Item deletion analysis identifies which low-selling products may be safely removed from a retailer's range, in order to free up stockroom space for faster-selling lines. It takes account of other criteria, such as seasonal differences, effects on associated products and the preferences of valuable customers, to ensure that deleted items will have minimal impact on store performance. The process is descriptive rather than predictive and does not employ advanced methods; however, the results are highly actionable for users.

In contrast, price optimization and markdown pricing are analytical processes that many retailers integrate with their other systems. With their wide applicability in mind, the next two sections discuss these two approaches in turn.

Finally, forecasts of consumer demand are essential for retailers (and others) to manage their businesses. The last section overviews techniques that may be used in retail to forecast base demand – the regular demand for goods from existing customers.

Price optimization

The importance of price

It is widely accepted that pricing is the most important aspect of a business – for the simple reason that businesses exist to generate value, and pricing is the 'exchange rate' that is used to convert products into value.

Out of all the decisions that a business can make, pricing has the greatest and fastest impact on maximizing profit. A study by Marn et al (2003) at McKinsey & Company, looked at 500 American companies in the S&P stock market index; the study found that, on average, a 1 per cent price rise resulted in an 8 per cent increase in operating profit, assuming no reduction in the volume sold. The impact of price was nearly 50 per cent greater than that of a 1 per cent fall in variable costs and more than three times greater than the effect of a 1 per cent increase in volume.

In this section we outline an approach to price optimization, which is designed to find the optimal price point for each product. We assume that a retailer is seeking to optimize the profit on selling each item, where profit is defined as the *difference between value of sales and cost of purchasing the units sold*. We first describe a straightforward method of price optimization, and then refine the method to take into account interdependencies with other products.

Price elasticity

As we all know, there is usually a relationship between price and demand – typically consumers will demand more of a product at a lower price, and less at a higher price. This relationship is quantified by the price elasticity (PE) – the price elasticity of demand represents the percentage change in demand for a product, resulting from a 1 per cent increase in its price.

PE values vary from sector to sector and from product to product. Where a 1 per cent increase in price causes a greater than 1 per cent decrease in demand, then the product is responsive to price, and demand is said to be *relatively elastic*. Where a 1 per cent price increase causes less than a 1 per cent decrease in demand, then demand is said to be *relatively inelastic*. If a 1 per cent price increase causes exactly 1 per cent decrease in demand, then demand is said to be *unit elastic*.

Since raising the price of a product will generally cause demand to reduce, PEs are usually negative values, typically just below zero for more essential products (relatively inelastic demand) and less than –1.0 for more discretionary items (relatively elastic demand).

While the PE for a product can vary according to its price, we often assume for simplicity that the product has a constant PE over its range of possible prices. We will make this assumption when discussing how PEs may be calculated.

Calculating PEs from transaction data

Knowledge of PE values is essential for price optimization because, if we know the PE for a product of interest, then we can predict the effect of a price change and apply a simple method to locate the optimal price.

Ignoring other factors that can affect demand, the basic relationship between demand and price is assumed to be:

$$D = k * P^{PE}$$

– where D = demand, P = price, PE = price elasticity and k is a constant. This equation is often simplified by taking the logarithm of each side, which gives:

Equation 10.1:

$$\ln(D) = c + (PE * \ln(P))$$

– where ln( ) = logarithm to base e and c is a constant.

Then, if we had records containing product price and demand for a series of time periods, we could apply regression analysis (see Chapter 4) to fit this model to $\ln(D)$; the PE value would be given by the regression coefficient for $\ln(P)$.

However, it is far more likely that many other factors alongside price will also be having an effect on demand, such as promotions, advertising, competitive pricing and seasonality. If we ignored such factors, then we would be liable to obtain an incorrect estimate of the PE – for example, demand could appear to be highly elastic and driven by price, when actually it is being driven by something else.

For this reason, in order to calculate the true effect of price, we should take other factors into account in the model. For simplicity, we do this by assuming that Equation 10.1 holds as a linear model including other variables – this gives the following:

$$\ln(D) = c + (PE * \ln(P)) + (b_1 * x_1) + (b_2 * x_2) + ... + (b_n * x_n)$$

– where $x_1, x_2 ... x_n$ = factors that can be measured,
and $b_1, b_2 ... b_n$ = regression coefficients for the effects of those factors.

This model may similarly be fitted using regression analysis, in order to calculate the PE taking other factors into account.

There are several important points to bear in mind when calculating PEs from transaction data:

- PEs should be calculated at product-line level (also known as stock-keeping unit, or SKU level), as the effects of price can vary by pack size or by variety.

- Each row in the dataset will represent a time period; for FMCG, each row will typically summarize a particular week, and the dataset may contain 52 records for each SKU over the last year.

- The data must contain price changes – if the product price has been unchanged for the entire year, then it will not be possible to calculate the PE. Therefore, in the preliminary analysis before fitting the model, any product with a constant price would need to be identified and excluded.

- The signs of the PE and other coefficients should always be checked – only accept the model if the signs make business sense. For example, the PE should be negative and the coefficient for advertising should be positive. If advertising appeared to have a negative effect that would clearly make no sense! – in that case, advertising would need to be excluded from the model.

Approach to price optimization

Having calculated the PE for a product, it can be applied to predict demand for different price points and, from this, the sales revenue: demand * price.

Using the unit cost of the product to the retailer, then we can derive the expected profit obtained at each price point, this equals:

$$\text{sales revenue} - (\text{demand} * \text{cost})$$

The profit will typically vary by price, as shown in Figure 10.1. As we see, if the price is too low, then profit is not maximized because the profit margin on each unit item will be too small. At the other extreme, if the price is too high, then the result will be insufficient demand and so again profit is impacted. Between these two extremes, there should be an optimal price point at which total profit is highest.

The optimization is best done by first creating a list of eligible prices that could be realistically charged for that product, taking into account any existing business rules on the prices that can be set. Next, each eligible price is put into Equation 10.1 above, to predict demand (using the calculated PE value). Then, given the known unit cost per item, the predicted profit may be calculated for each price point. The price that gives the maximum predicted profit would be the optimal point.

Figure 10.1   Price optimization business problem

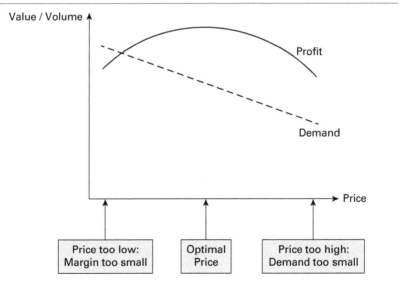

Taking product interactions into account

The above approach can and should be refined, if product sales interact significantly with sales of other items in the retailer's range. For example, beauty shoppers who purchase moisturiser are also likely to buy night cream. So if the price of moisturiser were increased, this would reduce the demand for moisturiser and therefore cause associated sales of night cream to fall as well. This effect should be taken into account – otherwise the repricing may be far from optimal.

There are two kinds of interaction between products that may be reflected by calculating cross-price elasticities (CPEs):

- If product B is cross-sold with product A, eg the same brands of night cream and moisturiser, then a price increase on A will *reduce* the demand for B. This implies calculating a *negative CPE* between A and B.

- If product B is a substitute for product A, eg two different brands of shampoo, then a price increase on A will *increase* the demand for B – the effect is also known as *cannibalization*. This implies a *positive CPE* between A and B.

If it is suspected that significant interactions exist between products, then they may first be identified with the help of association analysis (see Chapter 4).

The CPE is then calculated for each significant relationship that is discovered. For example, if product A is the 'target item' for which price is to be optimized and product B is the related product, then this calculation will involve building a regression model to predict the change in weekly demand for product B. The model will include a variable for the average price of item A – the regression coefficient obtained for this variable will be its CPE. This coefficient should be positive for a substitute relationship and negative for cross-sales.

Having obtained the CPEs, they may be included in the price optimization process. When each eligible price point for product A is being assessed, each CPE is applied to the price change on product A, in order to predict the impact on demand for each related product. The predicted impacts may then be converted to sales values and contributions to profit or loss from those products. The overall profit may then be calculated at each price point, resulting from the PE value for product A (as above) and its CPEs with related items, and the optimal position found.

Validating the results of price optimization

The final stage should be to validate the results of the price optimization process by carrying out a pricing test. This applies particularly if new prices are being planned for a large number of lines or product categories.

The test should involve putting the proposed new prices into operation – ideally for a small sample of pilot stores in order to minimize risks. The test will primarily monitor the impact on sales performance, but will also look out closely for other effects, such as any reactions from customers. The test should include a sample of control stores, carefully selected to match those in the pilot. The existing pricing strategy is maintained in the control stores, which are then used as a benchmark for interpreting sales changes in the pilot outlets.

If the test is being conducted in, say, 10 stores, then 10 matched control stores should be selected. The best way to achieve this is to first select 10 pairs of stores that are as similar to one another as possible and, across the 10 pairs, reflect the broad mix of store types and catchment areas across the chain. Within each pair, one store is randomly chosen as the test store and the other is used as its matched control.

The decision to use 10 pairs of pilot and control stores, in this example, is made on practical grounds. The sample size needs to be sufficiently large to be able to draw conclusions from the comparisons of change in product sales between each pair of stores, and not so large that an adverse result will have a serious impact on the product.

CASE STUDY

Price optimization by a pharmaceutical retailer

A price optimization study was carried out by a pharmaceutical retailer that wanted to examine the pricing of its own-brand products.

Price elasticity models were developed for 160 products and included factors for in-store promotions and seasonality. Cross-sales and cannibalization products were identified by means of association models, and then a series of cross-price elasticity models were built for the significant interactions.

The study found that, by adjusting prices, it was possible to increase revenues, profitability and share of demand for the retailer's own-brand products.

If the optimization had ignored cross-price elasticities, then one pricing decision in six would have been incorrect.

The retailer validated the findings by making price changes for 12 of the investigated products. For two-thirds of those items, the results were in accordance with predictions from the study.

Markdown pricing

The business problem

The need for markdown pricing arises in many sectors, for products reaching the end of their selling periods. Rather than not selling the item and having to lose its entire value, the retailer would prefer to reduce its price and so make it attractive to purchase, in order to obtain some of its value.

Examples of sectors facing this problem are:

- *Retailers selling fresh products* – retailers are constantly striving to maintain high product availability, in order to keep their customers satisfied. However, the downside is that wastage levels will be high on items passing their sell-by dates. Therefore, many retailers such as supermarket chains employ markdown systems in order to reduce their wastage losses.

- *Clothing retailers* face a similar challenge for fashion products. Although the selling periods on garments are longer than for fresh foods, stocks need to be sold by the end of the season – otherwise they may need to be written off.

- In the *airline industry* an equivalent process is employed, known as yield management, for managing the pricing of seats on a plane. The process is highly complex, because seats are sold through multiple channels, some of which will take longer than others to provide information on seat sales.

- The *hospitality industry* has a similar challenge when selling hotel rooms. However, high proportions of rooms are sold by intermediaries, thus making it difficult for the hotel operator to obtain accurate information and manage a markdown process.

The markdown pricing problem facing the retailer is summarized in Figure 10.2. If the price reduction is too small then the product will be unattractive to the customer and most of the stock will be unsold. Therefore the waste losses will be high. On the other hand, if the price cut is too deep, then the stock will sell out, however the retailer will have given too much margin back to the customer. Therefore, again, the retailer will incur heavy losses.

Figure 10.2   Markdown pricing – optimization objective

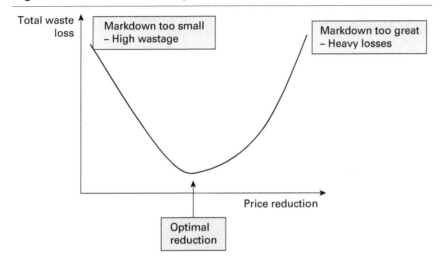

The business objective is to find the optimal reduction between these two points, where the overall loss is minimized.

Approach to a markdown pricing solution

The following steps outline a suggested approach for either developing a markdown pricing solution or improving on an existing system.

Step 1: understand existing markdown system

If the retailer already operates a markdown system and is seeking to reduce its wastage losses further, then the existing strategy and process first need to be fully understood, so that a new solution can be developed to fit in seamlessly. For example, for supermarkets selling fresh foods, the process is likely to involve repeated stock checks – identifying items that are about to reach their sell-by dates, making price reductions and potentially following up with further reductions. At the same time, data transfers are likely to be taking place between the data warehouse and the local store system. Therefore, the new solution will need to integrate with a complex process and produce markdown prices in an identical format.

Step 2: carry out preliminary analysis

A preliminary analysis should be conducted to examine the levels and patterns of current wastage losses. This should look at how losses vary by factors such as product type, price, day of week and outlet type. The analysis should help to understand how well the current markdown process is working, how many price reductions are being made, how much discount is being 'given' to the customer and whether the potential exists for the retailer to reduce its losses.

Step 3: calculate price elasticities (PEs) for products to be marked down

As we saw earlier in this chapter, PEs quantify the relationship between price and demand. If the PE is large in magnitude, for example –2 or less, then a small price reduction will stimulate demand and may be sufficient to clear the stock. If the PE is between 0 and –1, then a deeper markdown will be needed. PEs may be calculated by the approach outlined in the previous section, and the process could again require calculating cross-price elasticities for any significant substitute or cross-sale products.

Step 4: develop markdown strategy

For each product to be reduced, the opening stock and the regular average rate of sale should both be known at store level (or could be computed by the retailer). Putting these together with the PE, it becomes possible to address questions such as:

- How likely is the product to sell out without making a price reduction?
- Applying the PE, what level of reduction is required in order to increase the rate of sale sufficiently to sell out the product?
- By what point does this reduction need to be made, to allow sufficient time for the product to sell out?
- Is a further reduction required (having carried out a further stock check)? What level of reduction should be made and at what time?

Having developed analyses to answer these questions, it will become possible to develop a markdown pricing strategy for each product. The understanding of any existing approach (acquired in step 1) is essential in order to ensure that the new strategy will operate without requiring changes to systems or business processes.

The analysis should ideally also take into account the customer profile for each store. For example, in an affluent area, a small price reduction may be sufficient to attract the customer to buy that item – whereas, in a poorer area, a deep reduction may be needed to enable the purchase.

Step 5: simulate new strategy and measure benefits

The new markdown strategy is applied to recent trading days, to reprice each product on which markdowns were needed and predict the effect on sales by applying the PE models. The result will be a predicted outcome for each day – the quantity sold, at a new reduced price, the quantity wasted, and the wastage loss incurred. The predicted result may then be compared with the actual outcome in order to measure the potential benefit of the new strategy. For this assessment to be valid, a different trading period should be analysed from the time period used for building the PE models and developing the markdown strategy.

Step 6: carry out live test on effects and performance of new strategy

The simulation results will most probably suggest that there is a huge potential saving in losses to be made from introducing the new markdown strategy. The only way to establish the actual saving is to carry out a live test involving a small number of stores (or a sample of customers). Such a test is essential, in order to check that the new strategy will work in practice and will be accepted by customers. The test should include a matched control sample of stores for comparison purposes, selected by the approach described above (for validating the results of price optimization).

Key point

For the results to be valid, it is essential that the only difference between the test and control stores is the markdown strategy. In order to avoid biasing the results, all other procedures and processes must be identical in the two groups of stores.

Assuming that the test is conducted rigorously, it will provide vital real evidence to convince stakeholders of the benefits to be gained from the new strategy and its operational effects. The retailer will then be well placed to roll out the strategy across its business.

CASE STUDY

Reduced-to-clear pricing by a supermarket chain

A supermarket chain had been successful in growing sales and providing strong availability to its customers; however, this had resulted in wastage increasing at a faster rate each year. The retailer needed to slow down or stop the increase, and ultimately to reduce wastage losses.

At the outset of the project, sales and waste data were extracted from the retail data warehouse; the data were used to quantify how well wastage was being managed and answer various business questions. Using the understanding gained from the preliminary analysis, a model was developed to predict the success rate in clearing items reaching their sell-by dates, for each product/ store/day combination.

In parallel with the model development, an alternative pricing strategy was created for marking down the prices of 'reduced to clear' (RTC) products. The model was then applied to RTC items under the old and new strategies in order to predict the clearance rates and compare the business savings. The benefits were examined by products, stores and trading periods.

Finally, the benefits were validated by carrying out a store pilot over an independent time period. Senior management decided that the pricing strategy should be trialled in 10 stores of different formats and location types, for a period of 10 weeks. The pilot stores were measured against a set of 10 control stores of the same formats and with similar wastage losses. The pilot stores outperformed the control stores by a significant amount, with the pilot stores gaining a positive result and the control stores an adverse outcome against their average wastage rates.

However, the pilot also identified low compliance rates to both the retailer's existing markdown rules and to the new pricing strategy. With an improved compliance rate, business savings could have been significantly greater; therefore, the retailer decided to focus initially on investigating and improving compliance by each store to the existing process, and revisit the markdown strategy subsequently.

Forecasting base demand

Retailers, along with many other sectors and enterprises, require forecasts that enable them to plan for the future and also manage their business operations today. A host of different forecasting techniques are available, geared to the business problem. For example, different methods will be appropriate according to the forecasting horizon – that is, for how far ahead forecasts are required.

The forecasting horizon will depend on the business question to be answered, such as:

- What is the future potential demand for a new hypermarket that a retailer is considering building? This implies a long-term forecast looking ahead, say, 5–30 years.

- What resources will be required for delivering goods to customers of existing stores? This implies a medium-term forecast, say over the next 1–2 years.

- What will the consumer demand be for products sold by each store, for the coming sales cycle? This implies a short-term forecast, looking days to months ahead.

This section overviews several approaches to short-term forecasting, which may be employed to predict base demand – that is, the demand for goods (or services) that comes from existing customers. Base demand forecasts are used as input to supply chain and logistics systems, helping the retailer to avoid holding excess stocks and also not become out of stock. Other applications, such as availability analysis and markdown pricing (see above), also require base demand estimates amongst their inputs.

A large body of literature is available on forecasting techniques, covering all time horizons and approaches. For example, see either Makridakis et al (1998) or Hyndman and Athanasopoulos (2014) as starting points.

Overview of techniques

There are three widely used approaches that could be employed for producing forecasts of base demand – moving averages, exponential smoothing and forecasting models. Each is considered below, together with its main strengths and weaknesses.

Moving averages

The most straightforward of all techniques is to calculate a moving average, which is the average of a recent set of data points. For example, it could be the average of the most recent three values of daily demand for a product. As each new value of demand is observed, it gets included in the set, the earliest value is removed and the average is recalculated.

The moving average 'smooths' the variation in demand over the recent past; where demand is stable and not subject to external factors, the moving average will be a reasonable forecast of the next time period.

The main strengths of the moving average are that it is very simple to calculate and reflects recent demand for the product. However, the moving average suffers from three main weaknesses. First, it ignores seasonality in demand, and so will be unable to predict an impending increase or decrease due to a change of season. Second, all data points contribute equally to the average – often, the most recently observed demand will be more important than the earlier values in the set. Third, the forecast will tend to follow behind the actual demand.

Exponential smoothing

Exponential smoothing is a group of forecasting methods that smooth out fluctuations in base demand and overcome those weaknesses of the moving average. The choice of method will depend on the presence of trend and seasonality in base demand. By *trend* we mean that demand is showing a long-term increase or decrease, rather than being relatively stable. And *seasonality* implies that there are regular seasonal peaks and troughs in demand, occurring at the same time each year.

There are four main exponential smoothing methods:

- Single exponential smoothing – for forecasting a series that has no trend or seasonality. This method is similar to the moving average; the key difference is that, in calculating the forecast, each data point is weighted, so that the most recent value carries highest weight and earlier values carry less and less importance.

- Linear exponential smoothing – this method extends single exponential smoothing to enable forecasting of a series that contains a trend.

- Seasonal exponential smoothing – for forecasting a series that contains seasonal fluctuations but shows no trend.

- Trend and seasonality method – for forecasting a series that contains both a trend and seasonality. Seasonality may be modelled either as additive effects or as multiplicative factors.

The main strengths of exponential smoothing methods are that they are more accurate than the simple moving average and are relatively straightforward to compute. However, the methods involve calculating parameter values such as trend and seasonality effects, and so forecasting software or algorithms need to be used. This disadvantage does not apply to single exponential smoothing, which is sufficiently straightforward to be programmed or calculated in a spreadsheet.

Finally, these methods tend to require a long time series of demand values – typically at least two to three years – in order to estimate trend and seasonality effects.

Forecasting models

Forecasting models may be developed using *regression analysis* (outlined in Chapter 4), which allows factors that affect demand to be reflected in the forecast. For example, this could include a factor for whether the product is on promotion, or has limited stock, along with trend and seasonality effects.

A general assumption made in regression models is that the observations to be predicted are independent of one another, which may not always be the case when modelling a time series such as base demand.

A more sophisticated type of model, known as ARIMA (autoregressive integrated moving average), overcomes this assumption. For example, ARIMA models will handle auto-correlated time series, where one value of demand is highly correlated with the previous value. The ARIMA approach allows past values of demand and also previous forecast errors to contribute to forecasting the next value. ARIMA models may be built solely using the time series to be forecast, or may be combined with regression analysis in order to include explanatory factors.

The strengths of forecasting models are that they will handle complexities in the series to be forecast, while also reflecting trend, seasonality and external factors. However, the main drawback is that these are advanced techniques that require forecasting software to develop and deploy. They also require a long time-series of historic demand values – typically at least two to three years.

Choice of technique

In the last section we identified a number of forecasting techniques from simple moving averages through to sophisticated ARIMA models. Although a sophisticated approach is capable of delivering accurate forecasts, it also requires expertise and care to develop and continual monitoring to maintain its validity.

As a general rule, forecasts need to be robust if they are going to be input to operational systems. For this type of use, a simpler method that always produces credible forecasts is preferable to a complex system that may occasionally break down.

Large retailers may have thousands of products to manage and hundreds of stores to maintain – in which case they may be continuously generating millions of base demand forecasts. Therefore, they tend to prefer simple methods that they know will deliver robust estimates to their operational systems. For these users, moving averages or single exponential smoothing are likely to be adequate.

Retailers with smaller number of product lines and stores may prefer the greater accuracy of methods that allow for seasonality and external factors, such as regression models. Businesses dependent on a single product or service will want to forecast demand as accurately as possible, and so may be willing to invest in sophisticated techniques such as ARIMA models.

Conclusion

In this chapter, we have seen that:

- ✔ Retailers are heavy users of predictive analytics for product management, driven by operational decisions that continually need to be made.
- ✔ Price optimization harnesses the price elasticity of each product, to locate the price point that will maximize overall profit.
- ✔ If products have significant associations with one another, it can be worthwhile taking account of cross-price elasticities when optimizing pricing.
- ✔ Markdown pricing solutions aim to minimize the wastage losses incurred when products reach their sell-by dates. They seek to reduce prices on those items by just enough to make them attractive to consumers.
- ✔ When forecasting base demand for input to operational systems, the approach needs to be robust, rather than highly sophisticated.

How to benefit from social network analysis 11

Introduction

Thus far, we have mainly considered customer data in terms of attributes and transactions between the customer and the company, such as purchasing and usage. In this chapter, we widen the scope to look at links *between customers*, together with the insights that these can bring. Social network analysis (SNA) is primarily concerned with mapping those connections and measuring those relationships.

SNA is widely known in the context of social media sites such as Facebook and Twitter; however, it is not confined to online relationships. Any situation in which people have contact with one another may also be viewed as a social network and similar analysis techniques may be applied.

Much of this chapter focuses on the use of SNA for measuring relationships between customers. As we shall discuss, the results may be applied for network-based marketing or used to learn more about customers – to increase the power of predictive analytics. The closing section extends the use of SNA to social media sites such as Facebook.

The main aims of this chapter are to:

- Introduce the key principles of SNA.
- Identify its principal business applications.
- Discuss some of its uses for learning more about customers.
- Introduce online applications to social media platforms and recommendation systems.

Analysing social networks of customers

Early developments

The early applications of SNA may be found in sociological studies over 100 years ago, as a method of discovering which person in a group was most important to its communications and decision making.

One historic example of SNA concerned a study into the marriage links between families in 15th-century Florence. Social scientist John Padgett collected data on marriage relationships between 16 families (see Padgett, 1994) and more recently these have been converted into a social network of Florentine marriage alliances. The Medici family was unmatched in terms of its centrality in the network – the Medicis had alliances with six other families!

In the early 1930s, various pieces of systematic research started to appear that explored the social ties linking individuals. Freeman (2004) reviews these developments and the processes that resulted in a single approach to network analysis.

Performing SNA

When we hear the phrase 'social network' we automatically think of media such as Facebook and LinkedIn. Certainly, SNA is directed to the networks operated by such platforms, and we consider some of the applications later in this chapter.

In this section, we focus on the use of SNA as a tool for learning more about customers. In this context, SNA maps and measures the links within a group of people who could, for example, be customers of a mobile phone company or a group of bank accounts.

In online social media, networks create themselves – you make 'friends' with a group of people you know on Facebook, for example, and these users constitute your network. However, no such self-defining system exists to determine your network of 'mobile phone friends'. Instead, your network could be defined as all the people with whom you share calls or messages on a regular basis.

An appropriate metric is used to quantify the importance of each link. This could, for example, be the numbers of calls and messages made between a pair of mobile phone customers. In financial services applications, the metric could be the numbers of payments sent between a pair of accounts.

The metrics of SNA

As we saw when considering different types of customer data, in Table 3.1, a mobile operator will typically hold a set of behavioural data for each customer, including total volumes, values and durations of calls. This may include the customer's calling circle, often expressed as the number of other phone numbers that have been called in the last billing period.

Using SNA, the mobile operator is able to drill down more deeply into each customer's calling circle and examine issues such as:

- The customer's relationships with other people – each customer probably 'belongs' to several groups that have different types of relationships with one another, for example immediate family, work colleagues, close friends, sports club and so on.

- The extent to which the other people in those groups also have relationships with one another, eg a group of work colleagues.

- The importance of the customer to facilitating communications within the network, which could reflect their position within the group.

There are two main stages in extracting social network insights for each customer – computing the network and extracting SNA measures from it.

Stage 1: compute each customer's network

SNA entails identifying connections that indicate real relationships, based upon regular contacts over a period of time. This creates a network known as a social graph which includes nodes that represent people and links that summarize the relationships between them.

A small example of a social graph for customer Andy is shown in Figure 11.1, identifying Andy, who has direct links to Ben, Cal and Dan, and indirect links to the remainder of his network. The essential first stage of SNA is to compute this network; for mobile phone operators, it entails large-scale analysis of call detail records (CDRs) that summarize all calls and messages sent by each customer. Given that, for a mobile phone operator, the customer base is liable to contain millions of customers and billions of CDRs, this stage involves a huge amount of data processing, but nowadays this is practical to achieve.

Having generated the network, various metrics can be computed to describe relationships between people who are connected, eg Andy–Ben, Andy–Cal, Andy–Dan, and so on. For example, measures of relationships for Andy–Ben include:

Figure 11.1 Example social graph

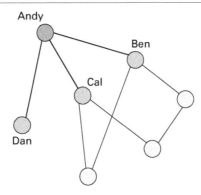

- Out of the last N weeks, in how many weeks has a communication taken place between Andy and Ben?
- What are the numbers and durations of communications between them over that period?
- What is the direction of communication between Andy and Ben, ie the ratio of outgoing to incoming calls?

These metrics may then be summarized at customer level and used within predictive and descriptive models, alongside other behavioural variables.

Stage 2: extract SNA measures

Having extracted the network, SNA is applied to obtain measures that describe each customer's importance or influence within it. Four such metrics are shown in Figure 11.2, for customer Andy – these are:

a Degree – the number of people in Andy's network.

b Betweenness – how essential is Andy for communications within the network?

c Centrality – how important is Andy to the network?

d Density – how well connected with one another are the people in Andy's network?

The measures such as these are included in the set of analytic data describing Andy's behaviour, and may be used for customer analysis purposes.

Figure 11.2 Some social network metrics

a) Degree

D1: Size of the degree 1 network
How many people are directly in Andy's network?

D2: Size of the degree 2 network
How many people are linked to those directly in Andy's network?

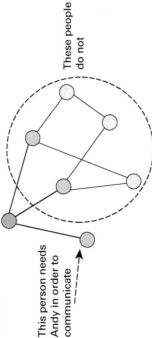

Degree 1 network

Degree 2 network

b) Betweenness

How essential is Andy to facilitate communication within his network?

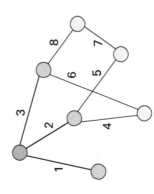

These people do not

This person needs Andy in order to communicate

c) Centrality

How 'important' is Andy in the network?

'High' is linked to 'engagement'
'Low' is linked to 'isolation'

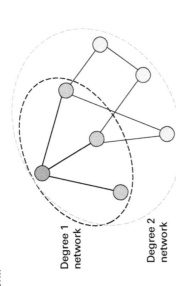

Highly central

Isolated

d) Density

How dense is the communications pattern within Andy's network?
Network contains only 8 links out of 21 potential links (7 * 6 / 2)

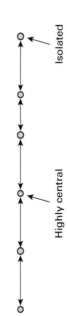

Business applications of SNA

Hill et al (2006) identify three ways in which a social network may be used for marketing:

- explicit advocacy – an individual in the network recommends a product to his or her neighbours;
- implicit advocacy – an individual in the network implicitly recommends a product through their actions, such as purchasing that product for themselves;
- network targeting – a product is marketed to the neighbours of an existing customer, if they can be identified.

These three modes may be applied either separately or in combination, to support business initiatives such as product adoption and customer retention. Bayer and Servan-Schreiber (2011) present many further business applications of SNA.

Product adoption

The take-up of some products, such as fashion items and new technology, may be viral in nature, and so would benefit from identifying influential adopters – customers who would recommend the product to their contacts, if they acquired it themselves.

Influential adopters may be identified by calculating a social networking potential (SNP) score for each member of the network, based on a combination of network metrics and relevant customer variables. If you can convince your most influential customers to purchase the product for themselves, then they will help you to spread its adoption.

An alternative, more reactive, approach is to compute the product take-up rate for each customer's contacts and include this measure along with other variables in your propensity model to target cross-sales. For example, returning to customer Andy's network: if two out of his three direct contacts already have the product, then that could increase the likelihood that Andy will also purchase it.

Of course, a great opportunity could be to go beyond your customer base and market the product online across social media networks. The extension of network analysis to online social media is discussed later in this chapter.

Customer retention

SNA may also be applied to customer retention, in two main ways – to help discover potential churners, and to identify influential customers who would lead others to churn.

One of the early applications of SNA has been to derive network metrics associated with churn, in order to improve the accuracy of churn prediction models. Such measures could be:

- size of first-degree network;
- proportion of calls or text messages to first-degree network with same phone company versus with other company;
- recent changes in either of these measures.

Having identified which customers are at greatest risk of churn, then you would make an offer designed to secure their loyalty.

The second approach is more preventive in nature – identify influential customers who would take others with them, if they churned. This can be aided by calculating the 'network value' for each customer – the expected loss from all customers who would leave, if this customer churned. Having discovered who your most influential customers are, for churn prevention, the approach is to ensure that they are well treated and looked after!

Applying SNA to learn more about customers

By gaining a better understanding of relationships between customers, it becomes possible to derive further useful information or fill in some of the gaps in the data that you hold. This will again depend on your sector; however, some examples follow.

Household composition and lifestage events

In the telecoms sector, it can be of great value to identify which individuals belong to the same household. For example, a household may contain several mobile phone users – some on post-pay contracts and others on pre-pay – as well as a fixed line for broadband. If a phone operator could form this picture of the household, then it could market its services more effectively, calculate its share of the household's telephony budget and work to increase this. For example, it could make better-targeted offers for providing phones to all users in the household.

SNA can provide valuable insights into household composition, as a large share of a customer's calls and messages are often with their 'nearest and dearest' – partner, children, parents and so on. Furthermore, the usage patterns tend to be characterized by frequent short calls and text messages, including at busy times of day.

Furthermore, SNA can be helpful in identifying life-stage events such as child leaving home, change of job or retirement – all of which are likely to be accompanied by social network changes for the affected individuals.

Identifying special communities

Staying in the mobile phone sector, SNA is useful for recognizing different types of communities such as workers, students and schoolchildren. Each of these groups is likely to have a different calling pattern, in terms of days of week, times of day, call numbers and durations, and use of text messages. By flagging the likely status of a customer, the use and tone of marketing messages may be altered accordingly.

Extending network analysis to social media

The interest in social media networks has grown enormously over recent years, with the rise in popularity of platforms such as Facebook and Twitter. Many books and papers have been written on social media marketing – see, for example, Ryan (2015), Chaffey and Ellis-Chadwick (2015). From a more technical perspective, Russell (2014) explains how to mine the social web and carry out network analysis.

Unlike customer networks, social media networks are defined explicitly, by one user 'following' or 'becoming friends' with another user. Therefore these relationships exist and do not need to be derived, as they are for customer networks.

However, the step to compute strengths of relationships and each user's position is essential for social network analysis. Similar measures, such as degree, betweenness, centrality and density, may be calculated in an equivalent way to customer networks.

By capturing more than just each relationship, the network can be made more useful. Therefore, depending on the content collected by the platform, features such as demographics, interests, activities and news stories may be captured and overlaid onto the network.

Rogers et al (2012) discuss network-based marketing on Facebook, which is currently the largest social media platform with 2 billion active users as at April 2017 (Statista, 2017). Rogers et al review methodologies for monitoring the impact of marketing strategies, by measuring the diffusion of messages through a network.

As Rogers et al explain, key data on the Facebook network may be obtained from the Facebook Graph API (Facebook, 2017). Public information, including wall posts/comments and fans who like particular news stories/products/brands may be extracted, while other attributes require permission from each user in order to obtain them.

Advertising messages on Facebook may be targeted to specific audiences according to location, demographics and interests. Also, advertising may be spread by 'word of mouth' through the network in the form of sponsored new stories.

Recommender systems (RSs)

Recommender systems are software tools and techniques that aim to identify interesting items – such as books, films or news stories – for an online user. For example, online retailer Amazon employs an RS to personalize the online store for each customer. Likewise, RSs play an important role in many other websites, including YouTube, Netflix, TripAdvisor and IMDb. RSs are closely related to network-based marketing, because both approaches exploit affinities between users; furthermore, RSs are a natural application of SNA.

The interest in RSs has grown over the last few years; many approaches to generating recommendations have been proposed and implemented for online use. For example, the handbook edited by Ricci et al (2015) collects together concepts, methodologies and applications in this field.

One of the most popular RS techniques is collaborative filtering, which is based on the premise that people who have had similar preferences in the past are likely to have similar preferences in the future. Content-based approaches overlay additional knowledge into the process, such as location of users or product genre, in order to improve the selection process.

Although recommender systems may be enhanced by overlaying information from interest graphs – networks that represent people's interests in relation to others – ultimately RSs tend not to take account of specific links between people in a network, which is a key difference from network-based marketing.

Conclusion

In this chapter, we have seen that:

✔ Social networks are not limited to online social media – in all sectors that involve interactions between customers, people form themselves into implicit networks.

✔ SNA involves building a social graph of significant relationships between customers and computing metrics that summarize each individual's position or involvement.

✔ SNA has business applications for product adoption and retention; both may involve identifying influential customers and targeting appropriate marketing activities at them.

✔ SNA may also be applied to infer more information about customers through understanding their relationships with others.

✔ Corresponding metrics apply to online social media and, in addition, networks may be overlaid with people's interests and activities.

✔ Recommender systems are online tools designed to identify interesting items for users of online retailers, movie sites and so on. RSs may be enhanced by overlaying information from networks based on people's interests, in order to offer the most relevant content to the user.

Testing the benefits of predictive models and other marketing effects

12

Introduction

As we have seen throughout this book, predictive analytics can create new ways of doing business – such as targeting best prospects, identifying influential members of a social network or optimizing prices in a retail store. *Testing* is a controlled approach to introducing different strategies, in order to understand their effects and manage the risk. It involves running a business experiment and interpreting the results in an objective, impartial way.

There are three overall stages in testing:

1 Design an experiment to test the changes that are being considered.

2 Construct a test sample, run the experiment and measure the results.

3 Interpret the results and draw conclusions.

The main aims of this chapter are to:

- Discuss the purpose of testing and its importance in marketing.
- Present five 'golden rules' that should always be followed.
- Describe the main components when designing an experiment.
- Explain how to plan the sample size for direct marketing tests.
- Plan the stages in constructing the test sample and measuring the results.
- Consider how the results from a direct marketing test may be interpreted.

- Overview the use of advanced experimental design for learning more from business experiments.
- Consider approaches to testing in the online world.

This chapter mainly focuses on business experiments carried out in direct marketing situations, eg for testing new predictive models. The same approaches may also be applied to direct e-mail campaigns, for example to decide whether a new version of an e-mail yields a significantly improved click-through rate. However, as the final section discusses, online marketing is best suited to different types of testing.

The purpose of testing

It is a fact of life that any new business activity with potential benefits will also have associated risks – and as the potential benefits increase, so do the risks. By carrying out an experiment, the level of risk may be managed at an acceptable level.

For example, in marketing any product or service, there are many factors that can affect the outcome – the marketer is constantly seeking which 'levers to pull' in order to achieve success or improve on past performance. These factors include:

- product design and quality;
- target audience and selection of prospects – for example, using predictive models;
- pricing, terms and incentive;
- creative treatment;
- timing of offer or campaign;
- sales channel and response mechanism.

Although the importance of testing is generally understood, many companies are either unwilling to invest in rigorous business experiments or are not geared up to run them. That was an overall conclusion by Thomke and Manzi (2014) from their studies in dozens of large companies. One company that is renowned for its continuous 'test and learn' strategy is Capital One. Richard Fairbank founded Capital One in 1988 based on his belief that the power of information, technology, testing and people could be combined to bring highly customized financial products directly to consumers (see Capital One, 2017).

Key point

Testing requires making an *investment* in how your company markets to its customers. Running an experiment implies comparing alternative approaches and accepting that some will perform better than others, in order to prove what works and learn from the results. This means being prepared to forgo some revenue and profit in the short term, in order to achieve proven success in the long term.

The benefits of this strategy may seem obvious; however, some companies struggle to make this kind of investment, as noted above. If the commitment to testing comes from the top, as in the case of Capital One, then the required culture will spread throughout the entire company.

As we shall see in this chapter, the size of each experiment is controllable and may be designed with the help of statistics, in order to deliver quantified confidence in the results for known investments in the sample sizes.

Golden rules

There are five important rules that should be followed when planning and running a business experiment, as set out below.

Rule 1: test the big things first

In other words, test the important marketing variables that will make a difference to your business, in preference to insignificant features. If a variable is not really of importance, then it should not be tested.

Rule 2: employ an adequate sample size

When you are testing how well consumers respond to communications, ensure that the sample size is sufficiently large to measure the statistical significance of the results and draw robust conclusions. In this chapter, we present a simple approach for calculating minimum sample sizes for direct marketing tests.

Rule 3: keep elements not being tested as constant as possible

For example, suppose that the purpose is to test whether a targeting model delivers an improved response over an existing selection method. In that case, the offer, creative treatment and all other factors need to be controlled – otherwise it will be impossible to decide whether a difference in outcomes was due to the model or some other factor.

Rule 4: keep the experiment simple and straightforward

Each factor being tested should be kept simple – ideally it should have just a small number of options, eg targeting model versus existing selection. However, more than one factor may be included in the same experiment, as we discuss in the next section.

Rule 5: be objective

Do not 'overstretch' test results or interpret them selectively. Interpretation of direct marketing tests is discussed later on in this chapter.

Planning a marketing test

There are two main types of test – predictive and comparative. Predictive testing is used to gauge the range of response that would be achieved from marketing to all customers, by first running the campaign on a smaller representative sample. Many tests and experiments, however, are comparative in nature, ie comparing results from two or more sample groups against one another, in order to measure the differences and assess which approach works best.

In order to assess the benefit of a new targeting model, a comparative test could contain two groups – also known as *cells*:

- Cell 1: a sample of customers selected by the model.
- Cell 2: a sample of eligible customers selected at random.

Alternatively, if the model has been built to replace an existing targeting model, the test could contain three groups:

- Cell 1: customers selected by existing model.
- Cell 2: customers selected by new model.
- Cell 3: customers selected at random.

In the first example, Cell 2 is essential to prove the benefit of the model – in this case, Cell 2 is known as a control group. In the second case, the random control group (Cell 3) is not strictly necessary, as the existing model can be the reference point for the new model. However, by including the random control, the benefits of both models can be evaluated.

Calculating the sample size required for a test

As Golden Rule 2 states, the sample size should be sufficiently large to draw robust conclusions from the test. In most situations, according to the method and objectives of the experiment, the minimum sample size may be calculated statistically. Then, provided that you use or exceed this sample size in your test, you should be 'safe'.

   We shall work through an approach to calculating minimum sample sizes for predictive and comparative direct marketing tests – ie for direct mail or e-mail campaigns. For other types of tests, different approaches are likely to be required and statistical advice should be sought.

Key point

There is a common belief that a larger sample size is needed for larger populations – that the sample should be, say, 5 per cent or 10 per cent of the population. This belief is a complete fallacy – market researchers would need sample sizes of millions for their surveys, if it were true. In fact, as we see below, test samples are generally in the realms of thousands.

   An important research issue is that any sample survey must be representative of its population – and exactly the same goes for direct marketing tests.

Sample size calculation for predictive tests

In order to calculate the minimum sample size, you first need to decide on values for three parameters:

- the approximate response rate that you expect will be achieved – suppose this is R per cent;

- the tolerance level, above or below the expected response, that you are prepared to accept as being 'no different' – suppose this is A per cent;

- the level of confidence you require that the true response rate, across the population, would be within A per cent of R per cent, ie fall between

(R – A) and (R + A). Usually, 95 per cent confidence is taken – we shall assume this confidence level throughout.

Based on these three criteria, the minimum sample size, S, may be calculated as:

$$S = \frac{3.8416 * R * (100 - R)}{A^2}$$

– where the value 3.8416 corresponds to taking 95 per cent confidence. This formula makes three important statistical assumptions:

- That the members of the targeted population will respond independently of one another; this might not always be the case in social media scenarios.
- That the response may be approximated by a normal ('bell-shaped') distribution. This assumption is reasonable provided that the expected number of respondents is at least five (ie that $S * R \geq 5$).
- That the test sample is drawn from a much larger population. If the sample is likely to be more than 1 per cent of the population size, then the formula should be adjusted by applying a factor known as a finite population correction (FPC). The effect will be to reduce the minimum sample size required for the test.

Also, the formula assumes that the tolerance level (A) is smaller than the expected response rate (R), which will usually be the case unless R is very small. The formula is demonstrated by Select Statistical Services (2017), which provides online calculators for obtaining minimum sample sizes in different situations.

Example A

Suppose that you are planning a predictive test with an expected response rate of 5 per cent (R) and a tolerance level of 0.5 per cent (A). Then the required sample size would be:

$$S = \frac{3.8416 * 5 * (100 - 5)}{0.5^2}$$

$$= 7{,}299$$

Therefore, by running a test campaign on 7,300 customers, you could be 95 per cent confident that a deviation of more than 0.5 per cent from the expected response rate of 5 per cent is a real effect and not due to chance.

Table 12.1 shows the minimum sample sizes, based on this formula, for various levels of expected response and tolerance. We can see that greater sample sizes are required for larger response rates and for smaller tolerances. If you are unsure about the response rate that will be achieved, it is better to err on the high side, in order to be sure of testing on an adequate sample size.

Sample-size calculation for comparative tests

In comparative testing, the key quantity to be measured is the difference in response rate between groups. For example, in the two group examples above, the difference between model group (Cell 1) and control group (Cell 2) represents the effect of the model. In the three-group example, there are three comparisons that can be made:

- difference between Cell 1 and Cell 3 = effect of existing model;
- difference between Cell 2 and Cell 3 = effect of new model;
- difference between Cell 1 and Cell 2 = improvement from introducing new model.

Table 12.1 Minimum sample sizes for predictive tests

Expected response rate	Tolerance level (+ or –)				
	0.25%	0.5%	0.75%	1.0%	2.0%
0.5%	3,100	N/A	N/A	N/A	N/A
1.0%	6,100	1,500	700	N/A	N/A
1.5%	9,100	2,300	1,000	600	N/A
2.0%	12,000	3,000	1,300	800	N/A
2.5%	15,000	3,700	1,700	900	200
3.0%	17,900	4,500	2,000	1,100	300
4.0%	23,600	5,900	2,600	1,500	400
5.0%	29,200	7,300	3,200	1,800	500
7.5%	42,600	10,700	4,700	2,700	700
10.0%	55,300	13,800	6,100	3,500	900

Note Based on 95 per cent confidence level and normal approximation to the binomial distribution.
Minimum sample sizes are rounded to the nearest 100.
Cells containing insufficient numbers of expected responders are shown as 'N/A'.
Cells where the tolerance level is greater than or equal to the expected response rate are shown as 'N/A'.

In any test, the result for each cell will be affected by random variation – in other words, a different result will be obtained from each possible sample of customers selected from the population, just due to chance. Furthermore, the difference in outcome between a pair of cells will be subject to a greater amount of variability than for a single-cell predictive test. For this reason, larger samples are needed for comparative tests, in order to cope with the greater uncertainty.

Assuming that the cells are to have equal sample sizes, the formula for minimum sample size, for each cell, is as follows:

$$S = \frac{7.6832 * R * (100 - R)}{A^2}$$

– where R per cent is the expected average response rate across the cells, A per cent is the tolerance level in the difference in response, and 7.6832 corresponds to being 95 per cent confident of detecting a difference of A per cent or more. The same statistical assumptions are made for this formula, as we saw above for predictive tests.

Example B

For example, suppose that you are designing a comparative test with an expected average response of 4 per cent (R) and a tolerance level of 0.75 per cent (A) – in other words, you want to be confident that a 0.75 per cent or more difference in response, between two groups, is real and not due to chance. Then the required sample size for each cell would be:

$$S = \frac{7.6832 * 4 * (100 - 4)}{0.75^2}$$

$$= 5,245$$

Table 12.2 shows the minimum sample sizes, based on this formula, for various levels of expected response and tolerance. Again, we can see that higher sample sizes are required for larger response rates and for smaller tolerances. Again, it is better to err on the high side with cell sizes.

As you can see, the sample sizes in Table 12.2 are double those of Table 12.1; this is because the difference between two groups will have twice the amount of random variation compared with the result from a single group.

Table 12.2 Minimum cell sizes for comparative tests

Expected average response rate	Tolerance level (+ or –)				
	0.25%	0.5%	0.75%	1.0%	2.0%
0.5%	6,100	1,500	N/A	N/A	N/A
1.0%	12,200	3,000	1,400	800	N/A
1.5%	18,200	4,500	2,000	1,100	N/A
2.0%	24,100	6,000	2,700	1,500	400
2.5%	30,000	7,500	3,300	1,900	500
3.0%	35,800	8,900	4,000	2,200	600
4.0%	47,200	11,800	5,200	3,000	700
5.0%	58,400	14,600	6,500	3,700	900
7.5%	85,300	21,300	9,500	5,300	1,300
10.0%	110,600	27,700	12,300	6,900	1,700

Note Based on 95 per cent confidence level and normal approximation to the binomial distribution. Minimum sample sizes are rounded to the nearest 100.
Cells containing insufficient numbers of expected responders are shown as 'N/A'.

Cell sizes in comparative testing do not necessarily need to be equal. The theory extends to unequal cells, which could easily arise if you are testing a new targeting model alongside an existing one, or if you are including a random control group in order to monitor the performance of your model.

When the cells are to be of unequal sizes, the formula for minimum *total* sample size, *across the two cells*, is as follows:

$$S = \frac{3.8416 * R * (100 - R)}{Q * (100 - Q) * A^2}$$

– where R per cent is the expected average response rate across the cells and Q per cent is the percentage of the test to be allocated to one cell, with (100 – Q) per cent allocated to the other cell. Again, A per cent is the tolerance level in the difference in response, and 3.8416 corresponds to being 95 per cent confident of detecting a difference of A per cent or more. The same statistical assumptions apply to this formula, as we have seen above.

Table 12.3 provides some examples of total test sizes implied by this formula, for various levels of expected response rate and tolerance, and

Table 12.3 Minimum total sample sizes for comparative tests with unequal-sized groups

Expected average response rate	Tolerance level (+ or −)	Proportion allocated to each cell				
		10% and 90%	20% and 80%	30% and 70%	40% and 60%	50%
1.0%	0.5%	16,900	9,500	7,200	6,300	6,100
2.0%	1.0%	8,400	4,700	3,600	3,100	3,000
5.0%	1.5%	9,000	5,100	3,900	3,400	3,200
10.0%	2.0%	9,600	5,400	4,100	3,600	3,500

Note Based on 95 per cent confidence level and normal approximation to the binomial distribution. Minimum total sample sizes are rounded to the nearest 100.

by different sampling allocations between the two cells. The right-hand column corresponds to equal cell sizes and therefore the results are double those shown in Table 12.2 – because Table 12.2 gives minimum sample sizes for each cell, whereas Table 12.3 gives total test sizes across the pair of cells.

We see from Table 12.3 that, as the sample allocation between cells becomes more unequal, the required total test size increases markedly. For example, this table demonstrates that running a 10 per cent control group could be uneconomic, unless you were prepared to allow a larger tolerance level in your test.

The test matrix

The above comparative test contains just a single factor – the method of targeting: this factor is known as the test dimension.

Each test that your marketing team runs will take time to set up, execute, collect results and interpret. Therefore, the learning process would be very slow if only one factor could be tested at a time. For this reason, tests often contain two or more dimensions and much larger numbers of cells. The layout of cells in a test is known as the test matrix – a complete test of two factors, such as targeting method and offer type, will contain cells for all combinations of those dimensions, as illustrated in the example of Table 12.4 for testing the method of targeting and alternative offer types.

In this example there are two dimensions, each measured by three groups, therefore the test matrix contains nine cells.

Table 12.4   Example two-dimension test matrix

	Method of targeting		
Offer type	**Proposed model**	**Existing model**	**Random control**
Offer 1			
Offer 2			
Offer 3			

Sample sizes for multidimensional tests

Continuing the same example, suppose that you want to plan the sample sizes for the test laid out in Table 12.4. Also, let us assume that you have calculated the minimum sample size per cell (in a comparative test) and arrived at 5,245 as in the example above – and, for safety, you have rounded this up to 6,000 per cell.

A full comparative test would cover all nine combinations of targeting method and offer types, with 6,000 per cell, as shown in Table 12.5a. This would be ideal if the two factors were believed to interact – eg to examine

Table 12.5   Examples of designs for tests on two dimensions

a) Where dimensions of test interact

	Method of targeting			
Offer type	**Proposed model**	**Existing model**	**Random control**	**Total**
Offer 1	6,000	6,000	6,000	18,000
Offer 2	6,000	6,000	6,000	18,000
Offer 3	6,000	6,000	6,000	18,000
Total	18,000	18,000	18,000	54,000

b) Where dimensions of test work independently

	Method of targeting			
Offer type	**Proposed model**	**Existing model**	**Random control**	**Total**
Offer 1	2,000	2,000	2,000	6,000
Offer 2	2,000	2,000	2,000	6,000
Offer 3	2,000	2,000	2,000	6,000
Total	6,000	6,000	6,000	18,000

whether the proposed model works best for a particular offer type – as the cell results could be compared to identify the combination that produces the best response. However, a total sample size of 54,000 would be required for this experiment, which might take up a large share of your marketing budget.

In this example, it could be reasonable to assume that the two dimensions work independently of each other, in which case there is no need to analyse how they interact. In other words, the objectives of the test would be to determine which targeting method to use, and which offer type works best. In that situation, the cell sample sizes may be reduced to give 6,000 for each *overall* targeting method and offer type – as shown in Table 12.5b – since the results will only be analysed for each dimension in total. This will cut the overall test size by a factor of 3, to 18,000 in total, and will still address the business objectives.

Further dimensions may be included in a test, however each additional dimension increases the number of test cells. For example, if we add a third dimension (with three levels) to the above test, then we will need 27 test cells. Adding a fourth dimension would require 81 cells, and so on.

Key point

For smaller businesses

If your business operates on a smaller scale or has fewer customers, then it may not be feasible to conduct tests using the sample sizes recommended in this chapter. However, this does not invalidate the concept of testing – it only means that you should not place too much reliance on results from individual tests, and that your tests should focus on major changes that cannot be examined by other methods.

Advanced experimental design

Factorial experiments

A test design that contains cells for all possible combinations of factors, such as in the two-dimension example of Table 12.5, is known as a factorial experiment.

The factorial experiment is a highly efficient design, because the entire test sample is used to analyse the results for each dimension. To see this, suppose that you need to test the effect of using a targeting model and also the offer type, and that each has two options. A simple test design could be:

Cell 1: No model, offer type 1 – 6,000 customers

Cell 2: Model, offer type 1 – 6,000 customers

Cell 3: No model, offer type 2 – 6,000 customers

This design would allow you to analyse and evaluate each effect:

Effect of model: Cell 1 vs. Cell 2 – total sample: 12,000

Effect of offer type: Cell 1 vs. Cell 3 – total sample: 12,000

However, the design is inefficient in the sense that one-third of the 18,000 customers would be unused in each evaluation.

Suppose, instead, that you ran a factorial experiment and tested all combinations of the two factors. To maintain the same overall sample size of 18,000, you reduce each cell to 4,500 customers, as follows:

Cell 1: No model, offer type 1 – 4,500

Cell 2: Model, offer type 1 – 4,500

Cell 3: No model, offer type 2 – 4,500

Cell 4: Model, offer type 2 – 4,500

In order to evaluate each effect, you would make the following comparisons:

Effect of model: (cells 2 + 4) vs. (cells 1 + 3) – total sample: 18,000

Effect of offer type: (cells 1 + 2) vs. (cells 3 + 4) – total sample: 18,000

Therefore, all customers contribute to each evaluation, increasing the analysis sample sizes by 50 per cent. Alternatively, of course, you could reduce each cell in the factorial experiment to 3,000 customers and achieve the same evaluation accuracy as in the simple test, while saving one-third of the test size.

A further benefit of the factorial experiment is that it allows you to test for the presence of interactions between the factors – where the combination of two (or more) factors has a significant impact on the outcome. Incomplete designs, such as the three-cell experiment above, cannot measure interactions.

As you increase the number of dimensions to learn more from each experiment, a point may be reached where the required number of cells exceeds either your budget or the number of customers available for selection. At this stage, you might wish to consider employing a different design to reduce the size of your test. Two possible ways to achieve this are the Latin square and the fractional factorial design.

Latin squares

The name 'Latin square' was inspired by the Swiss mathematician Leonhard Euler, who used Latin characters as symbols in his tables. A Latin square design is a way of testing three factors, for example, using the number of cells required for two factors.

Consider the two-dimension test shown in Table 12.4, for testing targeting method by offer type. Now suppose that we want to include a third dimension, creative treatment (creative A, B or C), in the same test. However, this would require 27 test cells, which might be too many for your marketing system. This number could be reduced by using a Latin square design, as shown in Table 12.6 – where each creative treatment is tested on all three options for targeting method and offer type.

As we see in Table 12.6, the Latin square is 'balanced' in the sense that each level of each dimension is used in three cells with different combinations of the other two factors. Therefore, by using a Latin square design in this example, the required number of cells has been reduced from 27 down to 9, a significant saving in test size.

However, the potential drawback is that, using a Latin square for the test, it would no longer be possible to identify interactions between the factors. Therefore, Latin squares should be avoided where interaction detection is one of the objectives.

Fractional factorial experiments

In some situations you may have many 'marketing levers' that need to be simultaneously tested – implying the need for a large number of test cells in your factorial experiment. If the number of cells exceeds the available

Table 12.6 Example Latin square design

| Offer type | Method of targeting | | |
	Proposed model	Existing model	Random control
Offer 1	Creative A	Creative B	Creative C
Offer 2	Creative B	Creative C	Creative A
Offer 3	Creative C	Creative A	Creative B

'space' or capacity, then the solution could be to carry out a fractional facto-rial experiment.

For example, suppose that you need to run an experiment on six factors, each with two levels, implying 64 (2^6) test cells. A quarter-factorial experi-ment would, instead, use 16 cells and would still allow you to test the effect of each factor (but not the interactions between factors). Hicks and Turner (1999) go into full details on fractional factorial experiments and advanced experimental design more generally.

If you are considering using an advanced design for your marketing test, such as a factorial, fractional factorial or Latin square, then statistical advice should be obtained – to plan the experiment and analyse the results.

Constructing and running the test

Sample selection

Having designed the test matrix, the next step in constructing a direct marketing test is to select a sample of customers and allocate its members to the cells in the matrix. While this step should be fairly mechanical, there are several points to keep in mind.

The sample should be selected from the population of customers who will be eligible to receive the subsequent marketing roll-out. In other words, any non-marketable groups need to be excluded from the test, just as they would be removed from the roll-out.

In order to use the test to draw valid conclusions, the sample needs to be representative of the population – it should not be biased to certain customer types or behaviour patterns. To guard against introducing a bias by accident, a suitable process of random sampling should be applied – a method of '1 in n' sampling is usually acceptable, as follows:

1 Identify the eligible customer population and count the number of customers – for example, suppose that this population size is 500,000.

2 Sum up the total test sample size, across all test and control cells – suppose this is 20,000.

3 Calculate the test sampling fraction = 20,000/500,000 = 1/25.

4 Select every 25th customer from the list of population members and assign to the test sample.

Note: technically this is a method of pseudo-random sampling and is not strictly random, however it works well in practice.

The sample of 20,000 customers, in this case, would then be allocated to the various test cells. For example, if the experiment contains four cells of 5,000, then customers should be assigned to cells in rotation, so that customers 1, 5, 9, etc go to Cell 1, customers, 2, 6, 10, etc go to Cell 2, and so on. This further stage of random allocation helps to avoid biases between the test cells.

CASE STUDY

Example – mortgage retention

As an example of how *not* to create a test sample, a mortgage lender once carried out an experiment to measure the effectiveness of a model to predict attrition on home loans. A test group was constructed, containing customers who were predicted would terminate their loans at the end of their fixed-rate period, and was compared against a control group. After running the experiment for six months, the test group was found to have a *lower* attrition rate than the control group. The company then checked into how the groups had been formed – customers had been assigned to groups using the mortgage roll number – the first 10,000 roll numbers were allocated to the test group, and the next 10,000 to the control group. However, as roll numbers are created sequentially, this meant that the test group tended to be older customers, who were more stable and therefore had lower attrition rates. For this reason, the test was invalid and had to be repeated using a randomized selection method.

Running the test and measuring performance

Define performance metrics

When setting up the experiment, a set of performance measures should be defined by which the results will be measured. If one of the test objectives is to evaluate a targeting model – say, for predicting response to a sales campaign – then the same metric should be used to judge success. In addition, other measures should also be included, such as conversion rates and sales generated. The model will hopefully be successful in delivering a higher response rate, but may sometimes have adverse side effects in other ways – depending on how carefully its use has been planned.

For example, in the mortgage retention case study, the model was eventually found to be a useful way to predict attrition; however, by contacting customers about their mortgages, it prompted more people to be aware that they could switch – therefore it helped to increase the attrition rate.

Running the test

If the experiment involves comparing two or more test cells, then care must be taken to ensure that cells are treated identically, in all respects other than the factor(s) being tested. Even the most subtle variation will be sufficient to cause an apparent difference in cell results, for example:

- If different methods of segmentation and targeting are being compared, they should all be applied to the same source list – otherwise the nature of the list will be sufficient to produce a significantly different result.

- If a revised procedure is being tested in a sample of retail stores, against a control sample that follows the existing procedure, then all stores in both groups should be briefed and managed in as similar a way as possible – otherwise, improved results from the new procedure may be due to the closer management and attention paid in those stores that introduced it.

A timescale should be agreed at the outset for running the experiment and all test cells should be monitored over exactly the same period. The testing period may take weeks or months, in which case interim results may be reported; however, the test should be allowed to run for the full term before carrying out a final analysis of the results – unless, of course, there is an overriding business reason for stopping early.

Ongoing tests

It may be argued that experimentation in business should be an ongoing process that should never end. This applies particularly in direct marketing, for list selection and model management. So, for example, once you have implemented a predictive model that improves response, it is best practice to maintain a small randomly targeted control cell in each campaign in order to keep a check on the performance of the model. In this way, you will be able to demonstrate the model's value and identify when this degrades – implying that a refresh may be required.

Analysing test results

Having conducted the experiment, the next step should be to analyse and interpret the results. In this section, we present methods for analysing the predictive and comparative direct-marketing tests introduced earlier in this chapter, and introduce a statistical technique that applies more generally. For methods applicable to other types of tests, see Hicks and Turner (1999) or Rasch et al (2007).

Placing confidence in results of predictive tests

Having conducted a predictive test – as discussed earlier in this chapter – and measured the actual response rate delivered, we can derive a confidence range for the response that may be expected in a future campaign or marketing roll-out. In performing these calculations, we are assuming that the test is representative of future marketing activity and that market circumstances do not change in a way that affects response.

Three inputs are required in order to calculate the confidence range:

- The test sample size, ie for the direct mail or e-mail campaign – suppose this is N.
- The response rate from the campaign – suppose this is P per cent.
- The required level of confidence – statisticians often select 95 per cent confidence, implying that you want to be 95 per cent certain that the future response rate will fall within the range that is calculated.

The first step is to calculate the standard deviation of the observed response rate, which is a measure of how much the response is likely to vary from one test to the next.

$$\text{Standard deviation, SD} = \sqrt{\frac{P * (100 - P)}{N}}$$

Then, for a confidence range with 95 per cent confidence, the lower and upper limits on response are calculated as:

Lower limit, $L = P - (1.96 * SD)$

Upper limit, $U = P + (1.96 * SD)$

– where the factor 1.96 corresponds to taking 95 per cent confidence. Other factors apply for different levels of confidence – the smaller the factor, the narrower will be the range, but the lower will be the confidence. The same statistical assumptions apply to these formulae, as we saw above for calculating minimum sample sizes.

We can apply these calculations to the predictive test designed earlier in this chapter, to obtain the confidence range.

Example A continued

Suppose that the predictive test has been run on 7,300 customers, as recommended, and achieved a response rate of 4.7 per cent.

Therefore the standard deviation of response will be:

$$SD = \sqrt{\frac{4.7 * (100 - 4.7)}{7,300}} = 0.25\%$$

Thus the confidence limits will be:

L = 4.7 – (1.96 * 0.25) = 4.2%

U = 4.7 + (1.96 * 0.25) = 5.2%

Therefore you can be 95 per cent confident that the future roll-out response will fall within a 1 per cent range, from 4.2 per cent to 5.2 per cent. This range is consistent with the expected response rate of 5 per cent that was used when planning the test.

Key point

Significance testing

The same logic may be used to test whether the achieved response differs significantly from a benchmark or expected value. For example, suppose that you have learnt that your competitor obtained a response rate of 4 per cent from a similar campaign – is your response of 4.7 per cent consistent with this?

Since 4 per cent falls below the *4.2–5.2 per cent* confidence range that you calculated for your experiment, you can conclude that your test delivered a significantly higher response.

Table 12.7 applies the same formulae as above, to give lower and upper confidence limits for different test sizes and response rates. We see that by increasing the sample size, the test becomes more accurate and the range narrows. As the response rate increases, so does the standard deviation and therefore the range becomes wider.

Table 12.7   Lower and upper confidence limits on response rate from a predictive test

Test size	Test response rate					
	0.5%	1%	2%	3%	5%	10%
1,000	0.06%	0.38%	1.13%	1.94%	3.65%	8.14%
	0.94%	1.62%	2.87%	4.06%	6.35%	11.86%
5,000	0.30%	0.72%	1.61%	2.53%	4.40%	9.17%
	0.70%	1.28%	2.39%	3.47%	5.60%	10.83%
10,000	0.36%	0.80%	1.73%	2.67%	4.57%	9.41%
	0.64%	1.20%	2.27%	3.33%	5.43%	10.59%
20,000	0.40%	0.86%	1.81%	2.76%	4.70%	9.58%
	0.60%	1.14%	2.19%	3.24%	5.30%	10.42%
50,000	0.44%	0.91%	1.88%	2.85%	4.81%	9.74%
	0.56%	1.09%	2.12%	3.15%	5.19%	10.26%

Note Based on 95 per cent confidence and normal approximation to the binomial distribution.

Key		Test response rate
Test size		Lower limit
		Upper limit

Analysing differences between cells in a comparative test

A similar process may be followed to calculate a confidence range for the difference in response between two test cells, and examine whether the difference is likely to be real. The inputs to the calculations are:

- The cell sample sizes – suppose that these are N1 and N2 for cells 1 and 2, respectively.
- The cell response rates – let these be P1 per cent and P2 per cent respectively.
- The confidence level we want to use – again, 95 per cent confidence is assumed.

Let D be the difference in response rates between the cells – using the above inputs:

$$D = P1\% - P2\%$$

First we calculate the standard deviation for D, which measures how much the difference in response is likely to vary from one experiment to the next. As both test cells contribute to D, its standard deviation combines the variability in both:

Standard deviation of difference,

$$SD(D) = \sqrt{\frac{P1 * (100 - P1)}{N1} + \frac{P2 * (100 - P2)}{N2}}$$

We start by assuming that there is no difference in response between the two cells, therefore D is expected to be zero. Based on this assumption, our confidence limits for D are:

Lower limit, LD = − 1.96 * SD(D)

Upper limit, UD = + 1.96 * SD(D)

If the actual value of D falls outside these limits, then the result is significant and it is likely that there is a real difference in response between the two cells. These formulae are again based on the statistical assumptions listed earlier. We can apply these calculations to the comparative test designed earlier in this chapter.

Example B continued

Suppose that the comparative test designed earlier was conducted using a sample size of 5,300 in each of the test cells. And the test delivered response rates of 4.4 per cent and 3.5 per cent for the two cells. The difference in response, D, was therefore 4.4% − 3.5% = 0.9%.

The standard deviation of this difference is:

$$\sqrt{\frac{4.4 * (100 - 4.4)}{5,300} + \frac{3.5 * (100 - 3.5)}{5,300}} = 0.38\%$$

Therefore the 95 per cent confidence limits are:

LD = − 1.96 * 0.38 = − 0.74

UD = + 1.96 * 0.38 = + 0.74

As D is greater than 0.74 per cent by a small margin, the difference between the cells is just significant and is likely to be real.

The above calculations are a useful way to analyse simple tests involving small number of cells. The method may be applied to experiments with more than two cells, by comparing cells on a pairwise base, i.e. Cell 1 vs. Cell 2, Cell 1 vs. Cell 3, and so on. For larger experiments, we need a more sophisticated approach – the method generally used is analysis of variance, and the following section introduces the concept.

Analysis of variance approach

Analysis of variance, or 'ANOVA' for short, is a statistical technique for analysing data containing many variables or factors on each customer, and developing a model that explains test performance. ANOVA may be applied to test outcomes – it is not limited to response rates, nor only to handling direct-marketing tests.

The ANOVA approach is essentially equivalent to regression analysis, which was introduced in Chapter 4. The key difference between the techniques lies in their purpose – ANOVA is generally used to model the test outcome and identify which factors should play a part in the model, rather than to make predictions for customers.

For example, suppose that ANOVA was being used to measure the response to the two-factor experiment on targeting method (TM) and offer type (OT). Then a possible ANOVA model would be:

$$\text{Expected Y} = \text{TM effect} + \text{OT effect}$$

– where Y is the response from the test.

ANOVA works by splitting the total variation in Y into separate components due to the TM and OT effects, as well as a residual component due to random error or 'noise'. ANOVA then measures the significance of each effect – if there really is a difference caused by targeting then the TM effect will have a large amount of variation that will be statistically significant.

If the experiment follows a factorial design, as in this example, then ANOVA can also test whether the interaction of targeting model and offer type is important in the model. In this case the model would be:

$$\text{Expected Y} = \text{TM effect} + \text{OT effect} + \text{TM*OT interaction}$$

Again, ANOVA will break down the overall variation into TM, OT, TM*OT and residual components, and test whether each element in the model accounts for a significant portion.

ANOVA software is included in most statistics packages and data-mining products (see Chapter 5). The technique is explained in many statistics text books, and its application to analysing experiments is discussed by Hicks and Turner (1999) and also by Rasch et al (2007).

Testing in the online world

We cannot leave this chapter without discussing some of the benefits and considerations of testing in the online world.

The applications of testing to online marketing are obvious. The owner of a website has control over the page displayed to each site visitor. If a new layout is being considered, or perhaps only a change to one part of the page, the owner can create two alternative versions, existing and new, and display each option to site visitors selected at random. Then the owner only has to conduct the test, measure the difference in conversion or click-through rates for those pages, and decide whether the new version produces a sufficiently worthwhile improvement for it to be implemented. This process is often known as A/B testing or split-run testing. The method extends to multivariate testing in which more than two options may be evaluated.

The main benefits of web-page testing are that it is straightforward to set up, measure the results, learn from the findings and proceed accordingly. So it is a highly actionable process.

Options for managing online tests

There are several approaches for managing online tests. The simplest option is to use classical statistics; the methods presented earlier in this chapter, for calculating minimum sample sizes and interpreting test results, all employ the classical approach. The same methods and formulae could be applied to A/B testing; however, they have disadvantages when used online.

First, the methods used for offline direct marketing tests employ fixed sample sizes, as we have seen. This works in the offline world, where direct mail campaigns (for example) require timescales of weeks or months before results can be measured. In contrast, the online world is highly dynamic – you are able to 'peek' at test results hourly or daily, and you certainly would not want to wait for a month to elapse before you could reach a decision.

As Johari et al (2015) explain, a statistical problem arises when users peek at online test results that employ fixed sample sizes, and then make decisions before allowing the test to complete. Essentially, peeking invalidates the test, in terms of the level of confidence that can be placed in the results.

The solution is to employ a sequential method of testing – in which the data are evaluated as they are collected and the test is stopped as soon as a decision can be made. Sequential tests can provide a valid measure of confidence whenever the user peeks at the results. Furthermore, sequential tests typically require smaller sample sizes than fixed-sample tests – therefore the user also benefits by reaching a decision sooner, thus saving time and costs. See Wald (2014) for an explanation of sequential analysis and the sequential-probability ratio test that he devised over 70 years ago.

A newer method for managing A/B testing, which Google employs in its Content Experiments system, uses an approach known as the multi-armed bandit. The method gets its name by supposing that you face a row of slot machines ('one-armed bandits') with potentially different expected payouts. You want to find the arm – ie web-page version – with the best payout rate, but you also want to maximize your winnings. This approach transforms A/B testing from a statistical experiment into an optimization problem.

Google employs mathematical models for managing the bandit problem when running an A/B content experiment. The Content Experiments Interface is described and multi-armed bandits are discussed within Google Analytics Help (2017). Scott (2010) from Google describes their heuristic for managing the bandit, which randomly assigns observations to arms according to the probability that each arm is optimal and uses Bayesian statistics (see Chapter 4) to compute those probabilities.

A key difference between multi-armed bands and sequential tests is that bandits adapt to the performance of the arms and, as the test proceeds, will allocate less of the sample to the poorer arm. So, for example, fewer site visitors will be shown the page version with lower click-through rates. On the other hand, sequential tests assign visitors randomly between the page versions, in equal proportions. The bandit approach should therefore achieve higher financial returns, but the unequal sample allocation might be less useful for analysing in more detail why one design gave a poorer outcome.

Conclusion

In this chapter, we have seen that:

✔ Business experiments are conducted by companies in order to introduce change and manage the risks.

✔ A culture of experimentation requires commitment from your management to invest in testing the available options, some of which will be less profitable, to learn from the results.

✔ Direct marketing tests may be designed to identify required differences in performance, with known levels of confidence.

✔ Advanced experimental designs can be applied to examine multiple dimensions within a single test, and maximize the information that will be gained.

✔ Analysis of variance (ANOVA) may be used to measure the results of multidimensional tests, to identify the important factors.

✔ Complex tests require careful design – statistical advice should be obtained!

✔ Online experiments, such as A/B tests, are best operated sequentially or adaptively using an approach such as a sequential statistical test or a multi-armed bandit respectively.

Top tips for gaining business value from predictive analytics

13

Introduction

In the preceding chapters we have reviewed a wide range of techniques and applications for predictive analytics. We hope that some of these will be either relevant to your business or at least new and interesting to you.

This chapter concludes with a reprise of main messages from the preceding chapters, together with some final suggestions for taking forward predictive analytics in your company.

Reprise of main messages

Data protection and privacy

✔ Compliance with data protection legislation is essential when processing personal data; at the same time, it is important to protect the privacy of the individual and gain their trust in how their data are being used. Make sure that your organization is 'squeaky clean' in all aspects of compliance and gaining the trust of your customers.

The data-mining process

✔ The data preparation phase is critical to the success of your data-mining projects – the predictive power of the data is more important than the choice of modelling technique. Therefore it is essential that all insights gained from the business and data understanding phases are fully leveraged, and that as much knowledge is 'squeezed out' of the data as possible.

✔ A successful project may not require a model – it may be that, by bringing data together in a novel way, a new insight is generated that obviates the need for a model. In that case, it is better to keep the project simple and apply the insight, rather than overcomplicate matters by building a model.

✔ Building and deploying the model are separate phases in the data-mining process. The build occurs once (until a model update is required), while deployment typically takes place many times over the model's lifetime. Therefore, ideally, the deployment method should be efficient, automated and self-monitoring.

Data

✔ Even though data science may have access to vast amounts of information and big data can provide many answers, the principles of statistics should continue to underpin data collection and analysis, to ensure the integrity of the results. Failure to consider statistical concepts can lead to flawed projects, irrespective of the impressive size of the big-data source.

✔ The most valuable data for predictive analytics will be the information you hold on your past, present and future customers. External sources are essential to fill in the gaps and for companies that do not hold consumer data.

✔ Some of the available external sources include *modelled* data – that is predicted data for each individual, obtained by the supplier using their own models. Modelled data are the supplier's best estimates for those variables, however, as with any model, will not always be correct. Therefore, keep in mind that *actual* data have been captured from the individual and so should be true (when collected), while modelled data will not be as accurate.

Analytical techniques

✔ The choice of technique should depend primarily upon the business problem, the available data, whether the data satisfy any key statistical assumptions, and whether your IT system is able to deploy the solution.

✔ In many projects, a combination of approaches is likely to work best. Each approach can yield insights that will help you towards the eventual solution.

Software solutions

✔ Analytical modelling requires logical thought processes and an understanding of statistics. No matter how automated the software tool might be, the analyst will need to apply it in a thoughtful and meaningful way, and interpret whether the results make sense and are useful.

✔ The Cloud makes large-scale predictive analytics available to a greater number of organizations than could be achieved using traditional 'in-house' solutions.

Predicting customer behaviour

✔ Framing the business problem to be modelled is an art, which can have a major impact upon the success of your project. Redefining the problem may significantly improve your results.

✔ When building a model, all predictors must be based on behaviours or attributes defined for a time period *prior* to the outcome period. The outcome must not be allowed to affect or taint any of the predictors.

✔ It is more important to use a smaller development sample that is representative of your model population, rather than a much larger sample that is known to be incomplete or biased. Modelling software cannot detect sampling biases, nor can it identify groups or behaviours that are missing from your data. It can only accept your data at face value.

✔ A model will always predict best on its build data, due to *optimistic bias*. To assess its performance more accurately, use a validation sample containing cases held back from the model's development.

✔ Models enable you to significantly reduce the number of contacts that need to be made to reach the majority of your target audience. This is the reason why predictive analytics makes excellent business sense. It means that a model does not need to predict perfectly for it to be useful. As long as the model delivers a small but consistent gain it can potentially save your company from making large numbers of unnecessary contacts.

✔ No matter how well the model appears to predict on its development and validation data, a live test should be conducted that deploys the model and uses a control group to evaluate its performance.

Predicting lifetimes

✔ Survival analysis focuses on analysing events that occur over time, such as customer attrition or churn. The technique allows for churners, whose lifetimes are known, and non-churners who have survived at least up to the current time.

✔ Survival analysis applications range from business planning, eg predicting future churn levels across the customer base, through to individual customer management, eg acting on a customer's predicted survival probabilities.

Customer segmentation

✔ There are many ways to create a useful segmentation. Segmentation is an actionable tool, rather than a theoretical solution, and should be developed using the data and techniques at your disposal, in order to meet your business requirements.

✔ The three basic requirements for a good segmentation are *identifiability*, *viability* and *distinctiveness*.

Applying predictive analytics in various sectors

✔ Predictive analytics has traditionally been applied in consumer markets, to analyse customers' bank accounts, shopping baskets, phone subscriptions and so on. It continues to extend into other markets, including the public sector for helping to manage citizens.

✔ Analytics in the B2B sector has primarily been used to support acquisition marketing. However, the same predictive analytics techniques could be applied as for B2C, allowing for the key differences in the way that business customers are recruited and managed.

Retail applications for product management

✔ Retailers are heavy users of predictive analytics for product management, driven by operational decisions that continually need to be made.

✔ Price optimization harnesses the price elasticity of each product, to locate the price point that will maximize overall profit. If products have significant associations with one another, it can be worthwhile taking account of cross-price elasticities when optimizing pricing.

✔ Markdown pricing solutions aim to minimize the wastage losses incurred when products reach their sell-by dates. They seek to reduce prices on those items by just enough to make them attractive to consumers.

✔ When forecasting base demand, for large numbers of products, for continuous input to operational systems, the approach needs to be robust, rather than highly sophisticated.

Social network analysis (SNA)

✔ Social networks are not limited to online social media – in all sectors that involve interactions between customers, people form themselves into implicit networks.

✔ SNA involves building a social graph of significant relationships between customers and computing metrics that summarize each individual's position or involvement.

✔ SNA has business applications for product adoption and retention; both may involve identifying influential customers and targeting appropriate marketing activities at them.

✔ Corresponding metrics apply to online social media and, in addition, online networks may be overlaid with people's interests and activities.

Testing the benefits

✔ Testing requires making an *investment* in how your company markets to its customers. Running an experiment implies comparing alternative approaches and accepting that some will perform better than others, in order to prove what works and learn from the results. This means being prepared to forgo some revenue and profit in the short term, in order to achieve long-term proven success.

✔ Direct marketing tests may be designed to identify required differences in performance, with known levels of confidence. Advanced experimental designs can be applied to examine multiple dimensions within a single test, and maximize the information that will be gained.

✔ Online experiments, eg A/B tests, are best operated sequentially or adaptively, using an approach such as a sequential statistical test or a multi-armed bandit respectively.

Final tips

Don't put off starting

Predictive analytics is a 'journey' and it is never too early to start planning or taking your first steps. Provided that your company holds customer data in a digital form, you will be able to learn from it – even if only to discover the quality of the information.

You may have a specific objective in mind for a predictive model; however, you may believe that your IT system is missing some of the key predictors. This should not put you off from building a first model using the currently available data; this will show how well you can do from your existing database – which could pleasantly surprise you – and will help you to justify developments to import further data sources.

Obviously, if your system does not hold the data required to construct the target variable for the model, then you will need to consider ways to obtain the missing information or a proxy for it. Your author once travelled some distance to advise an insurance company that wanted to build an attrition model. When he sat down with the client to examine the data, they found that the database only held records for live policyholders, because the IT department believed that there was no point in holding records for customers who had left! Therefore the first action was to restore lapsed customers onto the system and change the data retention policy.

Start with quick wins – follow the money!

Depending upon whether your company sells one product or many, and has one target market or several, your business may require many analyses and predictive models. Begin by constructing an analytics plan, listing all projects 'on the table', and then prioritize the list according to logical dependencies and expected benefits.

When embarking on the predictive analytics journey, start with quick wins from the 'low-hanging fruit', ie projects where the benefits are easier to obtain. And 'follow the money' – prioritize projects that will give greatest financial returns.

Publicize your findings and successes

By publicizing the findings from analytics projects – such as unexpected or interesting insights – you will generate interest amongst your colleagues, and they will wish to learn more. And nothing breeds future success better than past success – so by publicizing your successes, others will want some wins for themselves.

This tip assumes that you want the application of predictive analytics to flourish and grow within your organization. If that is not the case, or if you want to keep all the benefits for yourself, then please ignore this suggestion!

Learn from your failures

Occasional failures are bound to occur, especially with complex data-processing tasks; however, they can be a good way to improve processes and avoid the same mistakes being repeated.

Always investigate each serious failure in an open way, in order to understand what went wrong and put in place any mechanisms to avoid the same problem occurring again – and not in order to assign blame.

The value comes from implementing

Always remember that the value to your business comes when the analysis or model is implemented, and changes some way in which your company operates. This applies, no matter how great your predictive model may appear 'on paper' – the benefits have to be achieved when it gets applied.

Where to next? – operational analytics

Once you have established the benefits of advanced analytics and developed a firm analytics platform in your company, where to next? The ultimate phase is to embed analytical decision making into individual decisions or actions taken by your company. Bill Franks (2014) defines this situation as operational analytics; Bill explains the revolution in operational analytics that is taking place and how to join it.

Conclusion

Predictive analytics is a well-established discipline, closely related to data science and business intelligence. It has long passed the 'early adoption' phase and associated hype, and has been proven to deliver real business value in many sectors. This book has identified a small fraction of its applications that are likely to be of interest to marketers.

If your organization has yet to harness predictive analytics, then perhaps you should be asking 'Where would predictive analytics add value for us?' And if you are already a user, then the question could be: 'How can we get more value from predictive analytics, and how can we embed it within our operations, in order to maximize the benefits?'

Either way, we hope that this book has given you new ideas for benefiting more from predictive analytics, and we wish you every success on the journey!

BIBLIOGRAPHY

B2B Marketing (2016) [accessed 7 April 2017] Data Skills Benchmarking Report 2016–17, in association with Circleresearch [Online] https://www.b2bmarketing.net/en-gb/member-resources/data-skills-benchmarking-report-2016-17

Bauer, C L (1988) A direct mail customer purchase model, *Journal of Direct Marketing*, 2, pp 16–24

Bayer, J and Servan-Schreiber, E (2011) Gaining competitive advantage through the analysis of customers' social networks, *Journal of Direct, Data and Digital Marketing Practice*, 13 (2), pp 106–18

BEIS (2016) [accessed 10 April 2017] Business Population Estimates For The UK And Regions 2016, *Department for Business, Energy & Industrial Strategy* [Online] https://www.gov.uk/government/uploads/system/uploads/attachment_data/file/559219/bpe_2016_statistical_release.pdf

Box, G E P and Draper, N R (1987) *Empirical Model Building and Response Surfaces*, John Wiley & Sons, New York

Breiman, L (2004) [accessed 4 May 2017] Consistency For A Simple Model Of Random Forests, Technical Report 670, *Statistics Department, University of California at Berkeley* [Online] https://www.stat.berkeley.edu/~breiman/RandomForests/consistencyRFA.pdf

Breiman, L, Friedman, J H, Olshen, R A and Stone, C J (1984) *Classification and Regression Trees*, Wadsworth, Belmont

Breton, R, Flower, T, Mayhew, M, Metcalfe, E, Milliken, N, Payne, C, Smith, T, Winton, J and Woods, A (2016) [accessed 9 August 2016] Research Indices Using Web Scraped Data: May 2016, *Office for National Statistics* [Online] http://www.ons.gov.uk/aboutus/whatwedo/programmesandprojects/theonsbigdataproject

Brown, A and Haire, C (1998) Market Research and Database Marketing: Currently a blind date, but will it result in wedded bliss?, MRS Census and Geodemographics Group Seminar

Capital One (2017) [accessed 25 May 2017] [Online] https://www.capitalone.com/about/corporate-information/leadership/

Chaffey, D and Ellis-Chadwick, F (2015) *Digital Marketing*, Pearson Education, London

Chapman, P, Clinton, J, Kerber, R, Khabaza, T, Reinartz, T, Shearer, C and Wirth, R (2000) [accessed 13 June 2016] CRISP-DM 1.0 Step-by-step Data Mining Guide [Online] http://www.the-modeling-agency.com/crisp-dm.pdf

Cleveland, W S (2001) Data science: an action plan for expanding the technical areas of the field of statistics, *ISI Review*, 69, pp 21–6

Cox, D R (1972) Regression models and life tables (with discussion), *Journal of Royal Statistical Society: Series B*, **34**, pp 187–220

Curtice, J and Fisher, S (2016) [accessed 7 July 2016] How The BBC Will Be Benchmarking The Results On EU Referendum [Online] https://electionsetc.com/2016/06/22/how-the-bbc-will-be-benchmarking-the-results-on-eu-referendum-night/

Data Mining Group (2017) [accessed 7 January 2017] http://dmg.org/pmml/pmml-v4-3.html

Davenport, T H and Harris, J G (2007) *Competing on Analytics: The new science of winning*, Harvard Business School Press, Boston

Davenport, T H and Patil, D J (2012) Data scientist: the sexiest job of the 21st century, *Harvard Business Review*, October

Dillon, W R and Mukherjee, S (2006) Chapter 25 in *The Handbook of Marketing Research: Uses, misuses, and future advances*, ed R Grover and M Vriens, Sage, Thousand Oaks, CA

Facebook (2017) [accessed 27 August 2017] *Facebook Graph API* [Online] https://developers.facebook.com/docs/graph-api

Fenton, N and Neil, M (2007) [accessed 2 June 2017] Managing Risk In The Modern World: Applications Of Bayesian Networks, *London Mathematical Society* [Online] http://www.agenarisk.com/resources/apps_bayesian_networks.pdf

Fenton, N and Neil, M (2012) *Risk Assessment and Decision Analysis with Bayesian Networks*, CRC Press, Florida

Fox, J (2015) *Applied Regression Analysis and Generalized Linear Models*, 3rd edn, Sage, Thousand Oaks, CA

Franks, Bill (2012) *Taming the Big Data Tidal Wave: Finding opportunities in huge data streams with advanced analytics*, Wiley, New Jersey

Franks, Bill (2014) *The Analytics Revolution: How to improve your business by making analytics operational in the big data era*, Wiley, New Jersey

Frawley, W J, Piatetsky-Shapiro, G and Matheus, C J (1992) Knowledge discovery in databases: an overview, *AI Magazine*, **13** (3), pp 57–70

Freeman, L C (2004) *The Development of Social Network Analysis*, BookSurge Publishing, South Carolina

Furness, P (2011) Applications of Monte Carlo simulation in marketing analytics, *Journal of Direct, Data and Digital Marketing Practice*, **13** (2), pp 132–47

Google Analytics Help (2017) [accessed 25 May 2017] [Online] https://support.google.com/analytics/?hl=en#topic=3544906

Graham, A (2017) *Statistics: An Introduction, Teach Yourself*, Hodder Education, London

Harford, T (2014) Big data: are we making a big mistake? *Financial Times*, 28 March 2014

Hicks, C R and Turner, K V (1999) *Fundamental Concepts in the Design of Experiments*, 5th edn, Oxford University Press, New York

Hill, S, Provost, F and Volinsky, C (2006) Network-based marketing: identifying likely adopters via consumer networks, *Statistical Science*, **21** (2), pp 256–76

Hinshaw, M and Kasanoff, B (2012) *Smart Customers, Stupid Companies: Why only intelligent companies will thrive, and how to be one of them*, Business Strategy Press, New York

Hosmer, D W, Lemeshow, S and May, S (2008) *Applied Survival Analysis: Regression modeling of time to event data*, 2nd edn, Wiley, New Jersey

Hosmer, D W, Lemeshow, S and Sturdivant, R X (2013) *Applied Logistic Regression*, Wiley, New Jersey

Hyndman, R J and Athanasopoulos, G (2014) [accessed 24 January 2017] Forecasting: Principles And Practice, *OTexts.com* [Online] https://www.otexts. org/book/fpp

ICO (2017a) [accessed 21 April 2017] [Online] https://ico.org.uk/for-organisations/ guide-to-data-protection/

ICO (2017b) [accessed 21 April 2017] Big Data, Artificial Intelligence, Machine Learning and Data Protection, *Information Commissioner's Office* [Online] https://ico.org.uk/media/for-organisations/documents/2013559/big-data-ai-ml-and-data-protection.pdf

JICPOPS (2017) [accessed 4 May 2017] [Online] http://www.jicpops.co.uk/

Johari, R, Pekelis, L and Walsh, D (2015) [accessed 24 May 2017] Can I Take A Peek? Continuous Monitoring Of A/B Tests, *Stanford University/Optimizely* [Online] http://evalworkshop.com/eval_workshop_rj.pdf

KDnuggets (2017) [accessed 6 January 2017] [Online] http://www.kdnuggets.com/ software/suites.html

Kobielus, J (2010) The Forrester Wave™: Predictive Analytics And Data Mining Solutions, Q1 2010 (James Kobielus is no longer with Forrester)

Lazer, D, Kennedy, R, King, G and Vespignani, A (2014) The parable of Google flu: traps in big data analysis, *Science*, **343**, 14 March 2014, pp 1203–5

Lee, P M (2012) *Bayesian Statistics: An Introduction*, Wiley, Chichester

Leventhal, B (1997) An approach to fusing market research with database marketing, *International Journal of Market Research*, **39** (4), October

Leventhal, B (2016) *Geodemographics for Marketers: Using location analysis for research and marketing*, Kogan Page, London

Linklaters (2014) [accessed 21 April 2017] Social Media And The Law: A Handbook For UK Companies, January 2014 [Online] http://www.linklaters. com/pdfs/mkt/london/TMT-Social-Media-Report.pdf

Makridakis, S, Wheelwright, S C and Hyndman, R J (1998) *Forecasting: Methods and applications*, Wiley, New Jersey

Marn, M V, Roegner, E V and Zawada, C C (2003) The power of pricing, *McKinsey Quarterly*, McKinsey & Company, February

Mellon, J and Prosser, C (2016) [accessed 24 April 2017] Twitter and Facebook Are Not Representative of the General Population: Political Attitudes and

Demographics of Social Media Users [Online] https://papers.ssrn.com/sol3/papers.cfm?abstract_id=2791625

Mifflin M D, St Jeor, S T, Hill, L A, Scott, B J, Daugherty, S A and Koh Y O (1990) A new predictive equation for resting energy expenditure in healthy individuals, *American Journal of Clinical Nutrition*, **51** (2), pp 241–7

Mobile Today (2017) [accessed 4 May 2017] [Online] http://www.mobiletoday.co.uk/

Morgan, J, Daugherty, R, Hilchie, A and Carey, B (2003) Sample size and modeling accuracy of decision tree based data mining tools, *Academy of Information and Management Sciences Journal*, **6** (2), pp 77–91

MRS (2014) [accessed 21 December 2016] Code Of Conduct, *The Market Research Society*, London [Online] https://www.mrs.org.uk/standards/code_of_conduct/

MRS (2017) [accessed 5 February 2017] [Online] https://www.mrs.org.uk/standards/faqs/

Muthén, B (2001) Latent variable mixture modeling, in *New Developments and Techniques in Structural Equation Modeling*, ed G A Marcoulides and R E Schumacher, pp 1–33, Lawrence Erlbaum Associates, USA

New York University (2017) [accessed 3 January 2017] [Online] http://datascience.nyu.edu/what-is-data-science/

Ofcom (2016a) [accessed 28 March 2017] CMR 2016 Data Downloads [Online] https://www.ofcom.org.uk/research-and-data/cmr/cmr16/downloads

Ofcom (2016b) [accessed 28 March 2017] Communications Market Report [Online] https://www.ofcom.org.uk/research-and-data/cmr/communications-market-reports

Padgett, J F (1994) Marriage and elite structure in Renaissance Florence, 1282–1500, Social Science History Association Conference, Atlanta, Georgia

Patron, M (1994) A comparison of four profiling techniques, *Journal of Targeting Measurement and Analysis for Marketing*, **2** (3), pp 222–32

Quinlan, J R (1993) *C4.5: Programs for machine learning*, Morgan Kaufmann, San Mateo

Quinlan, J R (2015) [accessed 10 August 2016] Data Mining Tools See5 And C5.0, *RuleQuest Research* [Online] https://www.rulequest.com/

Radcliffe, N J (2007) Using control groups to target on predicted lift: building and assessing uplift models, *Direct Marketing Analytics Journal*, pp 14–21

Rasch, D, Verdooren, L R and Gowers, J I (2007) *The Design and Analysis of Experiments and Surveys*, 2nd edn, Oldenbourg, Munich

Rhodes, C (2016) [accessed 6 April 2017] Business Statistics, *House of Commons Library Briefing Paper* [Online] http://researchbriefings.parliament.uk/ResearchBriefing/Summary/SN06152

Ricci, F, Rokach, L and Shapira, B (eds) (2015) *Recommender Systems Handbook*, 2nd edn, Springer Science+Business Media, New York

Rogers, M, Chapman, C and Giotsas, V (2012) Measuring the diffusion of marketing messages across a social network, *Journal of Direct, Data and Digital Marketing Practice*, **14** (2), pp 97–130

Russell, M A (2014) *Mining the Social Web*, O'Reilly Media, California

Ryan, D (2015) *Understanding Social Media*, Kogan Page, London

Scott, S L (2010) A modern Bayesian look at the multi-armed bandit, *Applied Stochastic Models in Business and Industry*, **26**, pp 639–58

Select Statistical Services (2017) [accessed 23 May 2017] [Online] https://select-statistics.co.uk/calculators

Statista (2017) [accessed 31 May 2017] [Online] https://www.statista.com/statistics/272014/global-social-networks-ranked-by-number-of-users/

Struhl, S (2015) *Practical Text Analytics: Interpreting text and unstructured data for business intelligence*, Kogan Page, London

The Times (2012) The mathematics of weight loss, *Times Magazine*, 24 November

Thomke, S and Manzi, J (2014) The discipline of business experimentation, *Harvard Business Review*, Boston

Townend, J (2002) *Practical Statistics for Environmental and Biological Scientists*, Wiley, Chichester

Vidden, C, Vriens, M and Song, C (2016) Comparing clustering methods for market segmentation: a simulation study, *Applied Marketing Analytics*, **2** (3), pp 225–38

Vuk, M and Curk, T (2006) [accessed 10 May 2017] ROC Curve, Lift Chart And Calibration Plot, *Metodoloski zvezki*, **3** (1), pp 89–108 [Online] http://www.stat-d.si/mz/mz3.1/vuk.pdf

Wald, A (2014) *Sequential Analysis*, Dover Publications, USA

what-when-how (2016) [accessed 25 April 2017] BLOB Analysis (Introduction to Video and Image Processing) Part 1 [Online] http://what-when-how.com/introduction-to-video-and-image-processing/blob-analysis-introduction-to-video-and-image-processing-part-1/

INDEX

Note: *Italics* indicate a Figure or Table in the text.